IDEOLOGY
AND THE IDEOLOGISTS

Lewis S. Feuer

IDEOLOGY
AND THE
IDEOLOGISTS

Harper & Row, Publishers
New York, Evanston, San Francisco, London

© 1975 by Lewis S. Feuer

LIBRARY OF CONGRESS CATALOG CARD NUMBER:
74-10337

STANDARD BOOK NUMBER:
06-136168-2

To My Brother Abe

Contents

Preface

The revival of ideology which began early in the sixties has led questions to be reopened: what underlies the pattern of the rise and decline of the ideological mode of thought? what leads young intellectuals to search for an ideology? what accounts for the changes in ideological fashion, and the shifts from one set of philosophical tenets to another? what indeed are 'intellectuals'? and finally, has ideology contributed to the rational understanding and solving of political problems?

This book tries to answer these questions. I have explored the invariant structure in ideologies, namely, their common revolutionary myth, and also their wave-like alternation in philosophical tenets. Young intellectuals in generational revolt find in some version of the ideological myth a charter and dramatization of their emotions, aims, and actions. Since each generation of intellectuals tends to reject its predecessors' doctrines, a law of intellectual fashion arises,— the alternation of philosophical tenets. Ideology has inevitably made for an authoritarian presumption on the part of master-intellectuals and marginal ones, and for their antagonism to objective truth and science. Its quest for Community has contributed to the propensity of ideologists for such manifestations as anti-Semitism. One cannot predict an 'end to ideology'; one can say, however, that until intellectuals cease to be prophets and ideologists, and become instead men of intellect, the 'intellectuals', and their specific intellectual expression, 'ideology', will be a force increasingly hostile to the advancement of civilization.

CHAPTER I

The Structure and Ingredients of Ideology

The end of ideology has been prophesied, but the longing for ideology is recurrent and strong. The aim of this essay is to explore the social and emotional sources for the recurrent waves of ideological thought, and the laws which underlie their combinations of doctrine.

I. THE THREE INGREDIENTS IN IDEOLOGY

To begin with, we must as chemists of ideas separate the ingredients of ideology. If we examine the ideologies which today attract intellectuals, ranging from the varieties of Marxism, fascism, structuralism, Marcuseanism, Bakuninism, to African Negritude, and when to this inventory we add the classical ideologies of the nineteenth century, it becomes clear that every ideology (as a first approximation) is composed of three ingredients, the first, an invariant myth, the second, a compound of philosophical doctrines which alternate cyclically in the history of ideology, the third, a historically determined decision as to a chosen class of the time. These three ingredients, an invariant mythological structure, an alternating set of philosophical tenets, and a historically determined chosen group are inherent in every ideology. To understand their workings is to understand the motivations and evolving modes of ideology.

2. THE MOSAIC REVOLUTIONARY MYTH: THE INVARIANT INGREDIENT

Every ideology in some fashion repeats the Mosaic myth,—the dramatic story of the liberation of the Hebrew tribes by Moses. The Mosaic myth is invariant through all ideological transformations. There are many themes of myth,—those of creation, the sexes, the rivalries of brothers, the origins of technology, societies, and languages. But the one which is the prototype for the ideologies of intellectuals is the Mosaic. Especially does it give 'meaning' to the lives of the younger generational intellectuals. The Mosaic myth can be stated in its most elemental form as a series of situations and incidents:

(1) A people is oppressed;

(2) a young man, not himself of the oppressed, appears;

(3) moved by sympathy, he intervenes, and strikes down an oppressor's henchman;

(4) he flees, or goes into exile;

(5) he experiences the call to redeem the oppressed people;

(6) he returns to demand freedom for the oppressed;

(7) he is spurned by the tyrannical ruler;

(8) he leads the actions which, after initial defeats, overwhelm the oppressor;

(9) he liberates the oppressed people;

(10) he imparts a new sacred doctrine, a new law of life, to his people;

(11) the newly liberated people relapse from loyalty to their historic mission;

(12) almost disillusioned, their leader imposes a collective discipline on the people to re-educate them morally for their new life;

(13) a false prophet arises who rebels against the leader's authoritarian rule, but he is destroyed;

(14) the leader, now the revered lawgiver, dies, as he glimpses from afar the new existence.

The Mosaic myth is the drama of the young revolutionary intellectual. Moved by selfless idealism, by pure generosity (as he sees himself), he takes up the cause of the exploited; he suffers exile and imprisonment; but he leads his people to their historic victory; the people, however, are still slavish in their psychology, and incapable of realizing the new society; they require a preparatory period under a tutelary dictatorship; the revolutionary intellectual becomes their benevolent dictator; he quells factious elements; he dies, vouchsafed the sight of the new society, and living in the memory of his people. Thus Karl Marx in the wake of the defeat of the Revolution of

1848 wrote: 'The present generation is like the Jews, whom Moses led through the wilderness. It has not only a new world to conquer, it must go under, in order to make room for the men who are fit for a new world.'[1] Thus the adolescent Ferdinand Lassalle, fifteen years old, felt the stirrings of the Mosaic calling which he would later transmute into a more secular equivalent, the vocation of the revolutionist: 'Oh, when I yield to my childish dreams, it has always been my favorite idea to see myself sword in hand, leading the Jews to make them independent.' Ferdinand was ready to confront the scaffold itself could he but make the Jews a 'respected people'; he writhed in anger that the Jews humiliated in Damascus did not rise in revolt, and if necessary, 'meet death with their tormentors'.[2] The German Socialist leader, Wilheim Liebknecht, wrote: 'It was the God of the *Jews*, Jehovah, and the *Jewish* heroes, with the Maccabees at their head, who impelled Cromwell to fight for liberty—whereas no war was ever waged in the name of Christianity for the liberation of peoples, but rather for their subjugation. The only country where the struggle for the liberation of the people has borne a religious character is England—and in England it was not the *New Testament*, but the *Old*, which furnished the moral strength for the struggle.'[3] In the United States the Abolitionist-ideologist white colonel of a black regiment, the idealistic Harvard intellectual, Thomas Wentworth Higginson returning from the Civil War felt they had passed 'through a Red Sea which no one would have dared to contemplate', and 'attained the Promised Land by the sublimest revenge . . .'[4] America's most famous Communist

[1] Karl Marx, *The Class Struggles in France (1848-50)*, ed. C. P. Dutt (New York, n.d.), p. 114.

[2] Edmund Silberner, 'Ferdinand Lassalle: From Maccabeeism to Jewish Anti-Semitism', *Hebrew Union College Annual*, Vol. XXIV, 1952-3, pp. 157-8.

[3] Wilhelm Liebknecht, *Souvenirs*, Paris, 1901, p. 184. Cited in Edmund Silberner, 'German Social Democracy and the Jewish Problem Prior to World War I', *Historia Judaica*, Vol. XV, (1953), pp. 18-19.

[4] Tilden G. Edelstein, *Strange Enthusiasm: A Life of Thomas Wentworth Higginson*, New Haven, 1968, p. 297.

advocate, Lincoln Steffens, wrote a whole book *Moses in Red* to show that *Exodus* was the classical model for all revolutions with Jehovah personifying nature, and 'Moses as the uncompromising Bolshevik'; the Mexican and Russian revolutions, he asserted, followed the Mosaic pattern in evolving into autocracies.[5] The mythological ingredient is essential to ideologies; without it their historical use and attractive power cannot be understood. It is altogether inadequate to define an ideology, as Talcott Parsons does, as 'a body of ideas that is at once empirical and evaluative' with respect to the states of a social system.[6] An essay in economics which set forth the causes of unemployment, and then outlined the measures to be taken to alleviate them, on the stated assumption that material want, insecurity, and enforced idleness were evils, would scarcely be regarded as ideological. What is distinctive in ideology is the drama it sets forth as the 'meaning' of the historical process, together with its assignment of the roles of leadership elite, chosen-class, and historical culmination. There is no dualism of fact and value in ideology but only because both are transfigured (and *aufgehoben*) in myth.

Sometimes the Mosaic myth grates on the socialist in a mood for economic realism and straightforward sense. Thus Bernard Shaw complained in 1896: 'Socialism wins its disciples by presenting civilization to them as a popular melodrama, or as a Pilgrim's Progress through suffering, trial, and combat against the power of evil to the bar of poetic justice with paradise beyond; . . . with the fullest conviction that we have attained a Pisgah region far above such Amalekitish superstitions.'[7] But without the drama, and the Mosaic role of leadership, even if it fails to take one beyond Mount Pisgah to the Promised Land itself, in short, without ideology, socialism would be devoid of intellectual disciples.

[5] Ella Winter and Herbert Shapiro, eds., *The World of Lincoln Steffens*, New York, 1962, pp. 77, 81, 86.

[6] Cf. Philip Rieff, ed., *On Intellectuals: Theoretical Studies, Case Studies*, Garden City, 1969, p. 22.

[7] Bernard Shaw, 'The Illusions of Socialism', in *Forecasts of the Coming Century*, ed. Edward Carpenter, Manchester, 1897, p. 171.

3. THE JACOBIC MYTH OF THE ELECT

The vocabulary of ideology always includes such words as 'mission' or 'vocation'. The historic 'mission' of the intellectuals, for instance, as it is conceived from Lenin to Marcuse, with their forebear in Plato, is to bring communist ideology to the ordinary people, and then to serve as philosopher-kings. A second type of myth, which we might call the Jacobic myth, is interwoven with the Mosaic; what it does is to explain or justify the 'mission' conferred on the intellectuals. Some Biblical myths revolve around the theme: who will inherit the birthright? who will have the father's blessing? Thus Jacob conspires (with his mother's aid) to deprive his brother Esau of the birthright, for it will decide who will be chosen among the peoples. Thus Joseph's brothers hated him for they saw he was his father's favorite. Jacob and Joseph preeminently were 'intellectuals' as compared to their brothers; Joseph, the interpreter of dreams, the planner for the reorganization of the Egyptian agricultural economy, felt the vocation to rule. The Jacobic myth, too, invariant in all ideologies, evokes deep strains in the unconscious,— all the longings and anxieties of the child to be the favorite of its father. The theme echoes in children's fairy tales; Cinderella, rejected by a stepmother, but chosen by a surrogate fairy godmother, like the voice of history, is a figure beloved by children because she embodies their sadnesses and hopes. And when ideologies, the continuators of myth, assure intellectuals that they are the bearers of a unique historic mission, the latter feel like favored children. Their quarrel with history is appeased; they will be the most indulged, the most favored. The Jacobic myth narrates simply:

(1) There was a father with several sons;

(2) the sons contended for the father's blessing, which would determine their place in the world's hierarchy in future times;

(3) the intellectual son, the younger, is forced by his brothers to undergo ordeals;

(4) the intellectual, younger son secures the historic birthright.

Whereas the Mosaic myth is one of revolt against the Pharaoh, the established order, the Jacobic myth clarifies the nature of the

B

historic mission; the intellectual favored son is fulfilling the mandate of a Higher Established Order. The revolutionary son is exculpated, for he is indeed the most conservative, the most obedient to the primal mandate. The primary content of the Mosaic myth is revolt against injustice; that of the Jacobic myth is the emergence of a new elite, or new class, in the political cosmos.

4. THE MOSAIC MYTH AMONG THE CLASSICAL IDEOLOGISTS

Through the permutations of ideology, the components of the Mosaic myth repeat themselves. Marx, averring in his youth: 'The emancipation of Germany will be an emancipation of man. Philosophy is the head of this emancipation and the proletariat is the heart,' was casting the philosophers such as himself in the role of Mosaic redeemers.[8] Bakunin with his vision of 40,000 student-intellectuals, guided by himself, and leading the 'uncivilized' Russian peasantry to revolutionary triumph was assigning different values to the same structural equation.[9] Leon Trotsky varied the vocabulary somewhat, and wrote of the Bolsheviks as the Jesuit elite of the socialist movement.[10] But when the Russian masses acquiesced to the rule of a new idol, the Soviet autocrat Stalin, Trotsky finally asked at the end of his life, as Moses had asked of the Hebrew ex-slaves, whether perhaps he had overestimated the psychological capacities and the historical heroism of the proletariat;[11] the latter, singularly impervious to their presumable historical mission were like actors indifferent to the play in which they have been cast, and finding the ambitious playwright a tedious fellow.

[8] Karl Marx and Friedrich Engels, *Basic Writings on Politics and Philosophy*, ed. Lewis S. Feuer, New York, 1959, p. 266.

[9] G. M. Stekloff, *History of the First International*, trans., Eden and Cedar Paul, London, 1928, p. 166. Max Nomad, *Apostles of Revolution*, rev. ed., New York, 1961, p. 133. Shlomo Avineri, 'Feuer on Marx and the Intellectuals', *Survey*, No. 62, January, 1967, p. 154.

[10] Leon Trotsky, 'Their Morals and Ours', *The New International*, Vol. IV, June 1938, p. 164.

[11] Leon Trotsky, 'The U.S.S.R. in War', *The New International*, Vol. 5, No. 11, (November 1939), pp. 327, 329.

During the last decade, ideologists beginning with C. Wright Mills have given a fresh version to the Mosaic myth; they have perceived the intellectuals as clearly called upon by history to make the revolution, abetted by their allies located among the colored races of Asia, Africa, and Latin America, the Third World. Structuralism, an ideology with a more academic background, has given an even more primitivist interpretation of the Mosaic myth. The primitive peoples of the world emerge in its view as the innocent, uncorrupted exploited; the oppressors are the men of industrial societies, especially the capitalist directors; modern bourgeois technological society has allegedly warped men's souls, while the dwindling primitive tribes constitute the last bastion of the human spirit; primitive mythic thinking is held to be every whit as valid as that of the bourgeois scientific enterprise, indeed, it is more continuous with the inner character of nature itself. The mission for saving the primitive peoples, and preserving their mythic thinking and emotion as an exemplar for modern men, rests with social anthropologists. Where Marx wanted every intellectual to be a critical economist, a master of the law of motion of capitalism, the structuralist wants every intellectual to be an anthropologist; the fashion becomes 'the anthropologist as hero', and 'every intellectual an anthropologist'.[12]

A primitivist variant to the Mosaic myth has become ascendant in current ideology. On the classical Marxian version, technology, the mode of production, was the chief guidepost in the advancement of humanity. We are now however witnessing the birth and spread of ideologies which through using Marxian language, express a 'failure of nerve' peculiar to contemporary times. Technology, science, and civilization are held up to contumely; regressive emotions, neo-tribalism, astrology, and a consciousness which is the by-product of hallucinogenic drugs rather than the reasoning processes are extolled. Greek society in the third century B.C. experienced a similar

[12] Susan Sontag, 'The Anthropologist as Hero', in E. Nelson Hayes and Tanya Hayes, eds, *Claude Lévi-Strauss: The Anthropologist as Hero*, Cambridge, Mass., 1970, p. 184.

'failure of nerve' (the phrase is Gilbert Murray's),[13] and Roman society in the fifth century A.D. had its confidence in its own values finally undermined into an obeisance before the life-patterns of the Huns and Vandals.

5. THE MOSAIC MYTH IN NON-MARXIAN IDEOLOGY

a. *African Negritude*

The African ideology of Negritude, formulated in recent years, also shares the existentialist–structuralist animus against civilization. It originated too in Paris, among black student intellectuals seeking to define their identity, that is, the locus for their generational revolt. Léopold Senghor described it as their 'passionate quest' for a 'Holy Grail', inspired by a 'handful of crack intellects—writers, artists, ethnologists, prehistorians—who make the cultural revolutions in France'. The young black intellectuals were said to have 'as their mission the restoration of black values in their truth and excellence, . . .', and the overthrow of the values of the European Pharaohs: 'we threw ourselves like an unleashed sword into an assault on European values that we summed up by the trilogy: discursive reason, technology, the market economy, i.e. Capitalism'.[14] The ideology of Negritude celebrated the demotion of reason; its poet-founder, Aimé Césaire, wrote:

> Hurray for those who never invented anything . . .
> Hurray for those who never explored anything
> But who, in awe, give themselves up to the
>   essence of things.[15]

[13] It was J. B. Bury, however, who first used the phrase 'failure of nerve' in conversation. Cf. Gilbert Murray, *Five Stages of Greek Religion*, third ed., New York, 1955, p. xiii.

[14] Cf. Irving Leonard Markovitz, *Léopold Sédar Senghor and the Politics of Negritude*, New York, 1969, pp. 53, 50.

[15] Ulli Beier, 'In Search of an African Personality', *The Twentieth Century*, Vol. 165, No. 986, April 1959, p. 347. Léopold Sédar Senghor, *On African Socialism*, tr. Mercer Cook, New York, 1964, pp. 37-8, 76.

African ideologists, with a simple transformation equation, replaced Marxist terms of 'class' and 'class struggle' with those of exploited and exploiting races and their struggle; the mission of the black intellectuals was to impart ideology to black masses, and serve them as their political elite. The Mosaic myth remained the invariant structure through all the ideological invention. The causal world-line in the history of ideology also exhibited the invariance of the Mosaic myth. Kwame Nkrumah, haunting obscure Trotskyist circles as a student in the United States, 'learned how an underground movement worked . . . I read Hegel, Karl Marx, Engels, Lenin and Mazzini', he wrote.[16] Then he was fired by the writings of Marcus Garvey, a West Indian black intellectual who first raised the slogan of Africa for the Africans, and who boasted that he had discovered fascism before Mussolini.[17] Nkrumah replaced Marxist terms with Garveyite ones. Then with fellow-students in England, he organized a 'vanguard group', the Messianic elite, The Circle, it was called, and he became its chairman. Every political myth seeks to reinforce itself in behavior by an appropriate ritual; thus, Nkrumah's party in the Gold Coast availed itself of the practices of oath-taking; the primitive rites of tribal unity and tribal consciousness infused fresh blood into the Marxian structures.[18] But even in the tribal setting, the Mosaic mission of the intellectuals was affirmed. It was 'the educated intellectual minority' who were catalyzing their fellow African tribesmen, wrote Jomo Kenyatta, later Prime Minister of Kenya, in his doctoral thesis in anthropology; he pleaded before a British parliamentary committee for a sympathetic attitude toward such a Kikuyu custom as female circumcision; a few years later Mau Mau rituals were syncretized with Marxist myth.[19]

[16] Ghana: *The Autobiography of Kwame Nkrumah*, New York, 1957, pp. 45, 61.

[17] In 1937, Garvey told a friend: 'We were the first Fascists . . . Mussolini copied Fascism from me but the Negro reactionaries sabotaged it.' E. David Cronon, *Black Moses: The Story of Marcus Garvey and the Universal Negro Improvement Association*, Madison, 1955, pp. 198–9.

[18] Richard Wright, *Black Power*, New York, 1954, p. 228.

[19] George Delf, *Jomo Kenyatta*, New York, 1961, pp. 77, 92, 98.

b. *Fascism*

The Mosaic myth is not restricted in its domain to so-called left-wing ideologies. It appears in every revolutionary mode of thought, where the ideology is regarded as the metapolitical charter for the rule of a new, young generational intellectual elite. The ideology of Italian Fascism, for instance, was a simple variant of the Mosaic myth. The fascist regime was founded by a journalist, and carried on by journalists, noted one observer.[20] Every ambitious young fascist aspired to have his own journal, to be a full-fledged ideologist. Fascist juvenile rituals 'turned the whole country into a college fraternity'. The fascist anthem, *Giovinezza*, was an adapted student song. The young student intellectuals, according to fascist ideology, were assigned the role of redeemers of their suffering, exploited people. Early fascist politics had the character of a sport, even as that sport took on sadistic hues, and later fascist politics still retained 'many of the characteristics of a student movement'. The alleged mission of the youth was to rescue the people from selfishness, materialism, indiscipline, and to restore a sense of their ancient Roman vocation and pride; the era of the scheming, calculating politicians who had cynically despoiled the people would end. The 'March on Rome' was the equivalent of the miracle at the Red Sea, as the path to power opened before the elite. 'All Italy is but twenty years old today,' said Mussolini.[21]

According to the fascist mythology, Italy was literally a divinely chosen country, and Rome the holiest of cities. Italy had guided Europe into a civilized existence; rapacious capitalist powers now however exploited its people, regarding them as proletarians, as fit only to be laborers, to build them new cities and new factories; but the new fascist elite would restore dignity to the humble proletarians; Italy would be resurgent.

This cult of the New Rome with its mysticism and call to heroic action was often described as a ' "myth" in the Sorelian sense',[22] yet every Sorelian myth was but a variant on the primal Mosaic proto-

[20] Herbert W. Schneider, *Making the Fascist State*, New York, 1928, p. 237.   [21] Ibid., p. 250.   [22] Ibid., p. 229.

type; even the Sorelian vision of a 'general strike', which would overturn the old order and inaugurate the new, was a re-projection of the general strike of the Hebrew slaves, the first such recorded strike in history, when they refused to continue work on the Egyptians' construction sites. Georges Sorel, the ideologist of syndicalism, and the originator of the theory of political myths, wrote his first book on the Bible, and returned to the subject in later whole volumes. The Bible, he declared at the outset, was 'the sole book' which could initiate people into 'the heroic life'. The Hebrew Bible, he later wrote, was 'the book of a peasant democracy'; the Old Testament was 'a book written for workers; the Jews, more than any other nation, had an admiration for work . . .'. It was the Old rather than the New Testament, said Sorel, which had shaped revolutionary thought in the sixteenth and seventeenth centuries.[23]

And Mussolini evidently felt like Moses when the Italian people failed to rise to their historic mission. He was then filled with anger: 'Does not the sculptor sometimes break the marble in ire because it does not take under his hands exactly the shape which it had in his first vision?'[24]

c. *Nationalism*

The ideology of Nationalism in European history likewise conferred on the nation-group the same emotions which the proletariat receives in communism; its Mosaic myth furthermore conveyed a romantic appeal to the young, and a sense of mission.[25] The name of Joseph Mazzini, the apostle of nationalism, is today largely forgotten; but at one time, however, he was a living inspiration to intellectuals

[23] James H. Meisel, *The Genesis of Georges Sorel: An Account of his Formative Period followed by a Study of his Influence*, Ann Arbor, 1951, pp. 48, 65.

[24] G. A. Borgese, *Goliath: The March of Fascism*, New York, 1937, p. 191.

[25] Cf. Carlton J. H. Hayes, *Essays on Nationalism*, New York, 1926, pp. 104–5. Hans Kohn, *The Idea of Nationalism: A Study in its Origins and Background*, New York, 1944, pp. 330–1.

throughout the world.[26] It was the youth that Mazzini primarily addressed. Founder in 1832 of the society *Giovine Italia* (Young Italy) composed only of men under forty, intellectuals, Mazzini declared: 'Place the youth of the nation at the head of the insurgent masses; you do not realize the strength that is latent in these young men or what magic influence the voice of youth has on crowds. You will find in them a host of apostles for the new religion.' Over sixty thousand members flocked to Young Italy, for the most part university students and young intellectuals.[27] To unify Italy and elevate its moral stature was their mission. No thinker has ever made so central the idea of 'mission' as did Mazzini. 'Life is a mission. Every other definition of life is false, and leads all who accept it astray. Religion, science, philosophy, though still at variance upon many points, all agree in this, that every existence is an aim . . . Young brothers, when once you have conceived and determined your mission without your soul, let naught arrest your steps.'[28]

The whole scheme of history, according to Mazzini, resolved itself into a pattern of successive missions: 'Every epoch has a faith of its own. Every synthesis contains the idea of an aim, of a mission. And every mission has its special instrument, its special forces, and its special lever of action.'[29] The message of his ideology reached out to the youth of all nations; they would redeem their peoples; they were the chosen elite. 'Remember 1813: the youth of Germany abandoning their universities to fight the battles of independence; the cry that ran throughout the whole country at the cry of *nationality* . . .' It was the elders who had betrayed them with 'the circumlocution of constitutional opposition'.[30] To *Young Europe*, the universal association which Mazzini later organized, he assigned the mission of 'giving religious status to a principle of regeneration . . . "Young Europe" is creating a new philosophy, a new literature, a

---

[26] Gaetano Salvemini, *Mazzini*, tr., I. M. Rawson, New York, 1962, pp. 94–5.

[27] Ibid., p. 152.

[28] *The Living Thoughts of Mazzini*, ed. Ignazio Silone, Sec. Ed., London, 1946, pp. 111–13.

[29] Ibid., p. 72.   [30] Ibid., p. 60.

new political economy'.[31] The 'grey-headed men', the old liberals, 'distrustful of the young', were materialists, bred on the doctrines of the eighteenth century.[32] But Mazzini, coming to maturity in the romantic-idealistic awakening, cast his ideology in terms of an idealistic metaphysics in which God was the supreme moving agent. He took his philosophical tenets from the dominant current philosophical movements.[33] Aware of the romantic spirit of generational rebellion which was at the core of his ideology, Mazzini's political controversies almost seemed a footnote to literary ones. 'In 1827', Mazzini wrote, 'the war between classicists and romanticists was at its height, the former defending a literary despotism, . . . the latter struggling to escape that despotism. . . . We youngsters were all romanticists.'[34] And as such, they could write the most romantic mythical drama of them all,—the story of how they regenerated and led their people into a new and glorious nationhood. Though Mazzini was not a clear thinker, he articulated an ideology which, as Croce wrote, led him 'to a position of intellectual, moral and even political leadership in Europe'.[35]

6. THE HISTORICAL DETERMINATION OF THE CHOSEN CLASS

The Mosaic mythological structure thus ramifies through ideologies, whether of the so-called left or right. But ideologies are not merely structural invariants. The ideology-seeking temperament also responds to the social circumstances of his time; the latter pose various classes, groups, or nations who are respectively candidates for a place in the ideologist's consciousness as the chosen people of his time. Among the various peoples in the given period who are in various degrees oppressed, exploited, or deprived, the would-be ideologist selects one with whom he can most readily achieve an 'identification'. He finds in the members of that group the embodiments of the virtues he most prizes, and an absence of those defects which he most despises. The people, the proletariat, the peasantry, the Negro, the

[31] Ibid., pp. 56, 91.
[33] Salvemini, p. 88.
[35] Ibid., p. 21.

[32] Ibid., pp. 42, 50.
[34] Ibid., p. 8.

American Indian, the lumpenproletarian, the hobo, the Latin American guerrilla, the North Vietnamese, have been at different times the historically chosen in the ideological myths. On the part of the intellectual, this experience of identification has a conversionary emotional character. The union with the chosen people has a mystical quality; divisions within the intellectual's psyche are overcome; his feeling of weakness dissolves; he experiences a sense of manliness, strength, vigor. Karl Marx, taking part as a young man in 1844 in the meeetings of grouplets of Parisian workers, and nervously restless after nights spent in reading the history of the French Revolution, suddenly felt that these workers were mankind's highest representatives: '[W]henever you see the French socialist workers together,' he wrote, they are not merely 'smoking, drinking, eating, etc. . . .' 'the brotherhood of man is no mere phrase with them, but a fact of life, and the nobility of man shines upon us from their work-hardened bodies'.[36] Friedrich Engels was similarly moved in 1843 when he met in London several German workingmen who were 'the first proletarian revolutionists' he knew. 'I can never forget the profound impression these three men made upon me, a youngster at the time, just entering upon manhood.' One of them, a watchmaker, was a veritable 'Hercules': 'how often have I seen him and Schapper triumphantly defend the entrance to a hall against hundreds of assailants!', recollected Engels.[37] These tailors, shoemakers, furniture-makers, compositors, whom Engels met in small 'communes' in London and Paris seemed to him history's anointed heroes: 'These craftsmen, to their eternal honor, instinctively foresaw the future development of their class, . . .'[38] Engels' report was an example of what might be called 'ideological perception' wherein what one 'perceives' is already re-touched, as photographers often do, to subserve the emotional patterns of the Mosaic mythology. American intellectuals who made pilgrimages to North Vietnam in

[36] Karl Marx, *Economic and Philosophic Manuscripts of 1844*, tr., Martin Milligan, Moscow, n.d., p. 124.

[37] Frederick Engels, *Germany: Revolution and Counter-Revolution*, New York, 1933, p. 122.

[38] Ibid., p. 25.

the latter nineteen-sixties reported similar experiences. A novelist who had become filled with a loathing for the white race similar to that which Marx had for the bourgeoisie ('the white race *is* the cancer of human history:'),[39] transcribed her conversionary experiences in her diary: 'the North Vietnamese is an extraordinary human being, and in ways not accounted for by the well-known fact that any keen struggle . . . usually brings out the best . . . What is admirable in the Vietnamese goes deeper than that. The Vietnamese are "whole" human beings, not "split" as we are.'[40] Thus too Bakunin, exalting the Russian peasantry, had seen in their primitive instincts, a type of human being more whole than either the scientist or workingman. Marx, he wrote, had failed to recognize the irreducible importance for history of the 'temperament and particular character of each race and each people'. The Slavic and Latin races, he declared, were especially endowed with 'the intensity of instinct for revolt'. 'This is a fact altogether primordial, animal.' The 'civilized peoples' had it only to 'a feeble degree'. According to Bakunin, Marx, as an economic determinist, had entirely overlooked the psychological, instinctual source of revolutionary movements. Misled by his emphasis on the mode of production, Marx had misassigned the role of revolution-makers to the proletariat of the advanced, 'civilized' countries; but it was 'the peoples of the "inferior" races, Latin and Slavic, the one tired of bourgeois civilization, the other pretty much ignorant of it and despising it by instinct' who held the birthright of history.[41]

The ideologist, seeking to identify with a lowlier group, to find in their thought-processes a higher *organum* of truth, invariably casts aside some of his civilized, or bourgeois, or white rationality. The Western intellectual among the North Vietnamese documented this regression in her logical processes, 'For more than fifteen years',

[39] Susan Sontag, in 'What's Happening to America (A Symposium)', *Partisan Review*, Vol. XXXIV, Winter, 1967, pp. 57–8.

[40] Susan Sontag, *Trip to Hanoi*, New York, 1968, p. 77.

[41] Michel Bakounine, 'Lettre au Journal "La Liberté", de Bruxelles', in *Michel Bakounine et Les Conflits dans l'Internationale*, 1872, ed, Arthur Lehning, Leiden, 1965, pp. 162–5.

she wrote, the words 'capitalism' and 'imperialism' had seemed to her 'unusable, dead, dishonest . . .' Now she heard the North Vietnamese repeating them in a level, stylized fashion. 'Though my strong impulse is to resist their flattening out of language, I've realized that I must talk this way', 'with moderation', she added, as a saving grace of bourgeois integrity.[42]

[42] Susan Sontag, op. cit., pp. 16–17.

CHAPTER II

The Philosophical Tenets in Ideology:
the Law of Wings and the Law of Alternation

I. IDEOLOGY AND THE RE-ANTHROPOMORPHIZATION OF THE WORLD

Every ideology, in addition to its central Mosaic myth and its enunciation of a historically missioned group, clothes itself in philosophical, metaphysical, and epistemological premises. An ideology is more than a myth; it incorporates a myth but what it adds is distinctive; it tries to demonstrate the truth of its contained myth from basic philosophical and scientific premises. That is why an ideology can be defined as a blend,—a myth written in the language of philosophy and science. An ideology is never content with the narrative of the myth; the drama must be shown to be deducible from the laws of existence itself. As such, every ideology attaches to itself some combination of philosophical unit-ideas; the mythological drama, is regarded as derivable in some fashion from the latter. To accomplish this derivation, the laws of the universe are themselves 'ideologized', that is, the basic laws of the universe are held to be isomorphic, in other words, structurally similar with the patterns of the Mosaic myth. The social ideologist invariably becomes a cosmological ideologist. Thus Marx wrote in 1861 that Darwin's book was 'very important' and served him with 'a basis in natural science for the class struggle in history'.[1]

It is clear from what we have said that ideology aims to re-anthropomorphize the world. In this sense, ideologies, for all their use of philosophical and scientific language, are an attempt to reverse the de-anthropomorphizing motif which has been essential to the development of science. The ancient Greek philosopher, Xenophanes

[1] Karl Marx and Friedrich Engels, *Correspondence 1846–1895*, tr. Dona Torr, London, 1934, p. 125.

of Kolophon, in the sixth century B.C., articulated clearly the flaw in all anthropomorphic conceptions of the universe: 'Mortals deem that the gods are begotten as they are, and have clothes like theirs, and voice and form. Yes, and if oxen and horses or lions had hands, and could paint with their hands, and produce works of art as men do, horses would paint the forms of the gods like horses, and oxen like oxen, and make their bodies in the image of their several kinds.— The Ethiopians make their gods black and snub-nosed; the Thracians say theirs have blue eyes and red hair.'[2] The ideologist, enveloping his myth in scientific language, aims indeed to re-endow the universe with his political, or racial, or national traits. The Communist ideologist projects a universe which develops through revolutions, through qualitative leaps at critical nodal, quantitative points; if, in his view, all social forms and laws are transient, and none universal for all space-time, then by the same token he argues, an essential historicity pervades the laws of physics; the laws and constants of matter are themselves evolving in revolutionary transitions. The fascist ideologist perceives hierarchy and authoritarian control written into those orderly structures of the universe wherein life can emerge; the sun, controlling with its powerful force, the movements of the planets, reigning supreme in what is called in its name the 'solar system', is a cosmological authoritarian. The anarchist ideologist, on the other hand, like Bertrand Russell at the end of the First World War, claims that the theory of relativity is indeed a sort of confirmation of Kropotkin's anarchism for the cosmos as a whole. In formulating their respective political cosmologies, the ideologists avail themselves of the philosophical tenets which are the current fashion. When Marx, for instance, was developing the basis for his communism, he borrowed his philosophical tenets from the ideas which were then in generational vogue among the Young Hegelians, the university student circle with which he had been associated. A materialistic Hegelianism was thus made part of his Communist ideology, with an employment of such unit-ideas as the dialectical structure of historical sequences, the determinism of all events, and

[2] John Burnet, *Early Greek Philosophy*, Fourth Ed., London, 1930, p. 119.

the independent existence and causal primacy of the physical world. Behind Marx's view was the notion that sound political action must be founded on sound metaphysics, or theory of existence. And every ideology shares this conviction that politics must be based on a philosophy; thus Adolf Hitler maintained that the superiority of Naziism over liberalism was shown by the fact that in its warfare against Marxism, Naziism had at its command a *Weltanschauung*, a world-view.[3] When Marx polemicized in 1850 against other Communist leaders who wanted to make an insurrection in Germany directly and were disinclined to spend the next years reading in the British Museum Library while waiting for economic forces to bring forth a capitalist crisis, he charged them with being philosophical idealists rather than materialists: this faction, he maintained, 'substitutes dogmatism for the standpoint of criticism, and idealism for materialism. It treats pure will as the motive power of revolution instead of actual conditions.'[4]

From the sociological standpoint, however, no philosophical tenet, whether materialism, idealism, determinism, voluntarism, pantheism, deism, realism, positivism, empiricism, pragmatism, and so on, can be correlated through its history with any corresponding political or social standpoint. It is part of the 'ideological illusion' that it regards certain philosophical unit-ideas as linked necessarily to its political aims. The history of ideology shows on the contrary, that virtually every philosophical tenet has been used at some time or other by every ideology; the same philosophical idea in the course of its history generally moves through the political and social spectrum, from left to right, or right to left. What determines the prevalence of philosophical principles in their ideological use is, as we shall see, the working primarily of a cyclical law of generational fashion. Let us therefore first show how in the history of ideology the same philosophical ideas have been multi-potential as far as their use in ideologies has been concerned. We shall briefly review the ideological use of the principal modern philosophies and tenets:

[3] Adolf Hitler, *Mein Kampf*, ed. John Chamberlain *et al.*, tr. Alvin Johnson *et al.*, New York, 1940, p. 23.
[4] Marx and Engels, *Correspondence 1846–1895*, p. 92.

2. THE PRINCIPLE OF WINGS IN THE IDEOLOGICAL USE OF PHILOSOPHICAL IDEAS

a. *Kantianism*

The philosophy of Kant has in the course of its ideological career been at different times a postulate for attacking feudalism, and for advocating capitalism, socialism and cosmopolitanism, but on the other hand, it has been enlisted to justify the practices of rigid bureaucracy and the most anti-Semitic bestiality; it has been the rationale for both criticism and defence of violent revolution.

Kant, indeed, regarded the French Revolution (in G. P. Gooch's words) as 'the crowning event of his life'. Though he deplored the execution of the king of France, and recognized no right to revolution against the lawful sovereign, his republican and egalitarian sympathies were strong. 'He said all the horrors in France were unimportant compared with the chronic evil of despotism from which France had suffered, and the Jacobins were probably right in all they were doing.' 'He championed the principles of the French Revolution against all comers,' wrote a colleague of his, with 'boldness and fierceness . . . even against men of the highest position in the State.'[5] He took note in his *Critique of Judgment* that a contemporary Revolution had given a new meaning to the word 'organization' which fulfilled his ethical principle: 'In a recent complete transformation of a great people into a state the word *organization* . . . has often been fitly used. For in such a whole every member must be not only means, but end.'[6] Pupils of Kant then went on to work for the abolition of serfdom, an institution indeed in which men

[5] Cf. G. P. Gooch, *Germany and the French Revolution*, London, 1920, pp. 269–70.

[6] Gooch regarded Kant's passage as referring to the French Revolution, but the translator, J. H. Bernard, felt that it was the American Revolution which was intended. The date, 1790, a year after the adoption of the Constitution of the United States, and the passage as a whole with its mention of 'the regulation of magistracies', makes it likely that the second alternative is the true one. Cf. G. P. Gooch, op. cit., p. 266. *Kant's Critique of Judgement*, tr. J. H. Bernard, sec. ed., London, 1914, p. 279.

were often regarded as means only. 'My whole being shudders when I think of serfdom,' said one of them, the noted statesman, Schön. Feudalists have argued, however, that a sense of responsibility was shown toward serfs which exceeded that shown toward factory hands. At any rate, Kant became regarded as a spokesman for the developing middle class.[7]

Kantianism as it evolved in the mid-nineteenth century tended indeed to evolve into a doctrine of the right, a defence of traditional religion and rule. But in its first reception, it was perceived as radical in its consequences, as an ideology of the left. As Thomas Wentworth Higginson wrote in 1884: 'It is now difficult to recall the peculiar suspicion that was attached to any one in America, forty years ago, who manifested much interest in German thought. Immanuel Kant is now claimed as a corner-stone of religion by evangelical divines, but he was then thought to be more dangerous than any French novelist.'[8]

Intervening generations of ideologists were involved in waves of Hegelian, materialist, and Schopenhauerian ideas; among pure scientists, however, such as Hermann von Helmholtz, a persistent enclave remained loyal to Kant's phenomenalism and rejection of metaphysical speculation. One can distinguish between two generational waves of Kantianism; they were separated by the hegemony for thirty years of Hegelian ideology. The physical and natural scientists first began the assault on Hegelianism, though the Hegelian cycle, in its leftward phase, had its grandiose period in the Revolution of 1848. A Kantian academic movement subsequently appeared, more modest, more restrained, in their claims for philosophical knowledge. The Social Democratic movement, however, a new generation of revolutionists, looking back in the eighteen-eighties to the traditions of '48, and at odds with the academic and bureaucratic establishment, adopted the materialistic Hegelianism of Marx and Engels. Toward the end of the century, nonetheless,

[7] Reinhold Aris, *History of Political Thought in Germany from 1789 to 1815*, London, 1936, pp. 94–7.

[8] Thomas Wentworth Higginson, *Margaret Fuller Ossoli*, Boston, 1890, pp. 282–3.

C

socialist thinkers grew weary with the contemptuous rejection of ethical ideas on the part of Hegelian materialists. They felt that the human spirit was macerated when Marx and Engels ridiculed its ethical conceptions as 'modern mythology', and claimed to base their communist demands solely on the requirements of historical inevitability (making somehow into a categorical imperative: thou shalt cooperate with the historically inevitable). When Marx dictated the preamble of the program of the French Workers' Party, he threw aside the workers' statements of protest against 'injustice' and 'inhumanity' and their demands for 'equal rights'; he simply affirmed that the development of capitalism itself was dispossessing the small holders, producing a large-scale industry, and a proletariat which were being driven toward a collectivist society.[9] 'The men who had fought in the Commune' were aghast at this 'scientific socialism' which disregarded utterly the moral basis of their revolutionary tradition.[10] A similar repugnance to Marxist non-ethicism finally expressed itself in the writings of the gifted and respected Eduard Bernstein, Engels' testator and close friend, and in the 'revisionist movement' which he inspired. Bernstein felt that this aspect of Marxism was tending to corrupt the moral judgment of the working-class: 'And in this mind, I, at the time resorted to the spirit of the great Königsberg philosopher, the critic of pure reason, against the cant which sought to get a hold on the working class movement and to which the Hegelian dialectic offers a refuge.' In a Kantian spirit, one would perceive that the materialist tenet was itself the 'highest' but also the 'most misleading ideology', involving a 'self-deception' which based its 'contempt of the ideal' on a 'magnifying of material factors until they become omnipotent forces of evolution, . . .'[11] A whole section of the socialist movement felt drawn toward a Kantian ethical foundation. Hermann Cohen, a philosopher at the University of Marburg which became the center

[9] Paul Lafargue, 'Socialism in France from 1876 to 1896'. *The Fortnightly Review*, Vol. LXII, New Series, (1897), p. 451.

[10] Ibid., p. 452.

[11] Edward Bernstein, *Evolutionary Socialism: A Criticism and Affirmation*, tr. Edith C. Harvey, London, 1909, pp. 222–3.

for neo-Kantian ideas, had actually sought to base a socialist philosophy upon the principles of the Kantian practical reason. Kant, said Hermann Cohen, was 'the true and actual originator of German Socialism'.[12] His most famous socialist student was the journalist Kurt Eisner, who in 1918 led the revolution in Munich which for a brief period under his premiership saw an effort to establish a liberal Soviet Republic. Eisner was soon assassinated. A man of the highest moral character, he seemed an embodiment of the categorical imperative. He told a friend with whom he was discussing socialist revolution that 'at such critical moments it would be the Kantians, and not the Prussian Hegelians, who would act, and if necessary, die for social justice'.[13]

But for every Eduard Bernstein and Kurt Eisner, whose rich moral natures drew sustenance from Kant's philosophy, there were cold, impersonal administrators who found its universal laws coincided with bureaucratic rules, and that its moral imperative was a rationale for rigidity. Paul Tillich, a pastor's son, bred on Kant's writings, therefore declared: 'What Prussian "bureaucracy" means finds perhaps its clearest expression in Kant's *Practical Philosophy*: Superiority of the idea of duty over anything else, the valuation of order and law as highest norms, the tendency to centralize the power of the state and subjection to the military and civil authorities, and a conscious subordination of the members of the organic whole.'[14] 'A destructive revolutionary to many of his contemporaries, he [Kant] now seems almost wholly on the side of the conservatives,' wrote similarly John Dewey in 1924.[15] Kant's philosophy, he said, tended to make of morals 'an affair of formulas'; science itself became a

[12] Karl Vorländer, *Kant und Marx: Ein Beitrag zur Philosophie der Sozialismus*, Tübingen, 1926, p. 119. Hans Liebeschütz, 'Hermann Cohen and his Historical Background', *Publications of the Leo Baeck Institute, Year Book XIII*, (1968), pp. 14–15.

[13] Max Beer, *Fifty Years of International Socialism*, London, 1935, pp. 198–9.

[14] Paul Tillich, *The Interpretation of History*, tr. N. A. Rasetzki, New York, 1936, p. 10.

[15] John Dewey's *Characters and Events: Popular Essays in Social and Political Philosophy*, ed. Joseph Ratner, New York, 1929, Vol. I, p. 67.

separated 'technical occupation of an intellectual class', 'barren in morals'; Kant never looked at a fact of life or nature directly; all was refracted through the accumulated categories of professionals; his dualistic separation surrendered 'the concrete world of affairs to the domain of mechanism fatalistically understood; it encourages mechanical authority and mechanical obedience and discipline; . . .' '[T]he Great War was in some true sense a day of reckoning for Kantian thought, . . .' Dewey believed.[16] There is something far-fetched in Dewey's reasoning as he derives the horrendous political consequences from Kant's Practical Reason. Is this the same philosophy which stood for moral uprightness and respect for the human personality by which Bernstein, Cohen, and Eisner were inspired? In the United States, Kant's philosophy was the principal inspiration of Felix Adler, the founder of the Ethical Culture Movement, an indefatigable worker for social reform.[17] Can an ethics which teaches that every human being is an end in himself be transmogrified into a doctrine of tyrannical sadism? And yet Mussolini's chief legal philosopher, Giorgio del Vecchio, evidently found no difficulty in founding his Fascist ideology upon a neo-Kantian basis of 'human inviolability'.[18] From a sociological standpoint, moreover, the correlation upon which Dewey insisted has unfortunately received some confirmation in our own time. Adolf Eichmann, Nazi bureaucrat organizer of the extinction of hundreds of thousands of Jews, claimed at his trial that he had been attracted to Kant's categorical imperative; he did not affirm that it condoned the annihilation of a people, but nonetheless, its dictates evidently did not summon him to resist the orders of the Nazi machine.[19] The poet Heinrich Heine, endowed with uncanny foresight, had once warned against a German revolution which would be led by Kantians and transcendental-

[16] Ibid., pp. 66–8.
[17] Felix Adler, *An Ethical Philosophy of Life*, New York, 1919, pp. 9, 73.
[18] Cf. *The Legal Conscience: Selected Papers of Felix S. Cohen*, Ed. Lucy Kramer Cohen, New Haven, 1960, pp. 451–2.
[19] Lord Russell of Liverpool, *The Trial of Adolf Eichmann*, London, 1962, pp. 246–7.

ists: 'Because of these doctrines, revolutionary forces have evolved which are only waiting for the day that they can break forth to fill the world with terror and awe—. Kantians will emerge who will, without pity, use sword and axe to plough through the soil of our European life in order to eradicate even the last roots of the past . . . For . . . the hand of the Kantian strikes hard and without flinching, because his heart is not moved by any kind of traditional reverence.'[20]

The robot-like figure of a Nazi functionary, in a bizarre historical moment, gave a partial confirmation to Heinrich Heine's prophecy. At the end of the eighteenth century three Jews were preeminent in spreading Kant's ideas,—Marcus Herz, Solomon Maimon, and Lazarus Bendavid. What could they have thought of the notion of a Kantian Nazi? They saw the Kantian philosophy as the most durable basis for a rational universalism.[21] Never could they have dreamt that the categorical imperative, legislating its duties in supremacy over feelings, would be transformed into a device for categorical extermination. The so-called cunning of history masks its cruelty.

b. *Utilitarianism*

Utilitarianism, the assertion that the aim of men's actions should be the greatest happiness of the greatest number, went through the typical evolution of wings,—from left to right. Many years later, from the mid-nineteenth century onwards, it became the fashion for thinkers to attack utilitarianism as the ideology of the middle class. As late as 1920 John Dewey wrote that despite its social aim,

[20] Heinrich Heine, *Religion and Philosophy in Germany: A Fragment*, tr John Snodgrass, London, 1882, pp. 158-9 re-translated, in Jacob Robinson, *And the Crooked Shall be Made Straight: The Eichmann Trial, the Jewish Catastrophe and Hannah Arendt's Narrative*, New York, 1965, pp. 294-5.

[21] The attraction of Jews to Kant's philosophy is briefly discussed in Salis Daiches, *Aspects of Judaism: Selected Essays*, London, 1928, pp. tr John Snodgrass, London, 1882, pp. 158-9, re-translated in Jacob 52-65. A. A. Roback, *Jewish Influence in Modern Thought*, Cambridge, Mass., 1929, pp. 373-94.

'utilitarianism fostered a new class interest, that of the capitalistic property-owning interests, provided only property was obtained through free competition . . .'[22] It was widely held that Bentham's 'felicific calcus', the estimation of the pleasures and pains consequential on different actions, was in operational terms a bourgeois calculus of profits and losses. The words which Bentham invented like 'maximize' and 'minimize' were presumably tainted with bourgeois original sin.[23] The strict linkage between utilitarianism and the advocacy of competitive capitalism seemed obvious to many ideologists and social theorists.[24]

To be sure, the doughty Jeremy Bentham, Britain's most prolific reformer, felt, as did all his able friends, that the greatest happiness of England would be promoted by the abrogation of aristocratic privileges, and the expansion of competitive enterprise. That was indeed Radical doctrine in Bentham's time, when the landed aristocracy, extracting its tribute of rent, was characterized as the 'sinister interest'.

But there was nothing in utilitarianism that bound it intrinsically to the espousal of competitive capitalism. During the mid-nineteenth century the cold-hearted Gradgrinds were depicted as utilitarians; romantic ideologists decried the utilitarian pursuit of profit. And it was true that the spokesmen for the capitalist class in Parliament spoke in the utilitarian idiom. At the same time, however, socialists from Robert Owen on, had based their socialist demands precisely on their envisaged advancement of the greatest happiness of the community.[25] John Stuart Mill was the most outstanding among those who moved toward a socialist standpoint precisely because he

[22] John Dewey, *Reconstruction in Philosophy*, New York, 1920, p. 182.

[23] Charles Milner Atkinson, *Jeremy Bentham: His Life and Work*, London, 1905, p. 27, Wesley C. Mitchell, *The Backward Art of Spending Money and other essays*, New York, 1937, pp. 186–9.

[24] Mary Peter Mack, 'The Fabians and Utilitarianism', *Journal of the History of Ideas*, Vol. XVI, (1955), pp. 76–7.

[25] Robert Owen, *A New View of Society and Other Writings*, reprinted, London, 1949, pp. 17–18. Owen, as a left utilitarian, assailed Bentham's conception of human nature as a 'false principle'. Robert Owen, *The Life of Robert Owen*, reprinted, London, 1920, pp. 178–9.

felt that the system of private property had failed to advance the greatest happiness of the greatest number as much as he believed possible. As Sidney Webb wrote in the *Fabian Essays*: 'The publication of John Stuart Mill's "Political Economy" in 1848 marks conveniently the boundary of the old individualist Economics. Every edition of Mill's book became more and more Socialistic. After his death the world learnt the personal history, penned by his own hand, of his development from a mere political democrat to a convinced Socialist.'[26] Webb too had regarded utilitarianism as a doctrine for 'millowners and merchant princes'; he recognized, however, that British workingmen were turning toward socialism on the same utilitarian grounds as had Mill.[27] Socialism in England, he wrote, owed indeed its whole existence to Mill.[28] Perhaps a utilitarian lineage came naturally to Webb, for his father had been one of Mill's committeemen in Westminster.[29] But Webb, as a scientific utilitarian, as an enthusiast for Darwin and the new science of sociology, was at the same time a rebel against the philosophical idealism regnant in British universities.

If John Stuart Mill became the great proponent of individual liberties on the basis of utilitarian axioms, there were others who used those same premises to justify an authoritarian polity. Sir James Fitzjames Stephen believed himself a utilitarian, but he felt that Mill was led to his extreme liberalism and feminism by his want of virility, his lack of actual experience with life, his thinness of character. His own many years' experience in India had confirmed him in his view that a strong government was often necessary to guarantee both free trade and equality before the law; society, with its welter of harsh, conflicting impulses, he argued, could not be regarded as a Social Science Association. Stephen's book was well described by Sir Ernest Barker as 'the finest exposition of conservative thought

[26] G. Bernard Shaw, ed., *Fabian Essays in Socialism*, new ed., Boston, 1911, p. 52.
[27] Ibid., pp. 40, 50.
[28] Alexander Gray, *The Socialist Tradition: Moses to Lenin*, London, 1946, p. 389.
[29] Margaret Cole, *The Story of Fabian Socialism*, London, 1961, p. 28.

in the latter half of the nineteenth century'.[30] Thus, the history of utilitarianism has diffused through the various wings; with the later Mill and the Fabians it really entered on a second cycle, with its beginnings on the left. Whether a political ideology would attach the utilitarian tenet to itself depended largely on the given phase in the tenet's history. Young Marxists trying to differentiate themselves from an idiom which was virtually common to liberals, laborites, and conservatives, tried to define their ideology as utterly hostile to utilitarianism; Marx's cantankerous phrases against Mill, Bentham, and utilitarianism would be cited, though even Marxists were ill at ease with this rancor because almost every political speech they gave when it made sense, was cast in the language of human happiness. Indeed, from its inception there was an ambiguity in the attitude of Marxism toward utilitarianism. Friedrich Engels in his first book regarded himself as a left Benthamite. Bentham, he wrote, was the 'great practical philosopher' who was 'almost exclusively the property of the proletariat'.[31] Marx, however, felt a compulsion to differentiate himself from the utilitarians. Bentham, he asserted in *Capital*, was a 'genius in the way of bourgeois stupidity'.[32] Thus, Bentham, was alternately according to the working of the principle of wings regarded as a proletarian or bourgeois philosopher. Utilitarianism was a multi-potential tenet, available for ideological use by left, right and center.

c. *Pragmatism*

Where Kant's philosophy emphasized formal principles and a priori

[30] James Fitzjames Stephen, *Liberty, Equality, Fraternity*, ed. R. J. White, reprinted, Cambridge, England, 1967, p. 227.

Leslie Stephen, *The Life of Sir James Fitzjames Stephen*, London 1895, pp. 316–17, 308–9, 335.

Eric Stokes, *The English Utilitarians in India*, Oxford, 1959, pp. 281–9. Sir Ernest Barker, *Political Thought in England 1848 to 1914*, sec. ed., London, 1954, p. 150.

[31] Friedrich Engels, *The Condition of the Working Class in England in 1844*, London, 1936, p. 240.

[32] Karl Marx, *Capital*, New York, Modern Library ed., p. 668.

propositions, pragmatism was a philosophy which revolted against all such certainties and fixities. It regarded truths as themselves in flux, and verification as having a man-made component. The meaning of statements was equivalent to their consequences in human experience; the differences in statements were defined by their corresponding divergences in consequences, and the truth of a proposition was equivalent to its working. Within a generation this doctrine was put to ideological use from the left to the right; by the law of ideological fashions it fulfilled its generational vogue when it traversed the spectrum of the ideological languages from left to right.

America's great philosopher, William James, first introduced 'pragmatism' to the American people, giving it the stamp of his own individuality. A writer with an extraordinarily spontaneous sense of metaphor, James courageously spoke of the 'cash-value' of propositions, of the appointments and promotions that went to the man whose faith created its own verifications, and the God whose relations with men were those of a retailer rather than a wholesaler. At once critics began to charge that pragmatism was the ideology of the middle class, of American capitalist civilization. Within a few years, however, the French advocate of syndicalism, Georges Sorel, discovered James's writings, and declared that the myth of the general strike had a pragmatic truth. Young American socialists, moreover, such men as William English Walling and Walter Lippmann, found in the pragmatism of James and Dewey the natural philosophic basis for their ideology.[33] John Dewey meanwhile adapted pragmatism so that it would provide American teachers with a philosophy of democracy, conferring on them the Mosaic mission of leading America's children to the cooperative commonwealth.

James himself believed that events were moving toward 'the gradual advent of a socialistic equilibrium'.[34] But he scarcely welcomed this historic drift with hosannas. He came of that generation

---

[33] William English Walling, *The Larger Aspects of Socialism*, New York, 1913, pp. II–IV, 4 ff. Cf. Charles Wellborn, *Twentieth Century Pilgrimage: Walter Lippmann and the Public Philosophy*, Baton Rouge, 1969, pp. 14–15.

[34] William James, *Memories and Studies*, New York, 1911, pp. 286–7.

of Americans whose fathers had been involved in Fourierist, communistic schemes; to the sons, the fathers, with their Utopian conception of human nature seemed naïf; the sons had witnessed the hatreds unleashed by the Civil War. When H. G. Wells, embarking on an enthusiastic Fabian period, outlined a Utopia administered by a Samurai elite, James objected that the power-seeking drives of the elite would transform them into dictators: 'That I believe to be human nature's ruling passion.'[35] And after a week at Chautauqua, getting a foretaste of 'all the ideals for which our civilization had been striving: security, intelligence, humanity and order', James experienced an 'instinctive hostile reaction'; 'in this Sabbatical city' there was lacking the element of 'intensity and danger'; 'in this unspeakable Chautauqua there was no potentiality of death in sight anywhere, . . .'[36] The pragmatic philosophical tenet could coexist with the whole variety of views of human nature; it entailed no particular conception of man or emotions about him. That was why pragmatism was multi-potential in its ideological alignment.

Thus the career of pragmatism in Italy turned it into a catchword for fascism. Young Italians at the turn of the century were stirred by the pragmatic appeal to action; gone was the classical conception of the knower as a spectator; the knower was rather a doer, an actor. This doctrine filled a group of artists, painters, poets, and dreamers with a sense of spiritual liberation and vocation; they founded a generational organ *Leonardo*.[37] The message spread. Benito Mussolini, a journalist, socialist intellectual, found in pragmatism an idiom and emotion appropriate to fascism; the fascist pragmatist despised the rationalistic, verbalistic parliamentarians, and found in action the vindication of his ideology. To Horace M. Kallen, William James's favorite student, Mussolini said in 1926: 'Fascismo was

[35] *The Letters of William James*, ed. Henry James, Boston, 1920, p. 231.

[36] William James, *Talks to Teachers on Psychology: and to Students on Some of Life's Ideals*, 1899, pp. 268–73.

[37] Giovanni Gullace, 'The Pragmatist Movement in Italy', *Journal of the History of Ideas*, Vol. XXIII, (1962), p. 105.

turning the activism of James's philosophy into facts.' As Kallen noted, this 'might mean anything'.[38] But, curiously, this is exactly what happens when a philosophical tenet, put to ideological use traverses the spectrum from left to right, or vice versa.

During the thirties, pragmatism completed its cycle, as it became the generally accepted philosophy of liberals and statesmen in America. The president, Franklin D. Roosevelt was characterized as a pragmatist in the spirit of his teacher William James.[39] Sidney Hook proselytized valiantly for an understanding of Karl Marx which made Deweyan instrumentalism into a tenet of dialectical materialism. Among Trotskyists the most alert student section was converted to pragmatism, and was obliged to secede; among Communists the power of the party apparatus was invoked during the Stalinist era to crush the allure of Dewey's doctrine. The main drift, however, was toward Marxism. As Horace M. Kallen wrote in 1935, Dewey's pragmatism, 'so diffident of dogmatism and systems', offered 'little to the post-War generation demanding the indubitable certainties, . . .' Though Dewey, after the war, wrote extensively on socio-economic problems, 'the disturbed intellectuals would have none of him. They seek asylum from their anxiety in the aggression of Communism . . .'[40] Strangely enough, it was Dewey's articles in *The New Republic* written in 1928 when he was excited by his visit to the Soviet Union which won more intellectuals toward a sympathy for Soviet Marxism than any other writings in that decade. The great pragmatist wrote that 'the essence of the Revolution' was 'its release of courage, energy and confidence in life'. It was a 'liberation of a people to consciousness of themselves as a determining power in the shaping of their ultimate fate'. Here was the greatest of all social experiments, 'probably the first in the

[38] H. M. Kallen, 'Fascism: for the Italians', *The New Republic*, Vol. XLIX, 12 January 1927, p. 212.

W. Y. Elliott *The Pragmatic Revolt in Politics: Syndicalism, Fascism, and the Constitutional State*, New York, 1928, p. 316.

[39] Raymond Moley, *After Seven Years*, New York, 1939, p. 365.

[40] *American Philosophy Today and Tomorrow*, New York, 1935, p. 268, ed. Horace M. Kallen and Sidney Hook.

world to attempt scientific regulation of social growth'. Children were liberated in the Soviet Union as nowhere else: 'I have never seen anywhere in the world such a large proportion of intelligent, happy, and intelligently occupied children.' Scientists and teachers were the people's elite. Thus experimental, pragmatic logic merged at the left with Marxism. Right and center pragmatists could not share Dewey's enthusiasm. A few years later the pragmatic, experimental teachers whom Dewey so much admired were 'physically liquidated' by Stalin. The pragmatic cycle has been completed. 'Pragmatic' became the favored adjective of all American politicians; editorials were devoted to the 'pragmatic' politics of President Richard M. Nixon. The new ideological wave in the United States searched for a novel terminology, a new generational style.

d. Positivism

Perhaps of all philosophical doctrines positivism would seem to be the one that would be most lacking in any alleged political or social consequence. For positivism, as a theory of knowledge, affirms that our knowledge is founded on sense-perceptions, and that its content consists altogether of statements concerning such sensory phenomena or classes of them. What conceivable consequences could such an epistemological tenet have for one's political or social standpoint? Nevertheless this has been a doctrine which has been highly 'ideologically aligned'; its career shows it traversing through the customary left, right and center wings.

The founder of modern positivism, Auguste Comte, looked to the proletariat to help inaugurate the positivist society, and indeed, he had a devoted following among workingmen. Comte, however, had been a secretary and collaborator of the Count Claude-Henri de Saint-Simon, the original theorist of socialist managerialism. He had imbibed his share of the intellectual elitism which characterized the young engineers, industrialists, and Polytechnicians who surrounded Saint-Simon. Naturally then Comte ridiculed republican and democratic institutions, regarded the 'parliamentary metaphysic' as another obsolete mode of thought to be superseded in the scientific stage.[41] For if scientists rule, the vote of the multitude is as irrelevant to a scientific politics as it would be in deciding the truth or falsehood of Newton's laws or Darwin's theory. Therefore, Comte welcomed the *coup d'état* of Louis Napoleon, hoping the latter would institute a scientific, authoritarian society.

The Positivist movement, however, enjoyed no exemption from the law of wings. Comte's successors as its chieftains, Littré and Laffitte, felt the attraction of a new generation's leftism; they lent their positivist support after 1871 to the cause of the Third Republic, —setting aside the Comtist commitment to dictatorship. A later positivist group, however, reacting against what it regarded as republican 'decadence', and reviving the advocacy of dictatorship, allied itself to the monarchist, restoration-seeking Action Française.[42]

In Britain, on the other hand, no group worked so indefatigably for the cause of the Paris Communards as did the English positivists. Preeminent among them were Edward S. Beesly and the barrister Frederic Harrison. In 1862 the latter wrote to Beesly: 'The intimate alliance foretold by Comte between philosophers and the proletariat has undoubtedly commenced.'[43] Beesly, a professor of classics at University College, London, was chairman of the momentous meeting on 28 September 1864 at St. Martin's Hall which led to the founding of the International Workingmen's Association.[44] Marx sat on the platform that evening a silent participant. Six years later, with Marx's help and largely because of his desire, Beesly wrote the most important English article in defence of the International in

[41] F. J. Gould, *Auguste Comte*, London, 1920, pp. 41, 89.

[42] John Eros, '*The Positivist Generation of French Republicanism*', *Sociological Review* III, (1955), 255–77. W. M. Simon, *European Positivism in the Nineteenth Century*, Ithaca, 1963, p. 159. D. G. Charlton, *Positivist Thought in France during the Second Empire, 1852–1870*, Oxford, 1959.

[43] Austin Harrison, *Frederic Harrison: Thoughts and Memories*, London, 1926, p. 120.

[44] Royden Harrison, 'E. S. Beesly and Karl Marx', *International Review of Social History*, Vol. IV, (1959), p. 31.

The Fortnightly Review.[45] Frederic Harrison was Marx's chosen arbitrator when Marx became embroiled with a Communard inventor in the one recorded episode in which Marx tried to become a capitalist.

While English positivism was the creed of a small leftish sect, in Brazil and Mexico positivism became the ideology of movements for national liberation and scientific industrial reconstruction. The motto of positivism, *Order and Progress*, was inscribed on the national flag of Brazil, where positivism became a 'scientific Jesuitism', an ideology for a dictatorial presumably scientific elite. After all, August Comte himself had tried to enter into negotiations for an ideological union with the Jesuit order;[46] one recalls Trotsky praised the Bolsheviks as the Jesuits of the workers' movement. New bachelors of physics and mathematics from the technical schools led in the introduction of positivism. Mathematics was hailed as the new queen of the sciences, displacing theology from her wonted place. Engineers converting to Comtism, supplanted priests, in intellectual status. Positivist republicans, unlike metaphysical democrats, aimed to be a corps of technocrats.[47] Thus positivism became the ideology of a technical-intellectual elite which abhorred the meaningless prattle of democrats. Similarly in Mexico *los científicos*, the generation of positivists from 1880 to 1910, evolved in their ideological rule; partisans for independence in the struggle led by the constitutional president, Benito Juarez, they became during the next four decades, the bureaucratic agents for the rule of the dictator Diaz.[48]

Positivism has thus made the passage in its ideological career from

[45] Edward Spencer Beesley, 'The International Working Men's Association', *The Fortnightly Review*, Vol. VIII, (1870), pp. 529–30.

[46] F. J. Gould, *Auguste Comte*, London, 1920, pp. 106–7.

[47] João Cruz Costa, *A History of Ideas in Brazil*, tr. Suzette Macedo, Berkeley, 1964, pp. 129, 143, 86, 141, 88, 91, 96.

[48] Leopoldo Zea, *The Latin-American Mind*, tr. James H. Abbott and Lowell Dunham, Norman, 1963, pp. 270–2. Leopoldo Zea, *El Positivismo en México*, seg. ed., México, 1953, pp. 33 ff. Leopoldo Zea, *Apogeo y Decadencia del Positivismo en México*, México, 1944, p. 261.

left to right to center. At the beginning of the twentieth century, Friedrich Adler, physicist and philosopher, and a disciple of both Karl Marx and Ernst Mach, tried notably to base the generalizations and standpoint of historical materialism on a positivist theory of knowledge. Adler at this time was the close philosophical friend of Albert Einstein. His essays and example contributed much to the unique ideology known as Austro-Marxism, which endeavored to de-mythologize Marxism on the philosophical side while retaining the social dynamic. Its last adherents moved to America, merging with the pragmatists, while in England, Karl Popper, once a youthful Austro-Marxist, became the powerful critic of all historicist and leftist ideology. Ernst Mach himself, the founder of the modern empiricist standpoint in the philosophy of science, held to liberal and radical political and social ideas, but a later generation of such scientists, including the famed Heisenberg, formulator of the principle of indeterminacy, conjoined such a standpoint with Nazi sympathies. Vilfredo Pareto, an imposing figure in mathematical economics and sociology, was all his life a scientific empiricist; the same Pareto during one decade hailed the Swiss cantons as the best government man had devised, and in the next greeted the advent of Mussolini's Fascist regime in Italy. Thus, in the intellectual history of a single person, a philosophical tenet too could traverse the spectrum from left to right.

e. *Nietzscheanism*

The name of Friedrich Nietzsche is for many persons associated with the barbarities of Naziism. Adolf Hitler himself admitted Nietzsche into the temple of his prophetic forerunners. Nietzsche had inveighed against the 'slave-morality' of democracy, liberalism, Marxism, and Christianity, and affirmed the future of German culture as resting with the sons of Prussian officers. True, incidental remarks in his writings were favorable to the Jews, but these were conveniently deleted, and Nietzsche's books enjoyed a tremendous vogue in Nazi Germany. The 'superman' with his master-morality had been Nietzsche's version of the myth of the Mosaic redeemer;

his description of the superman in Nazi eyes seemed to fit, if not the storm trooper then the elite corps of the Schutzstaffeln.

The revolutionary right was, however, only one wing of the Nietzschean ideological movement; like all such intellectual waves, arising under the impulses of generational revolt, it spread through the left, center, and right of the co-generationists. As Crane Brinton wrote:[49] 'Ever since the young and the would-be young rebels of the nineties discovered him, Nietzsche has been a refuge and a hope for young men and women undergoing the manifold troubles of adolescence. To the bright and sensitive youngster who is just coming to appreciate with how little wisdom the world is governed, how dull, muddled, and un-enterprising his once-reverenced elders really are, how unending and unearthly are the hidden possibilities of life these elders have withheld from him, Nietzsche is an incomparable ally.'[50] The dramatic inspiration of Nietzsche's *Thus Spake Zarathustra* filled young socialists in England and young Zionists in Russia with a sense of mission and meaning in life. The Fabian socialist Bernard Shaw welcomed Nietzsche as a Diabolonian voice;[51] the Russian-Jewish graduate student, Chaim Weizmann, wrote to his betrothed: 'I am sending you Nietzsche; learn to read and understand him. This is the best and finest thing I can send you.'[52]

Weizmann spoke for countless young Jews; stifled by a system of persecutions which placed obstacles across their self-realization, they listened to a master whose words rang with an unquenched sense of self-hood. For every German barrackeer who paraded with

[49] Crane Brinton, *Nietzsche*, Cambridge, Mass., 1941, pp. 206 ff.

[50] Crane Brinton, op. cit., p. 233. A. Wolf, *The Philosophy of Nietzsche*, London, 1915, p. 36.

[51] Archibald Henderson, *George Bernard Shaw: His Life and Works*, Cincinnati, 1911, p. 455. 'Nietzsche's Zarathustra was the New Moses', writes David S. Thatcher, *Nietzsche in England 1890–1914: the Growth of a Reputation*, Toronto, 1970, pp. 271–3.

[52] *The Letters and Papers of Chaim Weizmann*, Vol. I, ed. Leonard Stein, London, 1968, pp. 341, 85: 'at the turn of the century there was a considerable vogue for Nietzsche among the Russian-Jewish intelligentsia'.

Nietzschean phrases, there was a Ghetto Nietzschean who found his life-spark kindled by the Nietzschean images.

Such doctrines as that of the Superman could be ideologically interpreted and aligned in the most diverse ways. Artists and writers could regard themselves as Nietzsche's elite, the rejectors of the 'bourgeoise compromise', who stood high above the mediocrities of the mass-man; the artists were the warriors against the past ascetic decade. Socialist intellectuals could see themselves as a vanguard of supermen, shedding the self-hatred of the Christian ethics and leading the workers to heroic victory; William English Walling, though basically a pragmatist, wrote a whole chapter to herald Nietzsche as the prophet of the new socialist morality: 'Nietzsche's test is: do the action and the motive of the action spring from a developing or from a degenerating personality, from an advancing or from a retrogressive mood?';[53] the socialist novelist Jack London was a disciple of both Nietzsche and Marx, depicting his mighty proletarians as cast in a superman's mould; 'Nietzsche was right. I won't take the time to tell you who Nietzsche was, but he was right. The world belongs to the strong—to the strong who are noble as well and who do not wallow in the swine-trough of trade and exchange,' said Martin Eden, London's protagonist. Maxim Gorki in Russia also gave his workingmen the posture of Nietzschean heroes.[54] H. L. Mencken, the American Nietzschean who was defining his mission as the shocking of the 'booboisie', called an imposing role of fellow-believers, ending with Shaw's admonition in 1906: 'Before long you must be prepared to talk about Nietzsche or retire from society.'[55] 'There is no escaping Nietzsche', declared Mencken. 'He has colored the thought and literature, the speculation and theorizing, the politics and superstition of the time. He reigns as king in the German universities—where, since Luther's day, all

[53] William English Walling, *The Larger Aspects of Socialism*, New York, 1913, p. 222.

[54] Alexander Kaun, *Maxim Gorky and his Russia*, New York, 1931, pp. 153, 241, 571.

[55] Henry L. Mencken, *The Philosophy of Friedrich Nietzsche*, London, 1908, p. 287.

D

the world's most painful thinking has been done . . .' Mencken
followed the German university fashion twenty years later in his
espousal of Adolf Hitler. Zarathustra was then identified with *der
Führer*; the will to power fulfilled the intellectual's longing for exalting hardness. This same note has reappeared in the writings of
the German New Leftist, Herbert Marcuse, wherein the Nietzschean
themes of an 'explosion' which will transvalue all values have over-
shadowed the Marxist.[56] Thus the Nietzscheans of the left and right
tend, in Hegelian fashion, toward a unity of opposites.

f. *Bergsonianism*

The Nietzschean fashion, which emanated from Germany, was very
soon followed by the Bergsonian which spread from Paris. Within
a few years the Bergsonian tenets were being absorbed, as the
Nietzschean had been, by ideologists from the left to the right.
'Like Hegel, Bergson has a Right and a Left', observed a leading
French socialist.[57] The Bergsonian intuition, overcoming the artificial, spatial separations of the intellect, seemed to provide the 'conservative and reactionary Right' with the means for defending the
mysteries of religion. But left-wingers, led especially by Georges
Sorel and his syndicalist associates, grasped at that same intuition to
give support to the proletarian urge toward a general strike, the
élan vital of the working class, which transcended the understanding;
the intellect, indeed was intrinsically corrupted in the practical,
bourgeois world. Though Bergson disclaimed responsibility for the
use to which Sorel had put his philosophy, he acknowledged that
Sorel was one who 'had read me attentively and understood me
perfectly'.[58] He wrote Sorel in 1908 that the latter's conclusions concerning violence 'frightened me, but I am very interested in the

[56] Herbert Marcuse, *An Essay on Liberation*, Boston, 1969.

[57] Charles Rapaport, 'The Intuitive Philosophy of M. Bergson', *The
New Review*, Vol. II, March 1914, p. 139.

[58] Henri Bergson, *Ecrits et Paroles*; textes rassemblés par R. M. Mosse-
Bastide, Paris, 1957–1959, 'Lettre à Gilbert Maire sur Georges Sorel
(1912)', Tome II, p. 370.

method through which you reach them'.[59] At the same time, however, the Bergsonian philosophy was becoming the ideology of young intellectuals who were finding the determinism of Marxism and positivism too desiccating a doctrine. Between 1900 and 1914, he became 'the teacher of the whole intellectual elite of the nation'; his doctrines were first espoused by young students, but then spread to their elders in various fields.[60] Charles Péguy, the bookseller, publisher, and Dreyfusard militant, from his shop on the Rue de la Sorbonne, led a younger generation of intellectuals in their ideological secession from the Establishment. At the Sorbonne, materialism and positivism reigned, but a few steps away, at the Collège de France, Henri Bergson was expounding his spiritual intuitionism to people's audiences. The young intellectuals walked those steps into a new philosophic universe, where reality was felt in its striving uncertainty and incompleteness, and where dialectical tricks and transitions were replaced by an empathetic hearing to the waves of existence.

In the United States, too, adventurous young thinkers turned to Bergson for a fresh idiom, all the more invigorating after the monotonous repetitions of the Marxist scholars with their formulae which mechanized every living impulse and movement. Walter Lippmann, the most gifted of the young socialists, wrote in 1912 that Bergson was 'the most dangerous man in the world. The spread of his teaching will put all institutions on the defensive'; Bergson's philosophy, in his view, was 'the deadly enemy of the stand-pat

[59] Rose-Marie Mosse-Bastide, *Bergson Educateur*, Paris, 1955, p. 94. Pierre Andreu, 'Bergson et Sorel', *Les Etudes Bergsoniennes*, Vol. III, Paris, 1952, p. 44.

[60] Mosse-Bastide, *Bergson Educateur*, p. 73.
'Bergson explained to us what we were already ready to feel,' said one young thinker. Bergsonism, wrote Julien Benda, 'came to tell contemporary society exactly what it wanted to hear'. *Sur le Succès du Bergsonisme*, Paris, 1914, pp. 165–6. Benda further suggested that the vogue of Bergson's conception of knowledge from within, overcoming spatial barriers, was founded on 'the desire of a perception of things which would be like a sort of sexual invasion'. *Ibid.*, p. 161.

intellect in all its forms'.[61] In a more academic setting, the older John Dewey, revered for marching by the side of the younger radical recruits, wrote—'who today is not reading Bergson . . .'[62] The Marxist faithful were alarmed by the Bergsonian incursion. Their most erudite theoretician, Louis B. Boudin, delivered a lecture in March, 1915 before the Harlem Socialist Forum entitled 'Bergsonism and Pragmatism as Special Cases of General Bourgeois Reaction'.[63]

Watching keenly the spread of the Bergsonian ideology at this time was Arthur O. Lovejoy whose work through the years, remarkable for its sweep of scholarship, analytic power, and imagination justly earned him the renown as America's greatest historian of ideas. Lovejoy perceived that underlying Bergsonian vogue were the workings of a periodic generational movement of ideas. 'The reasons for much of this vogue cannot be altogether obscure to anyone who has considered the history and the psychology of philosophical and literary fashions,' he wrote. 'There is a very evident touch of mystification about this philosophy; and the craving, which it has, in the more highly civilized ages, been one of the historic functions of philosophy to gratify. What the public wants most from its philosophers is an experience of *initiation*; what it is initiated into is often a matter of secondary importance . . . The need for a new sort of philosophic *Eleusinia* is recurrent among the cultivated classes every generation or two; it is a phenomenon almost as periodic as commercial crises.'[64]

Here indeed was the key to the understanding of the alternations

[61] Walter Lippmann, 'The Most Dangerous Man in the World', *Everybody's Magazine*, Vol. XXVII, (1912), pp. 100–1. Cited in Wellborn, op. cit., p. 20. Also Cf. W. Riley, 'La philosophie francaise en Amérique', *Revue Philosophique*, XCI, (1921), pp. 75–6.

[62] John Dewey, 'Perception and Organic Action', *Journal of Philosophy*, IX, (1912), p. 645. Reprinted in *Philosophy and Civilization*, New York, 1931, p. 202.

[63] Charles B. Mitchell, 'Bergsonism and Practical Idealism', *The New Review*, Vol. II, (1914), p. 193; also cf. pp. 224–7.

[64] Arthur O. Lovejoy, 'The Practical Tendencies of Bergsonism', *The International Journal of Ethics*, Vol. XXIII, 1913, p. 254.

of philosophical tenets in the history of ideologies. Not that the craving to be mystified is perennial, for it alternates with a craving for clarity and precision. A generation which imbibes a determinist, analytic creed from its fathers will in its revolt tend to attach to its political ideology voluntarist, anti-intellectual tenets. And that portion of the public which wishes to partake of the experience of initiation is characteristically composed of the intellectuals of the younger generation; the shared philosophical tenets in which their Mosaic myth is explicated, and from which it is derived, the shared tenet as to their method which gives them an insight into their 'mission' not vouchsafed by ordinary scientific method, the common discipleship in doctrines revelatory of a higher reality and a higher truth, superior to the commonplaces of their fathers and teachers, all this then becomes part of the ideological experience.

g. *Idealism and Transcendentalism*

Largely under the influence of Leninist ideology the view spread after 1929 that whereas materialism was a 'progressive' philosophy, idealism was a 'reactionary' tenet. American and British scholars moreover had earlier excoriated German idealism as having provided especially in Hegel's philosophy the rationale for a *Realpolitik* which led to the First World War.[65] The history of the ideological career of philosophical idealism shows, however, the typical pattern of diffusion through the political wings, left, center, and right. Absolute idealism has been the metaphysical tenet of the most selfless reformers as well as the world-postulate of the most egoistic reactionaries.

[65] John Dewey, *German Philosophy and Politics*, New York, 1915, pp. 109–19. George Santayana, *Egotism in German Philosophy*, London, 1916, pp. 6–7, 96. L. T. Hobhouse, *The Metaphysical Theory of the State; a criticism*, London, 1918, pp. 23–5. George H. Sabine, 'The Social Origin of Absolute Idealism', *The Journal of Philosophy*, Vol. XII, (1915), pp. 169 ff. *Collected Papers of Clarence Irving Lewis*, 'German Idealism and its War Critics', ed. J. D. Goheen and J. L. Mothershead, Jr., Stanford, 1970, pp. 55–65.

The transcendentalist philosophy in New England, an American variant of idealism, was the standpoint of its most devoted group of social reformers. Ralph Waldo Emerson, Theodore Parker, the co-operators of Brook Farm, the vegetarians, the clothing reformers who refused to wear woolen clothes because it was unfair to the shorn sheep, the variegated array of crack-pots with their crotchets, all believed themselves to be validated and certified in their action and beliefs by transcendentalist metaphysics. The abolitionist and first American socialist movements were baptized with transcendentalist principles. In his old age, Charles A. Dana, a Brook Farmer in his youth, then the managing editor of the socialist *New York Tribune*, and the benefactor and employer of Karl Marx, recalled the fervor of the transcendentalist, idealist socialists:

'In this party of Transcendental philosophers the idea early arose . . . that democracy . . . was not enough; . . . it should be raised up into life and be made social. The principle of equality should be extended . . . One of the things that the democratic philosophers particularly objected to was that while the master sat in the parlor upstairs, the servant sat in the kitchen downstairs. They ought to be on the same level; equality and democracy should characterize our social relations . . . That could only be accomplished by the reform of society; and this reform of society these people after long study and much discussion, determined it was their duty to realize. And that was what inspired the socialist movement which began about 1835 or 1838.'[66]

[66] Charles A. Dana, 'Brook Farm', in James Harrison Wilson, *The Life of Charles A. Dana*, New York, 1907, p. 521. Also cf. René Wellek, 'Emerson and German Philosophy', *The New England Quarterly*, Vol. XVI, (1943), pp. 56–62. Emerson wrote that Hegel 'dared not to unfold or pursue the surprisingly revolutionary conclusions of his own method; but not the less did the young Hegelians consummate the work, so that quickly, in all departments of life, in natural sciences, politics, ethics, laws, and in art, the rigorous Dogma of Immanent Necessity exterminated all the old tottering, shadowy forms'. *Journals of Ralph Waldo Emerson*, ed., Edward Waldo Emerson and Waldo Emerson Forbes, Vol. X, London, 1914, p. 460.

Southern apologists for slavery might profess themselves empiricists and Aristotelians, and justify their 'peculiar institution' by the empirical evidence of the low achievements of the Negro race. But Emerson and Parker were Platonists who appealed to the divine ingredient in the spirit of every man, partaker of the Oversoul, and not to be weighed in any calculus of additive pleasures and pains. Slavery, they felt, violated the intuited law of the equality of man even if it could be shown to make for the greatest happiness of the greatest number.[67] 'The American Revolution, with American history since', wrote Theodore Parker, 'is an attempt to prove by experience this transcendental proposition, . . .'[68]

Emerson and his fellow-Unitarian clergymen and friends in the Boston precincts quickly became transcendentalists of the left. But transcendentalist metaphysics was multi-potential in its ideological use. In the town of Burlington, at the University of Vermont, President James Marsh published Coleridge's *Aids to Reflection*, translated Kant, and together with several dour colleagues, zealously advocated transcendentalist philosophy. The Vermont transcendentalists were however conservatives, and had little respect for the social questioning of Emerson and his associates. 'The whole of Boston transcendentalism', wrote Marsh, 'I take to be a rather superficial affair.' He was sardonic about the experiment in collectivism at Brook Farm: 'The Colony is the theme of severe ridicule and sarcasm almost universally. These reformers hope to redeem the world by a sort of dilettante process, to purge off its grossness, to make a poetical paradise in which hard work shall become easy, dirty things clean, the selfish liberal, and the churl a churl no longer.'[69] The transcendentalists of the right found in their ultimate intuitions a rebuke to all doctrines of revolution and basic reform.

[67] Octavius Brooks Frothingham, *Transcendentalism in New England*, 1876, reprinted, New York, 1959, pp. XXV, XXVI. 115.

[68] Theodore Parker, *The World of Matter and the Spirit of Man*, Boston, 1907, p. 27.

[69] Cf. Lewis S. Feuer, 'James Marsh and the Conservative Transcendentalist Philosophy: A Political Interpretation', *The New England Quarterly*, Vol. XXXI, 1958, p. 23.

Hegelian idealists in Germany were numbered among the conservatives,[70] but in America, when the guns of the Civil War were first heard no group rallied to the Union cause with more of a freedom-loving spirit than did the St. Louis Hegelians. Henry C. Brockmeyer, a fugitive from Prussian militarism, put aside his Hegel for Hardie's *Infantry Tactics*, served as a colonel in the Union Army, and later as Governor of the state. Exiled German idealists helped organize the small army that won the first decisive battle for the Union at Camp Jackson; Grant and Sherman both in St. Louis at that time were still indecisive spectators.[71] Brockmeyer communicated to his fellow-Hegelians the secrets of 'the dialectic of politics and political parties'. Fort Sumter was the thesis, Camp Jackson the 'antithesis', and Lincoln's call for volunteers the 'synthesis'. Later, in the era of industrial expansion after the Civil War, the historical dialectic became an economic developer: the St. Louis real estate boom was the 'thesis', the founding of the Philosophical Club the 'antithesis', and the construction of the Eads Bridge the 'synthesis'. The St. Louis Hegelians were disappointed, however, as the city of Chicago rapidly surpassed St. Louis in population and economic importance. The dialectic seemed to have forgotten the place where it had attained its highest self-consciousness. Governor Brockmeyer died 'convinced that America was not yet ready for philosophy'.[72]

To Walt Whitman, who gave the word 'comrade' to the socialist movement, idealism seemed preeminently the ideology of the Ameri-

[70] J. S. Henderson, 'Hegel as a Politician: His views on English Politics', *The Fortnightly Review*, Vol. VIII, (1870), pp. 266-7.

[71] Henry A. Pochmann, *New England Transcendentalism and St. Louis Hegelianism: Phases in the History of American Idealism*, Philadelphia, 1948, pp. 8-15.

[72] Harvey Gates Townsend, 'The Political Philosophy of Hegel in a Frontier Society', Charles M. Perry, 'William T. Harris and the St. Louis Movement in Philosophy', George Rowland Dodson, 'The St. Louis Philosophical Movement', in *William Torrey Harris: 1835-1935*, edited by Edward L. Schaub, Chicago, 1936, pp. 25, 30, 44, 46, 76. Also cf. Frances B. Harmon, *The Social Philosophy of the St. Louis Hegelians*, New York, 1943, pp. 62-3.

can democratic spirit: 'What is I believe called Idealism seems to me to suggest, (guarding against extravagance, and ever modified even by its opposite), the course of inquiry and desert of favor for our New World metaphysics, their foundation of an in literature, giving hue to all.'[73] In Britain at the same time young idealists in the universities drew from their Hegelian metaphysics a devotion to liberal values and a vocation to serve the working classes. Edward Caird and T. H. Green were radicals, devoted to the Northern cause during the American Civil War, and admirers of Lincoln's democratic leadership. As metaphysical idealists, they affirmed that history was the self-development of an eternal spirit; its direction they believed, aimed through levelling all men to achieve their elevation. Caird helped found the Glasgow settlement, saying: 'Class distinctions have become purely artificial and must be broken down'. He tried to induce his brother to join Garibaldi's legion as a volunteer.[74] (Joseph Mazzini, the apostle of Italian nationhood was, let us also remember, a fervent believer in idealistic metaphysics.) Arnold Toynbee, the disciple at Oxford of Thomas Hill Green, felt the call to bring light and learning to the poor in Whitechapel, to lecture on history and political economy to classes of mechanics and workingmen.[75] The trend to philosophical idealism arose, said Bosanquet, from an 'enthusiasm' for the 'humanizing movement', not from 'Ontology'.[76]

The generation in Britain that was drawn to absolute idealism was not, however, of one ideological hue. As the doughty F. C. S. Schiller observed, a right-wing flourished at Glasgow, a left-wing, 'openly and exultingly anti-theological' at Oxford, and a center

[73] Walt Whitman, *Democratic Vistas and Other Papers*, London, 1888, p. 71.

[74] Sir Henry Jones and John Henry Muirhead, *The Life and Philosophy of Edward Caird*, Glasgow, 1921, pp. 34, 149. Also cf. G. P. Gooch, *Under Six Reigns*, London, 1958, p. 23.

[75] F. C. Montague, *Arnold Toynbee, Johns Hopkins University Studies in History and Political Science*, Vol. VII, Baltimore, 1889, P.11.

[76] Bernard Bosanquet, *Essays and Addresses*, London, 1891, pp. V. IX.

'silent or ambiguous'. These were wings, however, within an academic setting, defined primarily by differences in theology, quite dissociated from the philosophy of scientific evolutionism which had a tremendous vogue among average Britons and Americans. By contrast, the university ideologists were 'ascetics of the intellectual world', as Schiller described them, abnegating themselves before 'the Juggernaut Car of the Absolute'. Their dislike for scientific evolutionism and pragmatism was 'psychological in origin', related to a propensity for 'self-inflicted mutilations', their mode of initiation (in Lovejoy's phrase) to the 'absolute truth'.[77] Yet the university ideology was 'the most potent influence in Oxford', and was credited with the awakening of interest in social questions and the devoted labor of young idealists.[78]

During the first years of the twentieth century philosophical idealism rapidly declined in the United States. It had begun on the left with the transcendentalists but at the end of the nineteenth century was identified with conservatism. Josiah Royce upholding its banner was a staunch survivor, and in 1899, polemicizing against the critics of idealism, charged that it was realism rather which was 'the typical notion of socially respectable conservatism, whenever such conservatism begins to use the speech of technical philosophy'.[79] To his students, bent however on their realistic generational rebellion, and defining themselves as radical liberals, idealism seemed a lifeless doctrine; a man like Arthur Lovejoy felt that its denial of the reality of the time-process made meaningless all human aspiration for the improvement of the future society.[80] It was because a whole genera-

[77] F. C. S. Schiller, *Studies in Humanism*, pp. 14, 284.

[78] Samuel Alexander 'The Study of Ethics at Oxford', *The Ethical Record*, Vol. III, (1890), p. 82.

[79] Josiah Royce, *The World and the Individual*, First Series, New York, 1899, p. 91.

[80] Lovejoy used generational categories in explaining the transition from idealism to realism: 'With almost a whole generation of acute and powerful minds this [the idealistic tenet] passed for a virtual axiom. And with a great part of the succeeding generation of American and British philosophers the contradictory of this proposition has passed for a virtual axiom, . . .' Arthur O. Lovejoy, 'A Temporalistic Realism', in

tion of young philosophers had already been converted to realism, and the pendulum of philosophical ideas had swung to realism from idealism that a whole group of respected thinkers was able to convince many persons that philosophical idealism had been a primary factor in setting Germany into a militarist direction. Idealism, which had inspired Emerson and the young transcendentalists in 1837, was a captured and defeated German drill-sergeant in 1918.

A similar ambiguity of wings characterized the ideological alignments of idealism in Italy. Philosophical idealists were justly proud of the vigorous stand which Benedetto Croce took during the latter 1920s against Fascism. But then it was also conceded to be the case that 'Croce's philosophy from 1900 on gave powerful impetus to the anti-democratic wave that helped to lead to Fascism.' Croce's disciple, Giovanni Gentile, who became Mussolini's Minister of Education, declared: 'Young Fascists salute him [Croce] as their spiritual father, even if he, like many other fathers, does not want to recognize his sons.'[81] Indeed, until 1924, as G. A. Borgese writes, Croce 'had more or less heartily supported Fascism, and expected from it, somehow or other, the renovation of his country'.[82] And Mussolini had paid tribute to the 'clarity, sincerity and probity in research' which Croce had brought to his opposition to 'superficial positivism'.[83] Evidently positivism could be regarded as anti-fascist, while philosophical idealism vacillated, being presumably either consistently fascist or consistently anti-fascist; in short, the metaphysical tenet incorporated into the ideology was independent and arbitrary.

h. *Determinism and Historicism*

The books of Karl Popper have powerfully affected the philosophic

G. P. Adams and W. P. Montague, *Contemporary American Philosophy; Personal Statements*, Vol. II, New York, 1950, p. 85.

[81] Cf. Herbert L. Matthews, *The Fruits of Fascism*, New York, 1943, pp. 136–7.

[82] G. A. Borgese, *Goliath: The March of Fascism*, New York, 1937, p. 296.

[83] H. L. Matthews, op. cit., p. 136.

thought of the last twenty years. With much force Popper has argued that historicism since its beginnings has been a doctrine which eventuated in totalitarian political consequences; such, he maintained, was the lesson taught by the career of historicism from Plato to Marx, Lenin and Stalin. By historicism, Popper meant the doctrine that large-scale sociological laws can be known for societies as a whole so that one would be able to predict their future stages of evolution.[84] Historicism, as a species of sociological determinism, was said to have conditioned men's thoughts and feelings for submission to a closed society. The noted philosopher Isaiah Berlin wrote a vigorous essay against 'historical inevitability'. The moral outrages of Stalin's regime were associated in many people's minds with this dogma of sociological necessitarianism. If the horrors of the labor camps, the forced collectivization of the land, the judicial murder of the generation of old Marxists, were 'historically necessary', then it was historically meaningless to rail at their advent. The covert ethical principle of historicism was: Cooperate with the inevitable, or perish.

As an ideological tenet, however, historicism has had an oscillatory career, moving from left to right, and then after a voluntarist phase renewing its cyclical presence. Among the lay public and politicians as distinguished from the intellectuals, there is a certain lag in phases of philosophical fashion; for a time-interval is required for such changes to diffuse themselves through communication and education from intellectuals to laity. In any case, no sociological correlation binds historicism with totalitarian ideology. Indeed when liberal statesmen have wanted to speak in ideological language, they have averred the historical inevitability of the open society. Thus, in a memorable address on March 23, 1962, President John F. Kennedy counterposed a liberal historicism to the Marxist variety:

'Wisdom requires the long view. And the long view shows us that the revolution of national independence is a fundamental fact of our era. This revolution cannot be stopped . . .

[84] Professor Popper also argued that historicism tends to paralyze human initiative and action. Karl Popper, *The Open Society and its Enemies*, rev. ed., Princeton, 1950, p. 452.

'No one can doubt that the wave of the future is not the conquest of the world by a single dogmatic creed but the liberation of the diverse energies of free nations and free men. No one can doubt that cooperation in the pursuit of knowledge must lead to freedom of the mind and of the soul.'[85]

The historicist tenet diffused from the Marxist leftist to the liberal centrist to the conservative rightist. The conservative Republican leader Everett Dirksen, having guided the passage in the United States Senate of legislation for civil rights, was asked what had led him to do it. The Senator alluded to 'these forward thrusts' of history, and a statement of Victor Hugo's that 'no army can withstand the strength of an idea whose time has come'. The Senator said: 'It leads me to one conclusion: in the history of mankind, there is an inexorable moral force that moves us forward.'[86] Of course, this was an idealistic historicism rather than a materialistic one. The most diverse political standpoints, however, could avail themselves of the historicist tenet,—Kennedy's anti-Stalinism and Stalin's communism alike.

During the course of its career, furthermore, the doctrine of determinism moves from an activist emotional association to a passive emotional one. Determinism begins in a parricidal mood, as it decrees the end of old institutions and the triumph of the new; 'world-history is world-justice'. It ends, however, in a masochist mood, of resignation and submission under protest to a world one never made, with the consolation only that the men of evil are themselves only collections of events causally determined. When the latter stage is completed, the next generation of philosophers tends toward a return of voluntarism. The determinists of the French Revolution, as de Tocqueville observed in 1853, 'had an exaggerated and somewhat childish trust in the control which men and peoples were supposed to have of their own destinies. It was the error of those times; . . .' but then came 'the weary aftermath of revolutions, the miscarriage of so many generous ideas and of so

[85] *The New York Times*, 24 March, 1962.
[86] *The New York Times*, 20 June, 1964.

many great hopes . . .'[87] Whereupon the doctrine of determinism was conjoined with 'the opposite extreme . . . [N]ow we think we can do nothing; . . . This is really the great sickness of our age; . . .' Determinism begins by being revolutionary; it ends conservative. At that point, the search for a new philosophy begins. At first, the revolutionist, identifying with the determinist law of history, feels it confirms his Mosaic, messianic role; he sees himself the Agent of History and Existence, and his aggressive acts are sanctified.[88] Later comes the experience which the playwright-activist Georg Büchner described: 'I have been studying the history of the French Revolution. I felt myself crushed down under the ghastly fatalism of history. I find a horrible sameness in all human nature, . . . Individuals are so much surf on a wave, greatness the sheerest accident, the strength of genius a puppet play—a child's struggle against an iron law—the greatest of us can only recognize it, to control it is impossible. "Must" is the cursed word to which all human beings are born!'[89] Büchner had brooded over the saying of Danton and Vergniaud: 'The Saturn Revolution eats her own children.' And his determinism became post-revolutionary, masochist; perhaps the son destroyed the father, but only to be devoured himself.

Thus too in Britain, the Benthamite reformers were relatively optimistic determinists; Robert Owen looked forward to the achievement of the most basic changes in human nature through the reform of social institutions. By the latter part of the century, however, a gloom emanated from the determinist doctrine. It 'weighs like a nightmare, I believe, upon many of the best minds of these days', wrote Thomas Henry Huxley, for it banished 'spirit and spon-

[87] Alexis de Tocqueville, *'The European Revolution' and Correspondence with Gobineau*, tr. John Lukacs, New York, 1959, pp. 231–2.

[88] Leibniz observed: 'Even so do predictions often cause that to happen which has been foretold, as it is supposed that the opinions the Mahometans hold on fate makes them resolute.' Gottfried Wilhelm Leibniz, *Theodicy: essays on the goodness of Good, the freedom of man and the origin of evil*, tr. E. M. Huggard, London, 1951, p. 56.

[89] *The plays of Georg Büchner*, tr. Geoffrey Dunlop, Boston, 1927, p. 37. Also cf. Lewis Corey, 'The Vision of Heinrich Heine', *The New Leader*, Vol. XXXVI, 28 Sept. 1953, pp. 17–18.

taneity' from all human thought.[90] With determinism in its oppressive stage, the setting was prepared for a revival of voluntarism.

During the triumphant years of Naziism, old Marxists struggled to preserve the optimistic variant of sociological determinism. The most brilliant of the Central European Marxists, Otto Bauer, driven into exile, sought to affirm his faith in Marxist law: 'Though he slay me, . . .' The determinist doctrine, wrote Bauer, gave one 'the irreplaceable font of strength from which Socialist confidence issued'. Nothing else, he said, could inspire the underground parties in Fascist countries 'with unshakeable faith, with unbreakable will', based moreover, 'upon secure scientific knowledge'. His last book in 1937 still defended 'History's Iron Must'.[91] But when determinism was chiefly called on to explain one's own destruction by historical forces, the signal was transmitted to the next generation for the secession to a new philosophical tenet. Not that the old doctrine was logically refuted; rather its ideological users were exhausted and defeated. Even if determinism were true, the law of ideological cycles, reinforced in a declining phase by political defeat, decreed the doctrine's obsolescence.

A determinism–voluntarism cycle therefore characterizes the fluctuations of ideology, of socially moulded opinion. A thoroughgoing determinist like Emile Zola who had based his whole work as a novelist on that doctrine was thus aware as his last decade began that a new generational wave was rising of which he never would be part. He spoke in 1893 to the General Association of Students; aware of their malaise and striving, he wondered, 'with the youthful generation rising behind . . . What will become of our work in their hands, . . . My own generation was compelled to throw open brutally the window upon nature, . . . in accord with the long effort of the

[90] Thomas H. Huxley, *Methods and Results*, London, 1893, p. 160. Clarence Ayres, *Huxley*, New York, 1932, pp. 120–1. Also cf. Walter B. Houghton, *The Victorian Frame of Mind, 1830–1870*, New Haven, 1957, p. 337.
[91] Joseph Buttinger, *In the Twilight of Revolutionary Socialism; a history of the revolutionary socialists of Austria*, tr. E. B. Ashton, New York, 1953, p. 393.

positivistic philosophy, . . . I have been much the sectarian, . . . They
tell me that you are breaking away from us, recognizing moral and
social dangers in our tendencies, . . . You are undergoing a crisis,
the lassitude and revulsion of the end-of-the-century, after so fevered
a labor and so colossal, whose ambition it had been to know all, to
say all.' Zola's generation had declared with the critic Sainte-Beuve:
'Anatomists and physiologists, I find you everywhere.' But they had
written their Mosaic myth in the language of physiological determinism. For all the chemical hereditary mechanisms, Zola believed
'above all in a constant march toward truth', and he was a leader
in humanity's parade. 'The intellectual generation of the Second
Empire' had said with Renan: 'The world has no mysteries', and
with Taine that 'vice and virtue are chemical products like sugar
and vitriol'. But then on 18 August 1887, a generational revolt
arose against Determinism,—the 'Manifesto of the Five', directed
in the first place against Zola's naturalism. 'The rising generation',
it said, though mindful of Zola's achievement, 'the impetuous
breach made by the great novelist, the rout of the romantics', was
now however repelled by its consequences:- 'irrepressibly, disgust
spread, above all at the growing exaggeration of indecency, at the
filthy terminology of the Rougon-Macquart'.[92] The new generation
was resolutely anti-naturalistic and anti-deterministic. The romantic
metaphysics, indeed, was enjoying its cyclical, periodic revival. No
social, technological, or political developments can explain this
periodic movement, these recurrent waves of ideas. They are essentially inherent in the succession of generations.

America during the era between the two World Wars saw a
tremendous vogue of determinism. Hundreds of thousands of children were raised during the twenties on booklets which expounded
the proper methods of child-rearing according to the principles of
John B. Watson's deterministic behaviorism.[93] In the thirties determinism was part of the vogue of materialistic Marxism. When

[92] Matthew Josephson, *Zola and his Time*, New York, 1928, pp. 14,
378-9, 143, 117-18, 314, 355-7.
[93] Lucille C. Birnbaum, 'Behaviorism in the 1920's', *American
Quarterly*, Vol. III, (1955), pp. 18-29.

the First American Writers' Congress took place, 'the spiritual blacklisting of Sidney Hook' took place, according to one observer, because he rejected a 'deterministic logic to events'; Hook was an 'Arminian of the class struggle', a 'revolutionary free-willer', not a Calvinist.[94] The generational cycle terminated the prevalence of determinism after the Second World War.

i. Existentialism

The existentialist philosophy has probably influenced Western ideologies more than any other mode of thought during the twenty-five years after the end of the Second World War in 1945. The figure of Sören Kierkegaard, eccentric, haunted, detached, called by a few the 'Danish Socrates', virtually unknown in America for a hundred years, was recalled to philosophic significance in numerous articles and books. The thirties had been dominated by historical determinism; the influence of Marxism had ramified through every department of intellectual life; intellectuals spoke of 'systems', 'necessities', and 'inevitabilities'; the individual was an element in the system, a point of intersection of social forces, the ensemble of his social relations, as Marx said. As the war ended a new generation sought for a new emotion, the liberation of the individual from the trammels of system. Historical determinism had once seemed to bring a sense of heightened potency, of identification with triumphant forces of history. By the end of the thirties one might have said among the intellectuals and ideologists: 'We are all Marxists now'. And when this became true, an ideological generation was over. The situation was ripe for a new generational revolt in ideology.

To the new existentialists, there was at first a certain attractiveness in the very fact that Kierkegaard had been so indifferent to politics, a right winger, one might say. For Kierkegaard had denied any faith 'in the saving power of free institutions, obtained by political

[94] John Chamberlain, 'The Literary Left Grows Up', *The Saturday Review of Literature*, Vol. XII, No. 2, 11 May, 1935, pp. 4, 17.

E

means', and had avowed a 'suspicion' of them. He was no activist:
'I have never concerned myself with Church and State, these things
are too high for me, . . . I have never fought for the emancipation of
the Church, nor for the emancipation of women, or the Jews, or the
trade with Greenland.' Politics, he said, had nothing to do with
'eternal truth', and any political system which tried to bring the
eternal truth to bear upon actuality would, he wrote, 'prove itself to
be in the most eminent degree the most impolitic thing that can be
imagined'.[95] When existentialism became influential in pre-Nazi
and Nazi Germany, the metaphysical ideas it shared with Kierkegaard were soon employed to justify Nazi ideology. The rector of
the University of Freiburg, Martin Heidegger, promulgated the
decree in November, 1933, prohibiting awards to Jewish or Marxist
students, and giving 'special consideration' to students active as
storm troopers.[96]

During the Second World War, and the years that followed,
existentialism became a potent force among French intellectuals
especially from left to right. The previous Nazi involvements of the
doctrine scarcely perturbed the devoted existentialists. Such young
Parisian students as Jean-Paul Sartre and Simone de Beauvoir had
nurtured the doctrine during the thirties. Many of their generational
contemporaries were then rallying to Marxism, but Sartre and
Beauvoir stood aloof. The latter felt that 'it was our conditioning
as young *petit bourgeois* intellectuals that led us to believe ourselves
free of all conditioning whatsoever', and to reject the Marxist conception of the class determination of thinking and action.[97] But this
same petty bourgeois background in many cases provoked young
thinkers to adopt Marxism whole-heartedly. Clearly the causes for
the adherence of Sartre and Beauvoir to existentialist idealism were

[95] Cf., the citations from Kierkegaard in David F. Swenson, *Something about Kierkegaard*, ed. Lillian Marvin Swenson, Minneapolis,
1941, pp. 31–2.

[96] Raul Hilberg, ed., *Documents of Destruction: Germany and Jewry,
1933–1945*, Chicago, 1971, pp. 17–18.

[97] Simone de Beauvoir, *The Prime of Life*, tr. Peter Green, Cleveland,
1962, p. 22.

far more individual. They had 'a weakness for idealism', wrote Beauvoir; and Sartre, preferring the experienced reality of color to hypotheses about vibrations, disliking all general laws and concepts, was prepared to deny Science.[98] Then too his fellow student Raymond Aron brought the tidings from Germany of the 'phenomenological method': 'You see, my dear fellow, if you are a phenomenologist, you can talk about this cocktail and make philosophy out of it!'[99] Sartre turned pale at this revelation of an access to reality. It was only with the war and post-war years, however, that the philosophy became something of a generational creed. The philosophical cycle moved from a materialist to an idealist phase. Sartre felt early that in elaborating this philosophy he was fulfilling 'a duty to the "younger generation", and helping to obviate another "lost generation"; "the idea of the generations" concerned him, though he would accept a generational determinism as little as the class variant: 'One's generation forms part of one's given situation, like one's social class or nationality.'[100] There was no new argument or evidence which Sartre or Beauvoir advanced on behalf of their philosophical conception of freedom. They insisted that the experience of freedom was a given fact, that one's responsibility could not be evaded, that the human being always had alternatives from which to choose.[101] Determinists from Spinoza to Einstein have felt these experiences too; but they have not been able to forget, however, that the citations of personal experience were displaced by Copernicus and Galileo. What gave conviction however to the existentialist philosophy was what we might call the new 'generational postulate'. The determinist doctrine, which had enjoyed its vogue for a decade, seemed repressive, stifling; one had savored its historic sweep, but then one demanded that one's individual life affirm its reality, irreducible and apart from any Historical System.[102] Emotions craved a spontaneous rather than a regimented expression; the determinist vocabulary, which once seemed to fit the contours of concrete reality, now seemed abstract and lifeless. Left existentialists

[98] Ibid., p. 30.   [99] Ibid., p. 112.   [100] Ibid., p. 342.
[101] Raymond Aron, *Marxism and the Existentialists*, tr. Helen Weaver, New York, 1969, pp. 25-6.   [102] De Beauvoir, pp. 372-3, 435.

such as Sartre argued that the revolutionary experience itself, aiming in its consciousness to transcend social determinants, was incompatible with materialism. Right-wing existentialists on the other hand arose especially among those who had experienced the decline of the Marxist wave to its Stalinist nadir; to them authentic selfhood was to be re-discovered in social disaffiliation, and an Emersonian return to one's own spiritual life. The leading journal for intellectuals in the United States *Partisan Review* had begun its career in 1934 as a Marxist organ; in 1950 however, it published symposia on 'Religion and the Intellectuals', with an editorial noting that the significant tendency of our time, 'especially in this decade, has been the new turn toward religion among intellectuals and the growing disfavor with which secular attitudes and perspectives are now regarded . . .' And in the transition from the wings of Marxism to the wings of existentialism, with the repetitive distribution in the ideological spectrum from left to right, a law of alternating fashions was evidently at work: 'Intellectual fashions and fads are a matter we have all experienced, having all witnessed how these puffs of the *Zeitgeist* catch up the intellectuals for a decade or so only to let them down just as abruptly into disillusion and frustration.'[103]

3. THE PSYCHOLOGICAL BASIS FOR THE LAWS OF WINGS AND ALTERNATION OF IDEAS

Two principles have emerged from our brief history of the use of philosophical tenets by ideologies. We shall call them respectively the principle of wings, and the principle of the alternation of ideological tenets; the latter takes the form of a wave movement in the history of ideologies.

The principle of wings, as we have seen, affirms that every philosophic unit-idea in the course of its career makes the passage through the whole spectrum of ideological affiliations. A philosophical doctrine which begins at the left will move rightward, and if at the

[103] 'Religion and the Intellectuals: a Symposium', *Partisan Review*, Vol. XVII, (1950), pp. 103-4.

right, it will diffuse toward the left. In the course of its life-history, every philosophic standpoint and unit-idea will therefore be associated with contrary political standpoints. The time-period of this passage is the life-period of the given philosophical movement; from its point of origin with an insurgent generational group, the new emotional standpoint, the new perspective, the new imagery, the new metaphors and idioms spread to the more conventional sections of their own generation, then to their slightly older opponents and their relative elders. Thus, by the time that conservative Americans spoke of themselves as 'pragmatic', and virtually every American politician defined himself as a 'pragmatist', the word 'pragmatist' had become a cliché, and its span as a movement was done. A new insurgent generation would perforce have to explore novel emotions, images, and idioms in order to define its own independent character, its own 'revolutionary' aims against the elders. A new philosophical standpoint for the generation is then the order of the day. Thus, though the mythological structure of ideologies is invariant, the philosophical history of any given ideology, the succession in its sets of philosophical tenets conforms to an alternating wave pattern; the latter corresponds to the pattern which obtains in the overall intellectual history of the society.

The principle of wings sets forth the condition for the direction and completion of the wave of a philosophical movement as it moves through the ideological field. The principle of the alternation of philosophical tenets, on the other hand, enunciates a limiting condition for the pattern which the successor wave-movement will exhibit. We might describe this latter phenomenon as that of *generational counter-determination*. An emerging generation seeks to define itself in opposition to its predecessors; for example, young American intellectuals in the eighteen-twenties wanted to differentiate themselves in philosophy from the Lockean deists; they turned to transcendentalist idealism despite the conservative auspices under which it was first introduced in Coleridge's writings; innate ideas came back in fashion despite Locke's powerful polemic against them. But sheer counter-determination will not, however, fully account for the specific choice among philosophical tenets which is made. Every philosophy has at least several contraries. What determines which one among these contraries will evolve into the philosophy and ideology of the emerging generation? Another factor is involved which we might call the principle of the prime determining emotion. The next philosophical tenets will express those emotions which were most repressed by the previous philosophical scheme.

To explain: Every philosophical tenet, as it is held at a given time, represses some component in the human psyche. Determinism represses our desire for spontaneity; voluntarism is at odds with our desire for orderly explanation; empiricism represses the impulses to fantasy and world-creation; mysticism with its vague compenetrations offends our common sense of a reality of separated objects. Every philosophical tenet, if held consequentially, represses some emotional longing; that repressed emotional need, which by virtue of social circumstances in the life of the emerging generation, has been most dramatically ignited in its unconscious, will tend to become the prime determinant in the choice among successive contrary tenets.

The wave movements in ideological tenets are in their underlying logic not unlike the wave phenomena in the physical world. Underlying every such phenomenon are the elastic properties of objects, their reactions to strains and deformations, the operation of restorative forces. And every phenomenon of ideological waves is likewise the outcome of restorative forces of the human emotions, asserting themselves against the deformations imposed by an ideological tenet. The longing for free will wells up against the constraining determinist dogma; and if determinism has provided an ideologically aligned doctrine, that tenet must be abandoned or reconstructed; thus determinist Marxism is superseded by existentialist, voluntarist Marxism. No combination of philosophical tenets with its corresponding set of repressed and expressed emotions is ever in a state of stable equilibrium. The nature and development of the human psyche itself implies that every intellectual system will have its locus of instability defined by recalcitrant emotions. The Promethean determinist at the outset, enjoying an identification with a law of history which underwrites the downfall of those whom he hates and the triumph of himself and his comrades, finally becomes ill at ease with his own ideology; he longs for the restored sense of making his own law, choosing his own way. Thus one reaches too the generational source in the alternation of current ideas. The new generation always associates a received ideology with an indoctrination which is partially repressive; it has had none of the experiences which to its elders gave the ideology its liberative character; nowhere, moreover, does the ideology bear the stamp of the generations' own choice.

Why then, as William James asked, does 'every would-be universal formula, every system of philosophy' finally receive its 'inevitable critical volley from one-half of mankind', and then 'falls to the rear, to become at the very best the creed of some partial sect?' Because, answered James, either its net has left out something of the facts of nature, or has inflicted inconsistencies on our understanding, 'or else finally it has left some one or more of our fundamental active and emotional powers with no object outside of themselves to react-on or to live for'. Thus, noted James, 'from generation to generation' the sequence of philosophies perdures; when empiricism, for instance, runs dry in an emotional sense, it is replaced by 'generous idealism'; then . . . [104]

The component of repressed emotion, associated with every philosophical tenet, is obviously the crucial one in the history of ideology. We might call it the source of 'Jamesian waves' in the history of ideology. It is founded on one psychological postulate: that the goals and longings of human emotions do not constitute a consistent system; men are driven by both love and aggression; they alternate between competitive drives and cooperative aspirations; they seek both autonomy and self-donation; they hold fast to material interests even as they long for transcendent ideals. No ideological doctrine can satisfy these incompatible vectors, unless some powerful emotions have been super-added to repress partially one of them. But the repressed element always presses for an overhauling of the ideology. When is an ideology described as a dogma? When, having ceased to

[104] William James, *The Will to Believe and other Essays in Popular Philosophy*, New York, 1897, pp. 125, 128.

be the vehicle of rebellious feelings, it has become in turn experienced principally as a device of the previous generation for the repression of rejected emotions. The dogma is the revolutionary ideological doctrine of the past generation.

4. PERIODIC MOVEMENTS IN IDEOLOGY

The history of ideologies is thus a continuous document of a periodic, wave movement. Take, for instance, the sequence of the dominant intellectual fashions in the United States. A form of deistic materialism prevailed (with fluctuations) from about 1775 to 1815; then an idealistic reaction began, lasting from 1825 to 1860, with transcendentalism as its primary expression. Deistic materialism, one might say, was the Jeffersonian ideology of the American Revolution; idealistic transcendentalism that of the New England reformers in the pre-Civil War era. The post-Civil War years saw a recrudescence of materialism. The tenets of free will and the Oversoul were excess baggage in that era, despite the fact that powerful individuals were fashioning America's first industrial empires. Herbert Spencer, William Graham Sumner, John Fiske, deterministic evolutionists, with small regard for the efficacy of individual decisions, expressed the new temper. Then William James, toward the century's end, led the attack on the block universe and the large-scale impersonal determinism; the individual's will to believe also included a faith in his own freedom; the first act of freedom was to believe in freedom itself. This unit-idea, quite distinct from his pragmatism, was something like an American ideology, a philosophical basis for the New Freedom, a metaphysical counterpart to the political leadership of Theodore Roosevelt and Woodrow Wilson.[105] But with the end of the First World War, a new materialism became influential. Behaviorism, obliterating the individual psyche, became the fashion during the twenties, and in the thirties, materialism took a more leftward direction with the dominance of Marxism as the ideology of revolution. The years after the Second World War, as we have

[105] H. G. Wells, *Experiment in Autobiography*, New York, 1934, pp. 648–9.

seen, brought an idealistic revival in existentialist form. Thus, cyclical movement has characterized the evolution of American ideologies, with each intellectual wave having a period of roughly thirty years.

In France the fluctuations of ideology showed a similar cyclical pattern. The romantic movement, with its metaphysical striving for the infinite, its utopianism, and defiant affirmation of the individual will, was dominant during the eighteen-thirties and forties. The Revolution of 1848 was indeed its high political maximum; its decline proceeded rapidly after the class civil war of the June days and the failure of the political ministry of the romantic poet Lamartine.[106] Determinism then became the ideological fashion; Taine was its spokesman. A generation of determinism in social analysis, however, was a desiccating experience, even to Taine himself who wrote in 1892 toward the end of his life that he had 'probably made a mistake twenty years ago in undertaking this series of investigations; they are darkening my old age, . . .'[107] Others felt their lives thus darkened, and their manifesto of freedom came in 1889 with the novel by Paul Bourget, *Le Disciple*. Significantly Bergson's voluntaristic writings began too at this time. We need not recapitulate the subsequent Marxist materialist and existentialist waves.

The wave movements in ideology cannot be given a convincing explanation in terms of the 'logical' requirements of the novel social situation. Take, for instance, the development of transcendentalism. '[T]he younger generation of New England intellectuals naturally opened their eyes to discover what winds of new doctrine were blowing in the world', writes V. F. Parrington. They found John Locke's philosophy arid. Yet Locke's doctrines had inspired Thomas

[106] J. Salwyn Schapiro, 'Lamartine: A Study of the Poetic Temperament in Politics', *Political Science Quarterly*, Vol. 34, (1919), pp. 639–642.

[107] H. Taine, *Sa Vie et Sa Correspondance*, Tome IV, Paris, 1907, p. 338. Cited in Irving Babbitt, *The Masters of Modern French Criticism*, Boston, 1912, p. 246. Harry W. Paul, 'The Debate over the Bankruptcy of Science in 1895', *French Historical Studies*, Vol. V, No. 3, (1968), pp. 299–327.

Jefferson in the writing of the Declaration of Independence, and Jefferson, too, like the young Emerson, had found repugnant the Calvinist reiteration of the evil in man. There was no political, social, or moral reform that the transcendentalists advocated which could not have been phrased in the Lockean–Jeffersonian materialist language. But Emerson shuddered at the 'pale negations' of this doctrine. The Lockean doctrine of sensationalism was associated with the frozen, lifeless, mechanistic derivations in ideology of Condillac, and the Voltairean mockery at the human soul. The new young elite required a new set of philosophical tenets in which to formulate its ideology of the moral leadership of the American scholar.

To such a fully informed and wise observer as W. H. Channing, the rise of Transcendentalism in New England in 1839 'was as mysterious as that of any form of revival'. It was at once a reaction against 'materialists', 'Sceptics', and the 'Puritan orthodoxy'. The Transcendentalist 'gave himself up to the embrace of nature's beautiful joy, as a babe seeks the breast of a mother'. The Transcendentalists were 'critics and "come-outers" from the old'. 'The past might well be enough for those who . . . could yet put faith in common dogmas, . . . but for them the matin-bells of a new day were chiming, . . . The journal, the letter, became of greater worth than the printed page, . . . the "Newness" lifted her veil to her votaries . . . Thus, by mere attraction of affinity, grew together the brotherhood of the "Like-minded," . . .'[108] In this imagery of the young conquering the old, and recapturing the mother's nakedness, Channing described the movement which began in 1836 when four young Unitarian clergymen, Emerson, Hedge, Ripley, and Putnam meeting in Cambridge, shared their rebellious thoughts.[109] Their circle grew into 'The Transcendental Club', perhaps America's first society of intellectuals, or we might say, ideologists. It was clearly a movement of the young.

A leading spirit among the young Transcendentalists, James

[108] W. H. Channing, in *Memoirs of Margaret Fuller Ossoli*, Vol. II, Boston, 1852, pp. 12–14.
[109] Thomas Wentworth Higginson, *Margaret Fuller Ossoli*, p. 142.

Freeman Clarke, described how his revolt against the eighteenth-century materialists arose from obscure generational emotions rather than from logical considerations. 'The books of Locke, Priestley, Hartley, and Belsham were in my grandfather Freeman's library, and the polemic of Locke against innate ideas was one of my earliest philosophical lessons. But something within me revolted at all such attempts to explain soul out of sense, deducing mind from matter, . . .' He read a copy of Coleridge which had been published in his senior year. 'Then I discovered that I was born a transcendentalist; . . .' The generation of the American Revolution had been stirred by the reductive polemics of Locke and Priestley against idealistic notions such as innate ideas. Their descendants in 1830 found these polemics arid and unconvincing. '(A) certain enthusiastic expectation . . . at that time quickened the lives of all young people in New England.' A new generational postulate was in the making. The young New Englanders 'rushed into life, certain that the next half century was to see a complete moral revolution in the world . . . They were not quite sure what they were to do about it, but they knew that something was to be done. And no one rightly writes or reads the life of one of these young men or women, unless he fully appreciates the force of this enthusiastic hope.'[110] Thus the gestation of a new ideology took place in the womb of a new emotion of generational rebellion and self-definition.

In all these cases, the longing for a new generational philosophy arises after the previous doctrine has traversed the spectrum from left to right. In New England, Locke's philosophy, once the doctrine of ideologists in the American Revolution, had meanwhile become the philosophy of the well-established financial class and a conservative Unitarianism. In England, when Humean empiricism in Mill's formulations had passed from the aristocracy to the people's agitators of the left, the upper classes, hitherto Humean, felt the time had come for a new philosophy; idealism then became the fashion, and refutations of Mill from the idealist standpoint were welcomed. As

---

[110] James Freeman Clarke, *Autobiography, Diary and Correspondence*, ed. Edward Everett Hale, Boston, 1891, pp. 39, 87.

Mill wrote: 'Hume's scepticism agreed very well with the comfortable classes, until it began to reach the uncomfortable.'[111] With the empiricist tenets put to a leftist ideological use, the upper classes then realized that 'although men could be content to be rich without a faith, men would not be content to be poor without it, and religion and morality came into fashion again as the cheap defence of rent and tithes'. Yet as we have seen every doctrine is multipotential in its ideological use. The leaders of the laborite and trade unionist agitation were often the lay preachers in Methodist chapels, while the ideologically complaisant would be factual-minded empiricists, regarding socialistic ideals as verbal bubbles.[112]

5. THE LAWS OF WINGS AND ALTERNATION IN SOVIET IDEOLOGY

The alternation of philosophical tenets, the normal generational wave of ideas, can be dampened in a dictatorial, totalitarian society. In the Soviet universities and institutes, dialectical materialism alone is the permitted ideology. Powerful mechanisms of control, supervision, and censorship are used to prevent other philosophies from

[111] John Stuart Mill, *Essays on Ethics, Religion and Society*, Toronto, 1969, p. 80.

[112] 'The Methodist, whatever his shortcomings became a man of earnestness, sobriety, industry, and regularity of conduct ... It is these men who, in the mining villages, have stood out as men of character, gaining the respect of their fellows. From the very beginning of the Trade Union Movement among the mines, of the Co-operative Movement among all sections of the wage-earners, of the formation of Friendly Societies and of the late attempts at Adult Education, it is men who are Methodists, and in Durham County especially the local preachers of the Primitive Methodists, whom we find taking the lead and filling the posts of influence. From their ranks have come an astonishingly large proportion of the Trade Union leaders, ... They swarm on Co-operative and Friendly Society committees. They furnish today in the country, most of the working-class Justices of the Peace and Members of the House of Commons.' And the Methodist preponderant influence held as well for the 'silent solid membership of every popular movement in the country'. Sidney Webb, *The Story of the Durham Miners (1662–1921)*, London, 1921, p. 23.

arising. Yet despite the machinery of repression, the laws of ideological wings and alternation express themselves. Though all do obeisance to the official Marxist vocabulary, different factions, only tenuously joined, press their distinctive perspectives through the proper choices among Marxist texts. The young, often drawn to Western existentialism, have an avid interest in Marx's early writings, 'when Marx was not a Marxist', as an elder professor said; the young Marx wrote of freedom of the press and the alienation of man. A group of scientific realists, usually somewhat older, emphasize the fact that Lenin defined materialism as solely the belief in the reality of the external world; through the notion of truth as the correspondence of perceptions to external realities, they introduce such contemporary notions as isomorphism in structure. Also there are young pragmatists and positivists, often friendly to American democracy, who link dialectical materialism to Dewey, Peirce, and the logical empiricists. Curiously in the Soviet context, the spectrum takes one from the existentialists on the left to technocratic realists on the right.

For the generational alternation of ideas has now made philosophical idealism into a tenet of the emerging young Soviet dissidents. It would be possible, abstractly speaking, for the latter to present their demands within the Marxist framework, by using such notions as 'the withering away of the state'. But the old Marxist vocabulary has become tedious, lifeless, formalistic; in short, it is the idiom of a past generation, and its words, learned in the established schools, will never have the stamp of one's own emotional discovery, revolt, and self-definition. and since all the wings of materialism have been exhausted, the new dissidents make the radical break with materialism; philosophical idealism, a philosophy that only very old grandfathers can remember, experiences a rebirth. Whereas the official materialism held that there are no universal moral principles, the new Left Idealism holds that there are ethical truths eternally valid for all human beings in terms of which they can judge actions of the Soviet regime as evil. The social system ceases to be the arbiter, ordained by historical materialism, of conceptions of right and wrong, good and evil. The writers of *samizdat*, the literature of the underground, cite Pascal, Kant, Bergson, and the Book of Job; Solzhenitsyn and Sinyavsky set forth religious standpoints toward reality.[113] Thus the alternation of ideas asserts itself once more in Russian thought, as idealism struggles to revive despite the oppressive official materialism.

6. THE LAW OF WINGS IN ANCIENT IDEOLOGY: THE CASE OF STOICISM

The evolution of an ideology in modern times usually moves rapidly through the spectrum of wings. In ancient times the drift from left to right took place much more slowly. No philosophical tenets in antiquity had so unusual a political history as did those of Stoicism. When it was first expounded by its founder, Zeno of Citium, known as the 'Phoenician', it was a doctrine of determinism, 'an endless chain of causation', which was preordained however to culminate in a cosmopolitan, socialistic world-society.[114] The youthful Alexander the Great with his sense of an imperial mission was believed to be trying to realize the ideas of Zeno: thus he endeavored to be 'a mediator for the whole world', bringing together 'into one body all men everywhere', mixing them 'in great loving-cups, . . . men's lives, their marriages, their very habits of life'.[115] As Alexander's

---

[113] Lewis S. Feuer, 'U.S.S.R.: The Intelligentsia in Opposition', *Problems of Communism*, Vol. XIX, No. 6. Nov. Dec. 1970, pp. 10–13.

[114] As Plutarch describes it, Zeno in his *Republic* had set forth his political conception: 'all the inhabitants of this world of ours should not live differentiated by their respective rules of justice into separate cities and communities, but that we should consider all men to be of one community and one polity, and that we should have a common life and an order common to us all, even as a herd that feeds together and shares the pasturage of a common field. This Zeno wrote, giving shape to a dream or, as it were a shadowy picture of a well-ordered and philosophic commonwealth, . . .' *Plutarch's Moralia*, Vol. IV, tr. Frank Cole Babbitt, Cambridge, Mass., 1936, pp. 397–9. Diogenes Laertius, *Lives of Eminent Philosophers*, tr. R. D. Hicks, Vol. II, Cambridge, Mass., 1931, pp. 113, 137, 141.

[115] *Plutarch's Moralia*, op. cit., p. 399. Cf. W. W. Tarn, *Alexander the Great*, Vol. I, Cambridge, 1948, pp. 146–8.

empire collapsed, Stoics became the ideologists of the youthful left wing which nourished socialistic dreams. A Stoic philosopher, Sphaerus, a pupil of Zeno himself, was the ideological guide of the legendary effort of the king Cleomenes to restore communism in Sparta. Blossius, another Stoic philosopher, was adviser to the noble-hearted Tiberius Gracchus, who sought to reinstate agrarian equality in the Roman Republic while making it the ruler of the world.[116]

Revolutionary Left Stoicism was gradually transformed under the Roman Empire into an Imperial Bureaucratic Right Stoicism. The doctrine of determinism and the notion that reason regulated all, still persisted, but their ideological consequence was altered from one of revolutionary effort to acquiescence to the imperial despotism. And Stoic ideology, which had been philo-Semitic with Zeno and Alexander, became the ideology of anti-Semites in Roman times. Such was the life-cycle, or shall one say the death-cycle, in accordance with which Stoicism moved from the left to the right. By the time of Vespasian, it had evolved into an ideology of aristocratic elitism, the basis for the demand of the nobility that Rome be governed by the Senatorial class; the emperor retaliated by expelling all the philosophers (that is, ideologists) from Rome. An alienated, unreconciled Stoic opposition persisted under Nero, but the doctrine was transformed from an optimistic to a pessimistic determinism. Zeno's immense hope was replaced by the melancholy of Seneca, Nero's minister, who in studying 'the causes of individual sadness' wrote: 'one is sometimes seized by hatred of the whole human race'.[117] The early Stoics had been confident in the strength of the senses as conduits to knowledge; the later Stoics saw only their weakness and unreliability. Meanwhile, however, large numbers of the educated Roman Stoic youth were entering the service of the imperial bureaucracy. They renounced their elders' opposition, pursued their careers; by 96 A.D. a bureaucratic Stoicism became 'the recognized creed of

[116] Tenney Frank, *Roman Imperialism*, New York, 1914, p. 248.
Plutarch, *The Lives of the Noble Grecians and Romans*, tr. John Dryden, Modern Library ed., New York, pp. 973, 998.
[117] Seneca, 'On Tranquillity of Mind', in *Moral Essays*, tr. John W. Basore, Cambridge, Mass., 1935, Vol. II, p. 273.

the great majority of the educated classes at Rome, of all ages and ranks'.[118] It became the official imperial ideology much as dialectical materialism did in the Soviet Union but in so doing placed the emphasis on accommodation to the powerful order; the admonition of Epictetus expressed the new resignation: 'Do not seek to have everything happen as you desire but desire that they happen as they actually do happen.'[119] As zealous official ideologists became the spokesmen for Soviet anti-Semitism, so did Stoic ideologists, particularly in Alexandria, where Apion and Chaeremon polemicized against the Jews and Judaism.[120] Perhaps the principle of wings governed the history of ideologists according to a determinist pattern; Zeno the Phoenician might have wondered whether Reason ruled the world through its workings.

[118] E. Vernon Arnold, *Roman Stoicism*, Cambridge, 1911, pp. 144, 396–7, 401–2.

[119] Anthony Birley, *Marcus Aurelius*, London, 1966, p. 133.

[120] Norman Bentwich, *Philo-Judaeus of Alexandria*, Philadelphia, 1910, reprinted 1948, pp. 63–4.

CHAPTER III

The Generational Basis for Ideological Waves

I. GENERATIONAL REVOLT AS THE SOURCE FOR IDEOLOGICAL REVOLT: THE CYCLE OF THE NEW WAVE AND DE-IDEOLOGIZATION

An ideological wave always has its first followers among the young. The doctrine itself is often formulated by an elder thinker who stands in the relation of a 'master-intellectual', or 'youth-master', or 'father-figure' to the young. But it is young intellectuals who feel the need for ideology, for its assignment to them of a historic mission, for its charter of an opportunity to define themselves and their own ideas in rupture with the old. When Engels defined 'ideology', he said it was a mode of thought in which the impelling motives remained unknown to the thinker; these unconscious, impelling motives, he claimed, were in the last analysis, economic; hence, he said, ideology was a type of 'false consciousness'.[1] To which we might reply: that ideological thinking arises primarily not from an economic unconscious but a generational unconscious. Its underlying aim is to provide the dramatic outline, the myth, (the 'scenario' it is now called),[2] for its dethronement of the elders, (now Establishment figures), and for the coming to power of the new generation as an intellectual elite; the more reluctant the ideologists are to avow their latent goal, namely, the hegemony of the younger generational intellectuals the more do they stress their manifest goal, the historic mission of the class, race, or nation; and a variety of philosophical tenets, contemporaneously fashionable or coming to be so, are used to provide the metaphysical basis for the deduction' of the ideological conclusions. Immanuel Kant had an

---

[1] Marx and Engels, *Basic Writings on Politics and Philosophy*, p. 408.
[2] Walter Lippmann, with his expression 'Great Scenario', was evidently the innovator of this usage. Cf. *A Preface to Morals*, New York, 1929, p. 115.

F

elaborate stage-machinery for a 'transcendental deduction' of the categories of the understanding; every ideologist today has what might be called an 'ideological deduction' of the 'mission' of his generational elite and their appointed carrier class.

The first condition for a sound scientific hypothesis is that it must fit, or explain simply, the uniformities of the phenomena in question. Often these uniformities will not have been observed until the hypothesis is formulated. The hypothesis we are proposing explains certain overriding facts: every birth or revival of an ideology is borne by a new generational wave: in its experience, each such new intellectual generation feels everything is being born anew, that the past is meaningless, or irrelevant, or non-existent; hence also the periodic recurrence and vogue of the word 'new'. It began with the young Transcendentalists in 1841 who preferred to call their era 'the Period of the Newness'.[3] During the last half-century every ten years or so the younger generational elite has engaged in an ideological revolt, defining its mission and newness, excoriating the old, and founding its new magazines.

The New Republic, for instance, was such a generational organ in 1914. It propounded a New Psychology, a New History, a New Anthropology, a New Philosophy, a New Criticism.[4] A more established journal *The Dial* recorded the new phenomenon on 1 November 1914 in an editorial entitled aptly 'The Younger Generation':

'The younger generation has been slow to declare itself in America. Persons of an equable cynicism deny its existence . . .', but it was doubted neither by 'the young poets who imagine they have invented "poly-rhythmics", nor the young idealists who believe that the Industrial Workers of the World are about to establish the only true democracy . . . Just now the names of several able young men are linked by the announcement of a weekly paper, "The New Republic", which proposes to criticize politics, education, and the

[3] Anna Mary Wells, *Dear Preceptor: The Life and Times of Thomas Wentworth Higginson*, Boston, 1963, p. 36.

[4] William Wasserstrom, *The Time of the Dial*, Syracuse, 1963, pp. 2, 73.

arts . . . Mr. Croly [its editor] would say that in America we have no tradition of free intellectual discussion. The newspapers, the magazines, and even the universities are afraid of the public; their concern not to offend the majority commits them to the accepted view and prohibits iconoclasm. The result is that the younger generation faces not only all the handicaps it everywhere suffers, but also a well-supported taboo. The older generation holds all the vantage-points—the editorships, the professional chairs, the official positions —which have naturally fallen to it. That is a matter of course. But its success in suppressing the militant minority is peculiarly American . . . The question whether that bitter statement of the case is any more true of the United States than it is of England or of Russia is perhaps irrelevant. There is enough truth in it to give it poignancy . . . The spectacle of youth struggling to give itself is sometimes comic; but it is always a moving and . . . a significant spectacle.'[5] *The Dial* bade welcome to the new generational organs: *The New Republic, The Masses, The New Review, The International.*

The Seven Arts, a journal of the younger generation, in an article in 1916 by Van Wyck Brooks pondered the historic significance of 'Young America in the nineteenth century. It was the 'watchword of the new generation—Young Germany, Young Italy, Young Ireland', always purporting to represent 'a warm, humane, concerted and more or less revolutionary protest against whatever incubus of crabbed age . . .'[6] During the war years, however, a process of 'de-ideologization' took place among most of the pre-war young intellectuals. A roughly ten-year wave was completed; the ideology which had presided magisterially over their dreams withered into phrases like dry leaves. Almost all the leading socialist intellectuals discarded their ideology,—Walter Lippmann, John Spargo, W. J. Ghent, William English Walling, Robert Hunter,

[5] 'The Younger Generation', *The Dial*, Vol. LVII, (1 Nov. 1914), pp. 313–14. Also cf. Nicholas Joost, *Years of Transition: The Dial 1912–1920*, Barre, Mass., 1967, p. 42.

[6] Van Wyck Brooks, *The Early Years; a selection from his works, 1908–1921*, ed. Claire Sprague, New York, 1968, p. 163.

Charles Edward Russell, Robert Rives La Monte. The last named described the process in 1917:

'Most of us have realized at least subconsciously that we were at heart dreamers. And here was the irresistible strength of the appeal materialistic Marxism made to us. It gave or appeared to give us an absolutely scientific foundation for our romantic dreams. And so we eagerly and blithely swallowed whole Marxism—or whatever weird grotesque conception of Marxism we were able to form . . . We created fantasies that bore little or no resemblance to anything that ever was on sea or land, . . .'[7]

The process of de-ideologization, a counterpart of de-mythologization, characterizes the last years of the downward path of an ideological wave. But an emerging newer generation of intellectuals will hardly wish to define itself in terms of the de-ideologized phase of its predecessors. It embarks on its quest for a novel ideology. The postwar generation founded its new organs, such magazines as *transition, Broom, Secession*; in Greenwich Village a league of youth came into being in revolt against both puritanism and capitalism,— the symbiotic union of bohemian and radical. This new group was extremely generation-conscious, 'conscious of the difference between two generations', wrote Malcolm Cowley; the 'we' were those who had come after the war, while the 'they' antedated 1917.[8] This became a 'lost generation' because it failed to find a carrier class which would give credence to its myth. Scarcely anybody would listen to their anti-capitalist sermons; they felt themselves 'alien in the commercial world'; denied any political influence, they fell back on the Greenwich Village creed of personal free-expression, living for the moment and shocking the middle class. As a 'lost generation', that is, an ideological elite without a cohort of followers, some went into European exile to nurse the wound of their rejection.[9] They then

[7] Robert Rives La Monte, 'Socialists and War', *The Class Struggle*, Vol. I, July–August, 1917, p. 60.

[8] Malcolm Cowley, *Exile's Return: A Literary Odyssey of the 1920's*, 1934, Compass Books Ed., New York, 1956, pp. 4, 6, 9, 60, 66, 72.

[9] An article by Van Wyck Brooks in *The Freeman* on 10 August 1921, entitled 'Our Lost Intransigeants' told of this 'latest American

attributed their lostness to a disillusionment with the post-war world which had betrayed the ideals for which the World War had been fought.

Not dissimilar was the search for a new ideology which moved the younger generation in Britain at this time. It too was marked by a desire to de-authoritize the old, to show that they had betrayed the young. Often such a search is characterized by the discovery of one old man, the presumable exception among his generation who, despite temptation, remained uncorrupted; he heralds the new; he becomes, as we have mentioned, their 'master-intellectual'. Thus, for a while, John Maynard Keynes, with his book *Economic Consequences of the Peace*, 'gave enormous encouragement to a generation of idealistic undergraduates', wrote Kingsley Martin, later editor of *The New Statesman and Nation*. 'Most of us were pacifists of one sort or another, angry with the "wicked old men", ...'; Martin's friends were 'most of us young intellectuals who above all hated the wicked old men who we felt were responsible for the war and for the deaths of so many of our school friends'. When Keynes's book seemed to place him 'outside the financial and political Establishment, it made him a hero of the Left, ...' The later eminent Leftist editor was clear as to the generational roots for his ideological search: 'My father became less personalized, as it were. I was fighting the Establishment.'[10] Keynes, however, turned to the writing of *A Treatise on Money*, and rejecting Marxism and Communism, offered British intellectuals in the twenties no fresh vision. The Fabian Webbs at this time were attuned to a generational cycle which entailed alternating ideological phases. 'Now, on which side of us are you young people coming up now?', said Beatrice Webb to John Strachey in 1923. 'We notice ("the we" was always royal) that first a generation of young intellectuals comes up well to the left of us and then the next generation comes up well to the right of us.

generation of "young intellectuals" '. Cf. Van Wyck Brooks, *The Early Years*, p. 237.

[10] Kingsley Martin, *Father Figures: a first volume of autobiography 1897–1931*, London, 1966, pp. 100, 102, 188.

Now where are you, Mr. Strachey?'[11] By the thirties, John Strachey had very definitely taken up the Marxist Communist ideology. He was for several years the 'master-intellectual' of the Left in America, leading them in the revival of Marxist ideology, with which the Stalinist era began in the early thirties. His book, *The Coming Struggle for Power*, was the most influential ideological book among young American intellectuals at that time.[12]

In the early thirties, a generational division appeared in the ranks of the editors and writers of *The New Republic*, still the leading organ of American intellectuals. The younger were drawn to ideology; the elders were de-ideologized. 'The young men in the circle of *The New Republic*, unlike the older, cool-headed fellows..., were impatient for the coming of the Revolution; they talked of it, dreamed of it.' There was a contrast in 1931 and 1932 between such men as Felix Frankfurter, later Justice of the United States Supreme Court, and the ' "wild literary young men" ' in that circle, wrote Matthew Josephson, such as himself; the elders were planning to vote for the regular Democratic candidate for the presidency, while the younger ideologists were supporting the Communist candidate. What was paramount, wrote Josephson in July 1932, was 'to take the side of the extremists, the activists of all kinds, who may shake our inert society to awakening'.[13]

By mid-1935, the word 'revolution' had become a master-symbol of the new ideological generation. To be listened to on any subject,— whether in politics, morals, art, or science, one's stance had to be

---

[11] John Strachey, *The Strangled Cry and other unparliamentary papers*, London, 1962, pp. 185–6. Also Martin, op. cit., p. 114.

[12] Strachey's 'very trenchant essay... that season was the favorite reading of American and British intellectuals'. Matthew Josephson, *Infidel in the Temple: A Memoir of the Nineteen-Thirties*, New York, 1967, p. 315. The book 'was at the time the proverbial Bible of the more intellectually pretentious communists'. Charles Angoff, *The Tone of the Twenties and Other Essays*, South Brunswick, 1966, p. 233. 'Bertrand Russell once asked Strachey: "why are you a socialist? Did you hate your father, your childhood, or your Public school?" ' Strachey replied, ... "a little bit of all three." ' Hugh Thomas, *John Strachey*, London, 1973, p. 36.

[13] Matthew Josephson, *Infidel in the Temple*, pp. 103–4, 250.

that of 'revolution'. The poet Archibald MacLeish observed that year:

'The current literary fashion is The Revolution. And publishers have accepted it not only with enthusiasm but with a scientific objectivity which borders on the naive. That is to say that gentlemen who never met a communist in their lives . . ., members of the Union Club in solvent standing, have turned out books that fairly sizzle on the press.' For 'the publishers will follow the fashion . . . [O]ne has the sense that book shops take the hat shops for their models. The stylish numbers fill the windows . . . The Revolution rests upon a concept, in its essence poetic to the highest degree—the concept of mass destiny—of inevitable social overthrow—of the fatal preferment of an oppressed and exploited class.'[14]

'Revolution' went into a downward phase after the Second World War. In 1960 its value on the Ideological Exchange began anew to reach unprecedented levels.

2. THE POWER OF THE GENERATIONAL CIRCLE IN COMPELLING IDEOLOGICAL CONVERSION

The power of a spreading generational fashion in ideas, the sheer attractive force of the emotions and behavior of one's co-generationists, the desire to be one of them, to share their experiences and comradeship, to be part of the league of youth,—this power overwhelms intellectual resistances, shatters reservations and qualifications; through the generational unconscious, the network of emotional bonds shared by those of a common age and with a common experience against the elders, it turns scientists and philosophers into ideologists. The thinker surrenders his rational, independent response; rather repress one's independent judgment than cease to be one of the collectivity. The young Karl Marx, for instance, spontaneously and instinctively rejected the Hegelian tenets. But his independent judgment could not withstand the power of the ideological fashion among his co-generationists. He wrote his father in 1837 how the Hegelian philosophy made him sick when he studied it, how he detested it, and found it 'unpleasing':

[14] Archibald MacLeish, 'The Writer and Revolution', *The Saturday Review of Literature*, Vol. XI, (Jan. 26, 1935), pp. 441-2.

'I had read fragments of the Hegelian philosophy, and had found its grotesque craggy melody unpleasing. I wished to dive into the ocean once again ...

'I set myself to the main task, a philosophico-dialectical discussion of the godhead, ... My last thesis was the beginning of the Hegelian system, (... even I myself can now scarcely make head or tail of it), this darling child of mine, nurtured in moonshine, bears me like a false-hearted siren into the clutches of the enemy.' The young Karl Marx was then 'overwhelmed with vexation', 'for several days quite unable to think', 'like a lunatic'. He disliked the Hegelian doctrine intensely, finding it vapid and unreal, not unlike the reaction of his contemporary John Stuart Mill who regarded everything metaphysical that Hegel ever wrote as 'sheer nonsense'.[15] But the Hegelian philosophy was the common platform of the Doktorklub, the society of young students, instructors, and intellectuals at the University of Berlin to which Karl Marx belonged. They were Young Hegelians, and spoke its idiom; to it belonged his 'most intimate friend', the student activist and jail alumnus, Adolf Rutenberg. Marx read Hegel 'from beginning to end'; his rational resistances were strong, and he first hoped to 'escape' this 'contemporary philosophy'; in the struggle of his reason against the generational irrationality, he became ill: 'because of the futility of my lost labors, from intense vexation at having to make an idol of a view I detested, I fell sick, ...' He burnt his poems and sketches for novels; he hardened himself for enrolling as a Hegelian in contravention of his innermost feelings: 'a frenzy of irony had taken possession of me, as was natural enough after so many negations ... I could not rest until I had purchased modernity ...'[16]

[15] Georg Brandes, *Creative Spirits of the Nineteenth Century*, tr. Rasmus B. Anderson, New York, 1923, p. 194. Mill wrote in 1867 that he had 'found by actual experience of Hegel that conversancy with him tends to deprave one's intellect'. He hoped that 'the whole of German metaphysics' could be blotted out so as to prevent the waste of an immense amount of intellect. Cf. *The Letters of John Stuart Mill*, ed. Hugh S. R. Elliot, Vol. II, London, 1910, pp. 93, 369.

[16] Otto Rühle, *Karl Marx: His Life and Work*, tr. Eden and Cedar Paul, New York, 1929, pp. 20-2.

To purchase modernity,—in other words, not to follow the bent of one's own thinking, not to adhere unswervingly to one's own auto- nomous evaluation of the evidence, not to consider the alternative hypotheses and the rival arguments, but rather 'to purchase modern- ity', to be one of the club, to follow its generational fashion, to accept its generational postulates and language, even if it led to subscribing to a collective falsehood. Thus young Karl Marx described how he succumbed to the circumpressures of his generational circle. His experience was typical of conversions to ideology. Leon Trotsky as a youth was 'repelled' by the ' "narrowness" ' of Marxism and the unreality of socialist theory. But the power of the generational circle overcame the sense of logic and fact: 'I endeavoured to escape the personal influence of such young socialists as I would encounter. The losing battle lasted altogether a few months. The ideas filling the air proved stronger than I, especially since in the depths of my soul I wished for nothing better than to yield to them . . . I repudiated my assumption of conservatism and swung Leftward with such speed that it even frightened away some of my new friends.'[17] Thus generational ideology triumphed over science. The anarchist Peter Kropotkin similarly described how the power of his generational circle prepared him for his conversionary experience, that is, for an emotional state in which his rational, scientific doubts were over- come, and he joined in the 'collective representation', the group- emotionalizing projection, that is, in ideology. 'It is certainly true that our youth listened to the mighty voice of Bakunin', writes Kro- potkin, 'and that the agitation of the International Workingmen's Association had a fascinating effect upon us.' It had also begun in small circles of students, who had conceived the vision of their liberat- ing and teaching the peasantry, and overthrowing the Czar; they were at once candidates for rule and self-sacrifice. 'I was only work- ing with the tide which was infinitely more powerful than any individual efforts'; it was 'one of those mass movements which occur at certain periods of awakening of human conscience'. Bakunin was calling on young students to renounce science and scholarship, and give themselves to the emancipation of the people. In his *Words*

[17] Leon Trotsky, *My Life*, New York, 1930, p. 98.

addressed to Students, he ridiculed science, and extolled 'holy and wholesome ignorance'; 'give no thought to this useless knowledge in the name of which men try to tie your hands'.[18] Kropotkin, a true scientist, and a lover of research, could not become a worshipper of ignorance; but he did renounce his scientific career. He recognized that non-scientific forces were controlling his judgment; with his famed comrade, Stepniak, he observed that 'every revolutionist has had a moment when some circumstance, maybe unimportant in itself, has brought him to pronounce his oath of giving himself to the revolution'. The anarchist ideology troubled Kropotkin for 'many hours of my nights', he writes; he experienced a resistance to its sociological conception. But he spent a week among the simple, honorable Swiss watchmakers in the Jura Mountains; 'and when I came away from the mountains, after a week's stay with the watchmakers, my views upon socialism were settled. I was an anarchist.'[19] Thus the ideological myth is implanted by unconscious forces into one's consciousness.

From the Doktorklub which young Karl Marx joined to the collectivity of the Communist International, the generational circumpressure was paramount. It was underlying the will to ideology at the time of the organization of the Communist International after the First World War. The elder generation of Marxists in the various European Socialist Parties had become de-ideologized. Not so, however, the younger intellectuals: 'The majority of the youth in the Socialist and labor movements went over to Communism.' Everywhere the Socialist youth split with their parent Socialist party; the youth favored joining the Communist International while the elders opposed it. In France, Italy, Norway, Switzerland, Sweden, Rumania,—the phenomenon repeated itself. 'Nearly everywhere the "old"

---

[18] Emile de Laveleye, *The Socialism of To-Day*, tr. Goddard H. Orpen, London, 1884, p. 203.

[19] Peter Kropotkin, *Memoirs of a Revolutionist*, Boston, 1899, pp. 278, 289, 308. One could, of course, pursue the sources of Kropotkin's ideological revolt into the story of his relations with his father, always 'unkind and most unjust', and contemptuous of the new movement for 'schools for the people and women's universities'. Ibid., pp. 264–5.

and the "young" no longer spoke the same language.' The dividing line between Socialists and Communists was: 'Among the former, anyone under thirty was an exception, among the latter anyone over thirty.' Moreover, the latter, 'these young pioneers of Communism' were for the most part intellectuals: working-class people were rare, the overwhelming majority consisting of intellectuals and semi-intellectuals, with journalists, teachers, and lawyers predominating'.[20] The young ideologists were in the ascendancy, and when the Second Congress of the International took place in the summer of 1920, it was they, with the charter of their ideology, who purported to speak for the working class of the world.

3. THE RECURRENT WAVES OF THE DE-IDEOLOGIZATION AND THEIR IRRELEVANCE TO THE SUCCESSOR 'GENERATIONAL POSTULATES'

Even as young Karl Marx and the Young Hegelians experienced a need for ideology, an ideological hunger, so every generation of young intellectuals has felt this need. Virtually at the same time as the Young Hegelians the generational circle known as the Transcendental movement was arising in Massachusetts. It 'amounted essentially to this', wrote Thomas Wentworth Higginson, 'that about the year 1836 a number of young people in America made the discovery that . . . it was possible for them to take a look at the stars for themselves'.[21]

In the beginning was the emotion; then came the idea and last the deed. The emotional need for an ideology is the primary theme in the history of intellectuals; it is their longing for a generational myth of a mission, and of the validation of their claim to rule. It follows consequently that so long as there are new generations of young intellectuals, ideology, as a mode of thought, will be recurrent. Every so-called generation in politics, literature, or art will have its corre-

[20] Cf. Branko Lazitch and Milorad M. Drachkovitch, *Lenin and the Comintern*, Vol. I, Stanford, 1972, pp. 218–22.
[21] Thomas Wentworth Higginson, *Margaret Fuller Ossoli*, Boston, 1890, p. 133.

sponding ideology. Then what was the emotional source of the period of the so-called 'end of ideology' based?

An 'end of ideology' commenced indeed after the Second World War. The pre-war generation of Marxists were no longer youth; they had gone through the war years' drama, and had had their fill of dramatic thinking. Their experience was not unlike that of the Civil War generation. Many like the young Oliver Wendell Holmes, jr., had been, prior to the War, ardent abolitionists, and filled with moral fervor.[22] Like Holmes they went through the battle-years and measured their ideology in the camps and fields against the actualities of men and their motives. When Holmes returned to civilian life, he devoted himself with an exclusive cold passion to his professional studies and work, He had had his 'bellyful' of isms, he said, and he later remembered with displeasure the abolitionists, their fanaticism, and their abiding conviction in their monopolistic knowledge of the truth. He hated Communists such as Trotsky who reminded him of the Abolitionists. He had made the transition to an 'end to ideology'. Thus, Holmes the de-ideologized, who had learned to live without the illusion and self-deception of ideology, observed in his old age the new ideologists.

In 1918, reading of Bertrand Russell in an ideological phase, Holmes wrote of the 'emotional state' of 'the abolitionists in former days, which then I shared and now much dislike—as it catches postulates like the influenza'. Emma Goldman, the anarchist, led him to say: 'I had my belly full of isms when young'. As his young friend Laski moved further to the left, Holmes warned of 'the martyr spirit': 'The only thing I am competent to say from the experience of my youth is that I fear your getting into the frame of mind that I saw in the Abolitionists (and shared)—the martyr spirit.' '[I]n my day I was a pretty convinced abolitionist ... How coolly one looks on that question now but when I was a sophomore ...' Then in 1927: 'The abolitionists as I remember used to say that

[22] Higginson too rejected in later years central doctrines of the abolitionist ideology which he had militantly espoused before and during the Civil War. Cf. Tilden G. Edelstein, *Strange Enthusiasm: A Life of Thomas Wentworth Higginson*, New Haven, 1968, pp. 322, 378, 396.

their antagonists must be either knaves or fools. I am glad I encountered that sort of thing early as it taught me a lesson.' 'You put your ideals or prophecies with the slight superior smile of the man who is sure that he has the future—I have seen it before in the past from the abolitionists to Christian Science . . .' Trotsky reminded him of 'the tone that I became familiar with in my youth among the abolitionists, . . .' Holmes 'loathed' in the Communists what he did in the Abolitionists, 'the conviction that anyone who did not agree with them was a knave or fool'.[23] The generation of Marxists who went into the Second World War went through a similar experience; their ideological myths evidently dissolved in encounters with realities.

In the decade of the fifties, the stability of the social system and later lessening of the international tension corresponded especially to the mood of de-ideologization. Ideological issues seemed indeed to have withered away. The economy was sound; the revival of Western capitalism rebutted the Marxist argument for the inevitable decline of capitalism; the Leninist argument that it would collapse when imperialism ended was confuted by events. Problems of poverty, education, culture, obviously existed, but these raised no basic issues; liberals and conservatives, sharing common ends, felt they could agree as to the means best suited for achieving them. It became difficult to explain or find any differences between liberals and conservatives. Socialist measures themselves were regarded as purely economic devices which all might accept under certain circumstances as an efficient way of doing things,—as, for instance, the national development of atomic energy; such schemes of economic planning were quite devoid of any ideological aura of moral superiority. Then too Nikita Khrushchev in 1956 revealed the moral degradation of Soviet Communism under Stalin; the historic mission had destroyed its most devoted missionaries; a recoil took place in the latter fifties from masochist emotions. The process of de-ideologization in progress for several years reached its culmination. The Marxists of the thirties and forties, grown middle-aged,

[23] Cf., *Holmes-Laski Letters: The Correspondence of Mr. Justice Holmes and Harold J. Laski*, Ed. Mark De Wolfe Howe, Cambridge, Mass., 1953, pp. 164, 772, 893, 942, 948, 1265, 1291, 689.

basically lost the ideological need characteristic of the young; they had now become an elder generation themselves, and ideology, always an unconscious defence of generational revolt, simply no longer reflected their underlying emotions. They read authors who repudiated ideology,—Karl Popper, Isaiah Berlin, Camus, Raymond Aron. There was really very little that was new in the arguments of these authors. The scientific and ethical arguments against Marxism had been stated by previous generations of Marxists who had gone through the experience of de-ideologization,—Eduard Bernstein, John Spargo, Benedetto Croce, Max Eastman, Will Herberg, Sidney Hook, Arthur Koestler, Ignazio Silone. Bernstein had argued straightforwardly against the Marxist notion of historical inevitability: 'The materialist', he observed, 'is a Calvinist without God'.[24] Sidney Hook repeated the same argument for the thirties though not to much avail; sociologists and philosophers restated it for the fifties with much greater effect. Bernstein argued that Marxism was not a science,—'No ism is a science', he declared.[25] Max Eastman, thirty-five years later, reiterated the argument strongly for a later generation though with a little hearing; the same arguments were regarded as persuasive in the fifties. What is crucial is the particular phase in the generational cycle of ideas,—the phases of alternation in ideology, and the stages of de-ideologization which intervene between the alternations. Whatever the tremendous truth in the arguments against ideology, they will have virtually no impact on a young generation emotionally resolved for ideological experience. Bernstein, for instance, observed with discernment that so long as the working classes don't have their own strong economic organizations and an education in self-government, 'the dictatorship of the proletariat means the dictatorship of club orators and writers'.[26] Never was a more well-grounded and later confirmed prediction in social science ever made. But it scarcely affected ideological generations because a

[24] Eduard Bernstein, *Evolutionary Socialism: A Criticism and Affirmation*, tr. Edith C. Harvey, New York, 1961, p. 7.

[25] Peter Gay, *The Dilemma of Democratic Socialism: Eduard Bernstein's Challenge to Marx*, 1952, New York, 1962, p. 158.

[26] Bernstein, p. 219.

'dictatorship of club orators and writers' was precisely what the young intellectuals wanted. It was only during the stage of de-ideologization, with the overwhelming evidence of the fate of intellectuals under Stalin's regime, that intellectuals wondered whether ideology was the path to self-destruction. The new generation of ideologists is once again indifferent to Bernstein's Law; few films were so sparsely attended in the United States as Solzhenitsyn's 'A Day in the Life of Ivan Denisovich'. The 'generational postulate', arising from the generational unconscious, and expressing its striving for self-definition, liberation, and hegemony, has imposed its emotional veto on contravening evidence as the stale residuum of a past and irrelevant generation.

Thus, too, the charge that they were acting amorally has rarely affected a new generation of ideologists. One of the functions of ideology is precisely to suspend ordinary ethical considerations, and replace them by the prerogatives of the 'historical mission'. Marx ridiculed words like 'justice' and 'right', and regarded them as 'modern mythology'. As late as 1880, when he virtually dictated the preamble of the program of the French Workers' Party, he insisted on deleting all appeals to ethical ideas; he based the socialist demand solely on the assertion that given the inevitable disintegration of capitalism, socialism was the only alternative for the working class.[27] Eduard Bernstein, John Dewey, and Arthur Koestler have, at different times, argued that a political movement which eradicates its ethical sense becomes sadistic and self-destructive. Dewey argued with Leon Trotsky that the means chosen shape the character of the end achieved; to which Trotsky as ideologist replied that 'normative philosophy' was irrelevant to history and history-makers.[28] To the

[27] Paul Lafargue, 'Socialism in France from 1876 to 1896', *The Fortnightly Review*, Vol. LXII, N.S., (1897), pp. 451-2.

[28] John Dewey, *Liberalism and Social Action*, New York, 1935, p. 86. Leon Trotsky, 'Their Morals and Ours', *The New International*, Vol. IV, 1938, pp. 163-73. John Dewey, 'Means and Ends: Their Interdependence and Leon Trotsky's Essay on "Their Morals and Ours"', *New International*, Vol. IV, (1938), pp. 232-3. Leon Trotsky, *The History of the Russian Revolution*, tr. Max Eastman Vol. III, New York, 1932, p. 348. Leon Trotsky, *My Life*, p. 474.

ideologist as fixated generational rebel, ethics are always the 'ethics of the fathers', something to be overthrown, surmounted; ideology with its 'mission' legislates its own moral decree, confers its own legitimacy; the universal moral sense is something to be extirpated, after all; homespun, lacking in drama, it had no recipe for political power. The 'generational postulate' rejects moral principles in favor of ideology.[29]

Curiously, the process of de-ideologization has been far less studied than that of ideological conversion. Yet the evidence indicates that when intellectuals have shed their ideological myths, their achievement of realistic goals has thereby gained. Margaret Sanger first started writing articles about birth control in a socialist newspaper *The Socialist Call*; but her movement gained widespread support from all classes only when she dropped the unnecessary ideological integument.[30] Florence Kelley's notable career as a social and industrial reformer began only when she definitely put aside her associations with revolutionary ideologists.[31] William English Walling was a zealous socialist ideologist, but he shelved ideological doctrine when he became the chief agent in founding the National Association for the Advancement of Colored People. Roger Baldwin dropped the ideology of class struggle to organize the American Civil Liberties Union, originally dedicated to the civil liberties of all parties in discussion, not merely the leftist. Abraham Cahan became the most constructive editor of a Jewish newspaper in the United States because he courageously dropped one by one the components of Marxist ideology; finally he supported Roosevelt and Churchill in the war against the Nazis when Marxists of all sorts opposed American intervention. As early as 1911 Cahan brought down the wrath

[29] A neo-Communist ideologist thus wrote typically in 1970: 'Disillusioned former radicals praised the end of ideology. The young, however, need one'. Michael Myerson, *These are the good old days*, New York, 1970, p. 35.

[30] David M. Kennedy, *Birth Control in America: The Career of Margaret Sanger*, New Haven, 1970, pp. 110–12.

[31] Josephine Goldmark, *Impatient Crusader: Florence Kelley's Life Story*, Urbana, 1953, pp. 22–3. Dorothy Rose Blumberg, *Florence Kelley: The Making of a Social Pioneer*, New York, 1966, p. 97.

of ideologists upon his head when he published such articles as one advising a young socialist that he would not be violating his socialist conscience by saying the 'kaddish' prayer for his dead father, and another 'In Honor of Passover and in Honor of America', and an editorial, 'Free Thinkers, Don't be Fanatics!' He rebuked the young militants who staged dances on Days of Atonement to flaunt their atheism against the elders: was it God who was being dethroned, or the elders?[32] Walter Lippmann's powers of intellectual analysis obviously grew as he divested himself of ideological constraints; no ideologist could have written the path-opening *Public Opinion*. Carl Sandburg wrote his *Abraham Lincoln* after he renounced the identity of Charles Sandberg, socialist propagandist.[33] The most distinguished historian of the Russian revolutionary era, Bertram D. Wolfe, the unique exponent of religious existentialism, Will Herberg, and indeed the literary and social critics, Edmund Wilson and Max Eastman, did their most enduring work in their post-ideological phases.

4. CLUSTERS IN IDEOLOGICAL PERIODS AND IDEOLOGICAL MOBILITY

An age of ideology is never bounded by a single doctrine. It abounds in movements, causes, circles, and societies. For an age of ideology has its roots in a pervasive generational disaffection. An ideological period therefore overflows with eccentric doctrines and panaceas; youthful sects propagandize their doctrines for the rescue of society through special clothes, foods, personal habits; new faces, new gestures, new speech are advocated. The spirit of rejection of the old diffuses through society; the foods one imbibed at home, the garments in which one was clothed, are regarded as having been corrupt. Thus, in the eighteen-forties in America, though the anti-slavery movement was, as Higginson wrote, 'the profoundest moral element', still people spoke of ' "the sisterhood of reforms" '. 'It was in as bad taste for a poor man to have but one hobby in his head as for a rich

[32] Melech Epstein, *Profiles of Eleven*, pp. 86–7.
[33] Harry Golden, *Carl Sandburg*, New York, Crest ed., 1962, pp. 106–9.

G

man to keep but one horse in his stable.' Mesmerism and phrenology were cultivated; Bronson Alcott preached a ' "potato gospel" ', and opposed the use of fire in cooking; Graham denounced bolted flour and ate uncracked wheat. There were transcendentalists who froze in linen garments, because to wear woolen clothes was unfair to the shorn sheep. Edmund Quincy refused to serve the state as justice of the peace, while Edward Palmer wrote propaganda against the use of money. Young men proclaimed their radical allegiance by letting their beards grow; a beard was regarded as a manifesto.[34] Ralph Waldo Emerson described it in a classical passage in 'New England Reformers':

'In these movements, nothing was more remarkable than the discontent they begot in the movers ... They defied each other, like a congress of kings, each of whom had a realm to rule, ... What a fertility of projects for the salvation of the world! One apostle thought all men should go to farming; and another, that no man should buy or sell; that the use of money was the cardinal evil; and another, that mischief was in our diet, that we eat and drink damnation. These made unleavened bread, ... Others attacked the system of agriculture; the use of animal manures in farming; and the tyranny of man over brute nature; these abuses polluted his food ... Even the insect world was to be defended,—... With these appeared the adepts of homoeopathy, of hydropathy, of mesmerism, of phrenology, and their wonderful theories of the Christian miracles. Others assailed particular vocations, as that of the lawyer, that of the merchant, of the manufacturer, of the clergyman, of the scholar. Others attacked the institution of marriage as the fountain of social evils ...'

The projection of ideological rebellion in alterations of costume and personal appearance is, of course, the most observable trait of the era. Emerson noted in 1842 that 'men with beards' were in evidence at the 'Convention of Friends of Universal Reform'. Beards were so much an ideological manifesto, that when Charles Burleigh cultivated 'flowing locks' and an 'untrimmed beard', he seemed so much like the portraitures of Jesus that he was charged with blasphemy;

[34] Thomas Wentworth Higginson, *Margaret Fuller Ossoli*, Boston, 1890, pp. 175–6. *Cheerful Yesterdays*, Boston, 1901, p. 118.

James Russell Lowell was regarded as having announced his conversion to radical ideology when he allowed his beard to grow.[35] The beard, however, like a philosophical tenet, moved from left to right in accordance with the principle of wings. Perhaps, when Abraham Lincoln in the fateful days of 1861 allowed his beard to grow he was also announcing a potential conversion to a more abolitionist ideological standpoint than the one he had previously held. Within a few years, bearded presidents became the norm,—Hayes, Garfield, Harrison.

An 'ideological syndrome' has made Americans into collectors of 'causes'; a 'cause' is an aim pursued primarily because it provides an outlet for generational, ideological energies, satisfying the longing for a redeeming mission. Today's ideologists and enthusiasts, with their variety of schemes, exhibit, of course, the classical 'cluster effect'; enthusiasts for 'organically grown food', astrology, and communal sexuality; communards and the drop-outs from established occupations; mendicants, dynamiters, and thieves; opponents of cleanliness, and the practitioners of witchcraft, satanism, and assorted cults; the rebels against the 'Protestant ethic' and the seekers of charisma; all wish to stand the introductory textbook in sociology on its head.

The early eighteen-eighties in Britain were likewise a time of 'ideological cluster'. The younger generation were moved to experiment in every direction toward an alternative contrary to that of their Victorian elders. 'Hyndman's Democratic Federation, Edmund Gurney's Society for Psychical Research, Mme Blavatsky's Theosophical Society, the Vegetarian Society, the Anti-Vivisection movement, and many other associations of the same kind marked the coming of a great reaction from the smug commercialism and materialism of the mid-Victorian epoch, and a preparation for the new universe of the twentieth century.' One seemed to be borne, wrote Edward Carpenter, by 'a great new tide of human life over the Western world'. 'The Socialist and Anarchist propaganda, the Feminist and Suffragist upheaval, the huge Trade-Union growth, the Theosophic movement, the new currents in the Theatrical,

[35] Higginson, *Margaret Fuller Ossoli*, p. 176.

Musical and Artistic worlds, the torrent even of change in the Religious world—all constituted so many streams and headwaters converging, as it were, to a great river.' The year 1882 seemed to Carpenter the turning-point in time; 'It is curious that the same year (or 1882) saw the inception of a number of new movements or enterprises tending toward the establishment of mystical ideas and a new social order . . .'[36] The late nineteen-sixties shared this character with the eighteen-eighties and forties as a time of ideological cluster. It is noteworthy that the nineteen-thirties, the years of depression, had no comparable cluster. The pressures of economic reality and material want evidently tend to confine ideology to the economic domain.

All this was characteristic too of the age of 1848, and ours has the same flavor. These traits of an ideological age cannot be explained economically; no unconscious economic motives impel a drive toward Graham crackers or unleavened bread or astrology or mesmerism; the redistribution of the national income has no sociological interrelation with these divagations. Were economic crisis a central causative factor, its ideological consequences would rationally be primarily schemes for economic reconstruction. But in an ideological age, the impulse toward rejection embraces all the values, culture, mores and folkways of society. Sometimes this total ideological challenging is regarded as the by-product of an age of affluence. Our contemporary phenomena, however, replicate those of the eighteen-forties in America, and those were scarcely affluent times. This impulse for total rejection seems rather to arise from a recurrent heightening of the emotions of generational revolt. For whatever is perceived to express the elders' values is prima facie then a target for the younger generational attack. The 'totalism' in ideology has its source in the generational, emotional a priori; the relative independence of institutions is denied; a total systematic interdependence is affirmed of such a degree that the notion of a 'social system' becomes a kind of totemistic personification, a congelation of ancestral values.

An era of ideology, furthermore, is characterized by a pheno-

[36] Edward Carpenter, *My Days and Dreams: Being Autobiographical Notes*, 1916, Third Ed., 1918, pp. 240, 245.

menon which we might call 'ideological mobility'. 'Ideological mobility' denotes the movement of an ideologist from one given ideology to another presumably its contrary; the ideologist persists in the ideological mode of thought, but from being a communist he becomes a fascist, or vice versa,—or from being an internationalist he becomes a nationalist, or vice versa, and so on. For the essential similarity of pattern and emotional motivation which runs through all ideologies and ideologists makes possible the easy replacement of one set of values to the structural variables with another. Though 'ideological mobility' has been little studied there can be little doubt that it played a large part in the rise of fascism. As a sociologist with Fascist leanings, Corrado Gini, wrote in 1927: 'a fairly large part, if not, indeed, the very nucleus, of the Fascist movement has been built up of ex-Socialists . . . This observation is particularly true of the younger element in the Socialistic party, . . ., often restless in temperament, who had rallied to the Socialist party not so much because of its positive economic program, as because of its negative program of protest against the aimless individualism of the Liberal regime, and who found in Fascism the means for effectuating their desire to take a part and to reconstruct.'[37] The greatest of the anti-fascist novelists, Ignazio Silone, observed that many Communists during the years from 1930 to 1933 transferred their allegiances to the Nazis.[38] Thus too in the United States the most famous novelist to join the Communist Party, Theodore Dreiser, and the most famous publicist to lend it his support, Lincoln Steffens, were both enthusiastic admirers of Mussolini. Dreiser told a Harvard audience in the mid-thirties that Mussolini was trying to achieve the same goal as Stalin's,—but with slightly different methods.[39]

[37] Corrado Gini, 'The Scientific Basis of Fascism', *Political Science Quarterly*, Vol. XLII, (1927), p. 104. Also cf. John Strachey, *The Menace of Fascism*, New York, 1933, pp. 160–1.

[38] Ignazio Silone, *The School for Dictators*, tr. Gwenda David and Eric Mosbacher, London, 1939, p. 206.

[39] Lincoln Steffens, *The Autobiography of Lincoln Steffens*, New York, 1931, pp. 812 ff. The writer was present at this speech by Theodore Dreiser.

5. CONSERVATISM AND THE GENERATIONS

By middle age, most former ideologists have become de-ideologized. They have become scientific, and sceptical of ideological leaps. They are post -ideological, and if their outlook is conservative, they suspect any attempt to provide their outlook with an ideological basis. Some conservative intellectuals, however, evolve as ideologists. Generally, the conservative ideologist is one who in his youth has experienced the attractions of the revolutionary myth; his thinking may remain even in later years largely determined by his generational unconscious. His identification may merge with the fathers, and he sees the sons in lawless revolt. Who then will be the elite who will save society in its decline? A favorite theme in the Bible was God's discussion with a favored righteous man: what was the minimum number of such men for whose sake he would spare destroying a society? The myths of Noah and Lot told of a saved elite, who had remained immune to the corruptions of their societies. Noah and his sons entered into a Covenant with God; they entered into a pact of renunciations, they forswore murder and the eating of living animals; in return, God promised not to destroy the human race with some calamity. Often the conservative ideologist rewrites the myths of the covenant; the ideologist is the vanguard remnant; he pleads with his fellow-men not to destroy the fabric of society with murder, parricide, incest. From Edmund Burke, the classical conservative thinker to Coleridge, Wordsworth, and the able writers of *National Review* who were Marxists in their youth, all exemplify in large measure these patterns. Conservative ideology is thus the revolutionary Mosaic ideology as transformed when the generational coordinates are rotated. Ideology has not ended, however, for such a conservative thinker; neither a scientist, nor post-ideological, he has moved from one stage in the generational unconscious to a later. Conservative ideology, however, is a peripheral phenomenon; its appeal is limited to that group whose unconscious has been impervious enough to experiment so as to avoid de-ideologization.

Read, for instance, Burke's *Reflections on the French Revolution*, and ask: from what source does the emotive power of his key metaphors arise? To the revolutionist, wrote Burke, 'Regicide and parricide, and sacrilege are but fictions of superstition.' The state, he says, should be invested with all the emotions that sons have for their fathers; one 'should approach to the faults of the state as to the wounds of a father with pious awe and trembling solicitude'. Instead, the revolutionists, men of the 'mechanic philosophy' ('reductionists' would be the phrase today) use reason with sadistic intent: 'All the drapery of life is to be rudely torn off. All the super-added ideas, furnished from the wardrobe of a moral imagination, which the heart owns, ... as necessary to cover the defects of our naked, shivering nature.' The revolutionists aim to uncover the nakedness of their mothers and fathers. To these 'sophisters, econo-mists, and calculators, a king is but a man, a queen is but a woman; a woman is but an animal; and an animal not of the highest order'. The revolutionists, wrote Burke, would abrogate that 'wise preju-dice' by which 'we are taught to look with horror on those children of their country who are prompt rashly to hack that aged parent in pieces, and put him in the kettle of magicians ...' To the hackers of their fathers, those who wished to proclaim the dictatorship of a generation, Burke declared that the state was a partnership of all the generations, 'a partnership not only between those who are living, but between those who are living, those who are dead and those who are to be born'.[40]

A few years later Burke's polemic against the Revolution became even more elemental in character: 'With the Jacobins of France, vague intercourse is without reproach; marriage is reduced to the vilest concubinage: children are encouraged to cut the throats of their parents; ...' The sans-culotte philosophers were cannibals eating their fathers: 'the sans-culotte carcass butchers, and the philosophers of the shambles' were dividing them into 'rumps and sirloins, and briskets, and into all sorts of pieces for roasting, boiling, and stew-ing ...' 'To all this let us join the practice of cannibalism, which in the proper terms, and with the greatest truth, their several factions accuse each other. By cannibalism, I mean their devouring as a

[40] Edmund Burke, *Reflections on the French Revolution*, reprint, sec. Ed., London, 1923, pp. 68, 69, 83.

nutriment of their ferocity, some part of the bodies of their victims, . . .'[41]

To Burke, revolutionists are men driven in their unconscious by generational hatred; they are fanatics with murderous feelings against their fathers translated into hatred for the state, and a cruel readiness to 'sacrifice the whole human race to the slightest of their experiments.' The key metaphors,—'parricide', 'wounds of father', 'drapery rudely torn off', our 'naked nature', 'hacking the aged parents', boiling them in kettles, concubinage, cutting parents' throats, dismembering their bodies, eating them,—Freud could have incorporated whole paragraphs of Burke into the dramatic narrative of *Totem and Taboo*.

Thus Edmund Burke wrote in his sixties. In his youth, however, he had clashed vigorously with his father, and when twenty-seven years old, wrote *A Vindication of Natural Society*. It indicted the social order of Britain for the horrible slavery it imposed on 'upwards of a hundred thousand miners', 'unhappy wretches' who 'scarce ever see the light of the sun'. Politicians, says Burke, tell you that the people's servitude disqualifies them from the search of truth, but at the same time they deprive them of any means for raising their spiritual stature; these are the 'enfants perdus' of civil society, writes Burke. In middle age Burke was still prepared to hold that in all disputes between people and the rulers, 'the presumption is at least upon a par in favor of the people'. As a conservative ideologist he yielded to new myths, his own anti-science, his own resistance to scientific analysis. That was why men like John Morley felt that Burke's perception too had become ideological; the miseries of the French people were omitted in his pages.[42] Yet there never has been a political ideological movement which has genuinely felt itself Burkean. As Harold J. Laski, the noted British political scientist and later ideologist, wrote: 'He [Burke] was a member of no school of thought, and there is no influence to whom his outlook can be

---

[41] 'Letters on a Regicide Peace', in *The Works of the Right Honorable Edmund Burke*, Vol. V, London, 1889, pp. 211–12.
[42] John Morley, *Burke*, London, reprinted, 1928, p. 161.

directly traced.'[43] All this despite the fact that he was in Laski's opinion, shared with Morley, the 'greatest master of civil wisdom' in Britain. For no elite could truly be recruited in Burke's name; he offered no charter for hope or power.

In Benjamin Disraeli, however, conservatism found an ideologist who could delineate a myth for a youthful elite. Disraeli in 1833, prior to the beginning of his parliamentary career, already published the first Jewish historical novel, *Alroy*, a wildly imaginative tale of a medieval redeemer who comes out of the mountains in the Middle East to lead the Jews, in armed revolt against their Moslem oppressors. According to Cecil Roth, 'the young Benjamin identified himself with him in his thoughts, and looked upon himself too as the destined leader of a movement which would bring the Jews back, sword in hand, to Palestine'.[44] But Disraeli's Messianic elitism found a more suitable sublimative expression in the development of the Conservative Party and its ideology. The British Tories had begun after the year 1830 to call themselves Conservatives. Disraeli, in his first parliamentary candidacies, presented himself as a Radical with a bold program for parliamentary reforms. Later, however, he was filled with the dream of a redemptive aristocratic elite; 'Young England' as it was later called, preoccupied his imagination, and he saw himself as the teacher, the ideological guide of this group, though perhaps himself debarred by his Jewish origins from the highest political office. A little company of young aristocrats, fresh from Oxford and Cambridge, in 1840 about twenty-two years of age on the average, adopted the name 'Young England', and indeed recognized Disraeli as their leader. Romantic Tories, filled with dislike for the middle class, they regarded themselves as an elite which would bring joy back into the lives of the exploited laboring classes. Disraeli was their Moses; he wrote in 1842: 'I already find myself without effort the leader of a party chiefly of the youth and new members.' Scarcely a party, however, it was rather a manifestation

[43] Harold J. Laski, *Political Thought in England from Locke to Bentham*, London, 1937, pp. 172–3.

[44] Cecil Roth, *Benjamin Disraeli, Earl of Beaconfield*, New York, 1952, pp. 63–4.

of the swing of the generational pendulum from left-romanticism to right-romanticism. 'When Disraeli was a youth, romanticism had been flowing in the revolutionary channel prepared for it by Byron; it was now flowing strongly in the channel of reaction.'[45]

Disraeli's most influential novel, *Coningsby, or The New Generation*, published in 1844, was indeed the manifesto of Young England.[46] The Pharaohs in this new ideological myth were the middle-class manufacturers with their utilitarian creed, reducing human beings into numerical aggregates of profit and loss. The selfless, generous aristocratic youth, the natural leaders of the community bore the mission to rescue the suffering, exploited lower class from the calculating Benthamites. Disraeli's novel *Sybil, or The Two Nations* recounted the trials in this process of the union of the aristocratic elite and the lowliest class against the commercial exploiters. The new England on the horizon, would restore the sense of its community. Meanwhile, Disraeli reiterated his appeal to the youth as the redeemers: 'genius, when young, is divine. Why the greatest captains of ancient and modern times both conquered Italy at five and twenty! Youth, extreme youth, overthrew the Persian empire.'[47] And the Jew meanwhile, will be enabled to cast aside those leveller ideologies which he adopted only under the stress of persecutions which threatened to make of him a pariah. 'Yet the Jews, Coningsby, are essentially Tories', declares Disraeli's protagonist, Sidonia.[48] '[A]ll the tendencies of the Jewish race are conservative. Their bias is to religion, property, and natural aristocracy,' he wrote.[49] If the aristocratic elitism was clear and unmistakable, so were the moving passages in which Disraeli depicted the life of the poor to whom they would bring succor: 'It is that the Capitalist has

[45] William Flavelle Monypenny, *The Life of Benjamin Disraeli: Earl of Beaconsfield*, Vol. II, New York, 1913, pp. 166, 170.

[46] Georg Brandes, *Lord Beaconsfield: A Study*, tr. Mrs. George Sturge, 1880, reprinted, New York, 1966, pp. 120 ff.

[47] Benjamin Disraeli, *Coningsby*, reprinted, New York, 1948, p. 98.

[48] Ibid., p. 207.

[49] Benjamin Disraeli, *Lord George Bentinck: A Political Biography*, Tenth Ed., London, 1881, pp. 356–7.

found a slave that has supplanted the labor and ingenuity of man. Once he was an artisan; at the best, he now only watches machines; ...'[50] The words and illustrations were the same as those which Karl Marx that same year was writing in his *Economic-Philosophical Manuscripts*. But Disraeli would add that 'there is no error so vulgar as to believe that revolutions are occasioned by economical causes'. Both men were ideologists; both held to Mosaic myths, rewritten in the language of social science; they differed as to the stratum which would be cast for the redeeming role in history,—one chose the emerging intellectuals to displace the bourgeoisie, the other hoped the displaced aristocratic elite, fructified by Jewish genius, would carry out the same task.

[50] Benjamin Disraeli, *Sybil or the Two Nations*, reprint, London, 1930, p. 127.

CHAPTER IV

The Traits of the Ideological Mode of Thought: Logical and Psychological

1. THE EMPIRICAL INGREDIENT

If ideology were only a species of myth, it would scarcely have the power of attracting the intellectuals of the modern world. The Mosaic myth is an all-essential ingredient in ideology, but the myth, in modern times, must be embedded in scientific, empirical as well as philosophic arguments. An ideology must therefore enlist a certain minimum of sociological argument; it must at least avail itself of a minimum perception of social reality, some empirical facts which will lend at least a partial credence to its assertions; when the ideology proclaims a given class, nation, race, sex or group as chosen for a mission, it must preserve some minimal connection with reality; a myth altogether detached from reality can never do service in an ideology. This is the generative symbiosis in ideology of myth and science: an empirical content embedded in the ideology, yet always mythologized. How then can these two ingredients be separated and distinguished? In practice we can use a method of qualitative analysis in the chemistry of ideologies. Let us consider five empirical scientific propositions and their ideological counterparts in Marxism:

(1) (Scientific) The workingmen usually have lower standards of living than the upper or middle classes; their insecurities and unemployment are greater; often they have more resentments against the social system; their political behavior, in contrast to that of the upper and middle classes, then expresses this discontent.

(1^1) (Ideological) The workers have a historic mission to abolish capitalism.

(2) (Scientific) The capitalist system has been characterized by a cycle of prosperity and depressions; the latter have led to interventionist measures.

(2^1) (Ideological) The capitalist system is beset by insoluble growing contradictions which cannot be resolved within the framework of the system, but require a revolutionary qualitative transformation into another.

(3) (Scientific) A more democratically-minded government will equalize the opportunities for education.

(3^1) (Ideological) A classless society will emerge with all equally fit to govern.

(4) (Scientific) Moved by the discontents of people, political parties will propose programs for the reform of what they regard as injustices.

(4^1) (Ideological) Every society is pregnant with its contrary.

(5) (Scientific) The rate of social and political change varies in accordance with a variety of social circumstances; it tends to be violent when a crisis arises in a regime which is absolutist, totalitarian, without a democratic constitution.

(5^1) (Ideological) Force is the midwife of history.

Why have ideologies exerted a great influence on the development of the social sciences? Precisely because their myths told partially in the language of social science, are extrapolated, in compliance with a compulsive, emotional a priori, from a perception of social realities. The Marxist ideologist, desirous of proving that the workers have a historic mission to abolish capitalism will turn social scientist, and study painstakingly the miseries of working-class life and their political actions; always, however, there will remain an 'ideological leap' from the empirical facts and the testable social uniformities to the notion that history has conferred a 'mission' on the workers. When labor's political parties are elected as governments, they generally show as little consciousness of such 'missions' as the workers who elected them. Similarly the ideologist's leap from the evidence of industrial crises to the notion of 'inherent contradictions' acted as a powerful catalytic agent for scientific work on the phenomena of business cycles. Marxian ideology inspired likewise studies on the unequal opportunities for education in the different social classes; nevertheless it never built a bridge to replace the unparalleled leap to an ideological conclusion. None of the envisaged empirical consequences of equal educational opportunities ever included the proposition that in an emerging classless society every cook would be able to serve as a commissar. The scientific study of violence as an agency in social change was certainly stimulated by the Marxian ideology, yet 'force is the midwife of history' went far beyond the causal laws as to the relative frequency of violence in democratic liberal societies as compared to absolutist, totalitarian ones. Thus every ideology upon a minimal core of social fact super-imposes emotionally projective mythological formations; metaphors of the womb of the old society, the pregnancy with its contrary, force as the midwife, are all components of the myth of the birth of the hero, the class or group with the mission to destroy the old.

The ideologist, under the sway of his central myth, finally, how-ever, loses his sense of scientific method and verification. In 1852, for instance, Marx undertook to evaluate what his scientific achieve-ment had been. He wrote:

'And now as to myself, no credit is due to me for discovering the existence of classes in modern society or the struggle between them. Long before me bourgeois historians had described the economic development of this class struggle and bourgeois economists the economic anatomy of the classes. What I did that was new was to prove: (1) that the *existence of classes* is only bound up with *particular historical phases in the development of production*, (2) that the class struggle necessarily leads to the *dictatorship of the proletariat*, (3) that this dictatorship itself constitutes only the transition to the *abolition of all classes* and to a classless society.'[1]

Where in his writings was the 'proof' of these propositions? One found some items of evidence that different societies, with their respective economies and technologies, varied correspondingly with respect to their social classes, but virtually nothing, beyond the affirmation of a vision was adduced to 'prove' the necessary emer-gence of a proletarian dictatorship and its inauguration of a classless society. In Ideology, social science becomes possessed by a genera-tional myth.

[1] Marx and Engels, *Basic Writings on Politics and Philosophy*, p. 457.

2. ISOMORPHIC PROJECTION UPON THE UNIVERSE

No ideology, moreover is content with asserting its Mosaic myth in philosophical-scientific language. The ideologist wishes to derive that myth from the nature of the universe itself. If he is a revolutionary communist, he wishes to show that his quest for revolutionary experience is a special case of a general law of all existence,—that for the world as a whole, all the stages in the history of existents have been through revolutionary, discontinuous, abrupt transitions, and that the drive toward a classless consummation is the inherent culmination of successive equilibria and disequilibria. If he is a fascist, the ideologist will elaborate on the principle of hierarchy inherent in the nature of the universe,—in its solar and galactic systems, in the biological realms. If he is an anarchist, he projects a metaphysic of ultimately independent entities, or as Kropotkin did, describes the principle of mutual aid as a basic factor in biological evolution so that the anarchist trend emerges as a special case of the general biological law. No ideology, indeed, is satisfied with the status of a social myth. Georges Sorel stressed that myths were irrefutable and unverifiable, that they were solely emotional visions of movement. Not so an ideology which aims to be demonstrable. Ideology is driven toward 'deriving' its social myth from a world-view, a *Weltanschauung*. We might call this 'method' of world-mythologizing the method of 'isomorphic projection'. In other words, the same structural traits which characterize the social myth are projected on the world as a whole as a total myth. Then, after this projection has been accomplished, the ideologist claims to 'derive' his social myth as a special case of the world myth. Thus, the Marxist ideologist, in his full orthodoxy, is more than a historical materialist of human societies; he is also a 'dialectical materialist' for all nature. The universe as a whole adheres to his revolutionary ideology; it evolves through struggles of opposites, making qualitative 'leaps', at critical junctures to new qualitative epochs, negating previous stages with respect to their basic laws.

Anarchist ideology, which has been enjoying a revival, was noteworthy for the devoted efforts which Peter Kropotkin made for showing that it was a corollary of 'modern science'. His 'Appeal to the Young', published and republished since 1880, was the most stirring call to the energies of generational idealism, to the spirit of youthful comradeship. As a scientist, however, Kropotkin brought to anarchist ideology precisely that symbiosis of science with myth which is the essence of ideology. To provide a 'scientific foundation' for anarchism became his self-assigned, lifelong task. His book *Mutual Aid: A Factor of Evolution*, his pamphlet *Modern Science and Anarchism*, his volume *Ethics*, were all part of this labor. Young neo-anarchists revere these writings today. Scientific biologists however have found them embarrassingly naïve and ill-founded. Thomas Hunt Morgan, a great biologist and Nobel Laureate, remarked: 'Some years ago the famous and tender-hearted Russian, Kropotkin, wrote a charming book called *Mutual Help*. He made a valiant effort, by collecting many anecdotes about animals, to show that nature is often kindly, that animals perform acts of kindliness, and even cherish one another. However fine his intentions, the arguments he used will make most naturalists smile, while many of the anecdotes would do better in a child's fairy book.'[2] The eminent social biologist, Raymond Pearl, wrote restrainedly that 'never at any time did Prince Kropotkin win any great number of adherents among professional biologists for his mutual-aid theories, ...' Indeed, Kropotkin himself toward the end of his life, observing the realities of the Bolshevik Revolution, conceded a much greater significance to the 'rapacious instincts', those of domination, which 'unfortunately', he wrote, still survived in men, and his final conception of history was that of a conflict between two elements, the striving for justice as against the striving for domination over others.[3]

During the period in which Bertrand Russell was a fellow-traveller of anarchist ideology, he developed a theory of physics and metaphysics in which, appropriately enough, all reality seemed to

[2] Thomas Hunt Morgan, *The Scientific Basis of Evolution*, Sec. Ed., New York, 1935, p. 118. Melville Kress, 'Prince Kropotkin's Mutual Aid', *The New Republic*, Vol. LXXXIX, 30 Dec. 1936, p. 275.

[3] Prince Kropotkin, *Ethics: Origin and Development*, New Ed., tr. L. S. Friedland and J. R. Piroshnikoff, New York, 1936, pp. 263, 312.

exemplify Kropotkin's ideas. In 1919 Russell wrote his anarchist
credo: 'The best system', he declared, 'would be one not far removed from that advocated by Kropotkin, but rendered more
practicable by the adoption of the main principles of Guild Socialism.' State socialism, he felt, would fail to nurture the sense of
freedom; only those kinds of socialism 'which have absorbed what is
true in Anarchist teaching' would disenthrall men 'from the feeling
of oppression by a vast machine'.[4] During the next years, Russell,
studying Einstein's theory of relativity and formulating its philosophical consequences, decided that it exhibited Kropotkin's principles
on a cosmic scale. Whereas in the classical physics, 'the sun was like
a despotic government emitting decrees from the metropolis; in the
new', he wrote, 'the solar system is like the society of Kropotkin's
dreams, in which everybody does what he prefers at each moment,
and the result is perfect order'. 'If nature, as portrayed by Einstein
is to be our model, it would seem that the anarchists will have the
best of the argument. The physical universe is orderly, not because
there is a central government, but because everybody minds its own
business.'[5] Thus the physical world was declared to be isomorphic
with a Kropotkinite commune.

   At the same time Russell was constructing a philosophy of logical
atomism, a metaphysical projection of his anarchist emotions written
in the language of logic; D. H. Lawrence who for a period during
the Great War shared with Russell in his pacifist activities asked
one day: 'What does Russell really want?' Lawrence's answer was
that Russell was motivated by a desire to keep 'each separate little
ego . . . an independent little principality by itself'.[6] In metaphysics,
this became the notion of a universe composed of 'logically separable

   [4] Bertrand Russell, *Proposed Roads to Freedom*, New York, 1919, pp.
183, 192, 211.
   [5] Bertrand Russell, *The Analysis of Matter*, New York, 1927, p. 74.
'Relativity: Philosophical Consequences', *Encyclopaedia Britannica*,
Fourteenth Ed., Vol. 19, London, 1929, p. 100. *The ABC of Relativity*,
New York, 1925, p. 196.
   [6] *The Letters of D. H. Lawrence*, ed. Aldous Huxley, New York,
1932, pp. 250-1.
   H

particulars', more primitive 'events' ('happenings' one would say today) than the sub-atomic particles which occupied physicists. The classic of individualist anarchism, Max Stirner's *The Ego and His Own* was thus realized in cosmology, with order and law interpreted as 'human inventions' like catalogues superimposed on altogether independent entities. Einstein, unlike Russell, regarded the theory of relativity as the culmination of classical concepts of the field, and gave half his life to avoiding the quantum-indeterminacies, and to deriving atomic phenomena from all-comprehensive field laws. He felt that Spinoza's vision of Substance, or God as Nature, with order intrinsic to its character, came closest to the final philosophical consequence; he had no liking for the atomic disorder which Russell espoused. Indeed years later, Russell in philosophical discussions with Einstein could find no fruitful common ground.[7] During his anarchist phase Russell most exhibited the typical trait of the ideologist, the projection of his political longings upon the intrinsic nature of reality.

Why is 'isomorphic projection' so congenial to young ideologists? In the first place, it expresses the emotional resentment which so many experience with their first studies of science. At an early age the child is told to put aside the world of myths and fairy tales. There is an initiation, often traumatic, into the impersonal world of numbers and scientific laws. A de-personalized world replaces the personal. Religion discredited by science rarely provides among young intellectuals in modern times a domain for the expression of personalized emotions. But in ideology there is a 'return of the repressed'; the mythological longings are reinstated. A personalized drama is affirmed as inherent in the nature of things,—a drama, moreover, in which the ideologist is cast as hero. And for life, for reality to have meaning,—what is meant is that such a heroic role is assigned the individual. The myth restores the child to its primacy in the universe; instead of the discipline of scientific method which curbs and restrains one's emotions, one has an ideological myth which somehow can domesticate science itself. Ideology in this sense

[7] *The Autobiography of Bertrand Russell: The Middle Years: 1914–1944*, Bantam Ed., New York, 1969, pp. 326–7.

has a revolutionary directive against the old who de-personalized the world, but toward the science itself, it is something of a regressive counter-revolutionary.

In the second place, the young ideologist feels a certain insecurity about the cogency of his political drama. He knows that science has dismissed many dramatic human hopes. Again, the young ideologist experiences guilt as he challenges the *status quo*, and announces his plans for its overturn. He seeks to mitigate his presumption, to reduce his insecurity, to exonerate himself from all guilt. If he is revolting against the social super-ego, he can find no better ally than the cosmic super-ego. It tells him that he is acting with the warrant of cosmic approval, the highest court of existence, which overrules the judgments of the provincial courts of an elder generation. The young ideologist then knows that all existence is his ally, and he feels liberated from both doubt and guilt-experience. Every ideologist therefore tends to become a political metaphysician as he projects his social drama isomorphically on total reality.

All ideologists indeed as they engage in 'isomorphic projection' find themselves in pitfalls. Thus, if one postulates with Kropotkin a universal principle of mutual aid, how shall one explain how competitive and class societies could have arisen in the first place? If Nature is anarchist, communist, and revolutionary, then the segments of Nature which are hierarchical, destructive, and static become surds in the ideological picture.

Even Marx as an ideologist found himself in a contradictory situation when he adopted Darwin's theory of natural selection as a basis for his own doctrines. In *The Origin of Species*, said Marx enthusiastically, he had found 'a basis in natural science for the class struggle in history'. Yet if social struggles were an extension of the struggle for existence among plants and animals, what happened to Marx's argument that class struggles in humankind were not universal but arose only under specific historical, technological conditions, those which accounted for the origin of classes? And if social struggles were, in truth, a special case for men of the universal biological struggles, then the dream for the end of alienation vanished; for men's aggressive drives, as biological universals, would always clamor for satisfaction; a communistic society, with its frustration of aggression, would be a futile exercise in an ideology of exceptionalism to nature's universal struggle. As an ideologist, however, Marx leaped to adapt the latest advance in biological thought for his purposes. Most of the contemporary statesmen, like the philosopher Mill, were much too judicious to regard Darwin's theories as bearing on their political standpoints. They were content to work with the human scene. The ideologist, however, is restless till he has a doctrine of the 'totality' which underwrites his historical scenario and role.

3. TWOFOLD THEORY OF TRUTH

As unstable unions of a myth and science, ideologies tend to evolve a distinctive set of intellectual and emotional consequences.

Every ideology, in the first place, finds that its myth tends finally to contravene scientific evidence; therefore, as a defence-mechanism for its claims, it develops a theory of 'anti-truth'; it enunciates an organon higher than scientific truth and verification. Second, every ideology, averring, as it does, that the intellectuals are history's chosen elite, tends to become authoritarian; young intellectuals, often repudiated in democratic society, are drawn to ideologists who explicitly reject the democratic society which rejects them; thereby their status as an elite is reinforced against criticism. Third, every ideology by way of justifying its authoritarian rejection of scientific criteria tends to allege its own superiority by virtue of its 'totalist' conception of reality; its 'higher' knowledge precludes the comparative weighing of the consequences of proposed social changes. Fourth, since every ideology aims to inaugurate a *Gemeinschaft*, that is, an ideological community characterized by unity in emotion, (a neo-tribalism), and ruled by an elite, it is hostile towards any group which has resisted absorption into the surrounding community, especially so when such a group has prided itself on a rational, scientific, and individualistic tradition; hence, ideologists have almost invariably become anti-Semites. Lastly, in accordance with its rejection of the scientific approach to reality, and its quest for a neo-tribal community, every ideology tends to develop a primitivist tenet, a hostility to the ethics, requirements, and demands of civilization, and a return to presumably primitive modes of feeling, aggression, and thinking.

Let us briefly explain each of these five traits of ideology.

Every ideology, as we have seen, incorporates a variant of the Mosaic myth, a conception of an elite, a historically chosen class, and an emerging higher society. But the mythological propositions, in the course of time, are found to be plainly contravened by the scientific evidence. If so, says the ideologist, so much the worse for the evidence; under no conditions whatsoever will the ideologist renounce his ideology. Thus the master of European Marxism, Georg Lukacs, declared in 1967 that even if every empirical prediction of Marxism were invalidated, he would still hold Marxism to be true.[8] In other words, the higher 'truth' of Marxism transcends all commonplace scientific verifications. If the working classes, contrary to Marxism, fail to become more miserable in capitalist societies, but instead prosper more not only materially, but enjoy as well a higher and freer cultural life than they do in any of the world's communist societies, then the Marxist ideologist will say nonetheless that the workers are 'really' more 'repressed' than any class has ever been in history. No scientific criteria are ever provided for giving meaning to the ideological, non-empirical use of 'repressed'. Instead, the ideologist invokes a higher 'dialectical' conception of 'truth', a higher 'dialectical reason'. The latter may be defined as: the superimposition on observational facts of unverifiable auxiliary components, or their deliberate misreporting, in order to render them consistent with, or irrelevant to the ideological system.

Every ideological myth does violence to the reality-principle. The ideologist, however, unlike the scientist responds to such a conflict in accordance with the pattern of 'omnipotence of thought'. If reality is recalcitrant to mythological projection, then reality must be abrogated and a 'higher' super-reality 'posited' to conform to the

[8] Georg Lukács, *History and Class Consciousness: Studies in Marxist Dialectics*, tr. Rodney Livingstone, London, 1968, p. xxvi.

Ideological Ego. The methods of science are experienced as part of society's 'repressive' forces which contravene one's fantasies.

Every ideology thus tends to develop what historians of thought call a 'twofold theory of truth'.[9] A twofold theory arises under those social circumstances when a social schism has plainly developed between myth and science. Thus, the opponents of Galileo maintained that his cosmological theory might be 'mathematically true' but that it was 'philosophically false'. Thus, too, Soviet ideologists held that the theory of relativity might provide a convenient computational device but that it was nonetheless false from the 'dialectical' standpoint. Nazi ideologists similarly affirmed that the 'abstract' mathematical laws of the theory of relativity lacked the 'concrete truth' possessed by German science. Even the noble-hearted New England transcendentalists declared that if the material facts differed from the truth,—'so much the worse for the facts'.[10] The most influential form of the twofold theory of truth has been political; ideas or assertions which helped bring political power to one's ideological party are declared 'true'. This doctrine, wrote F. H. Bradley in 1911, 'now for a century takes its place in the thought of Europe. For good or evil it more or less dominates or sways our minds to an extent of which most of us, perhaps, are dangerously unaware.'[11]

The ideological conception of truth thus becomes a doctrine of 'anti-truth'. By one means or another, it tries to overcome or weaken the scientific conception of reality, and to cause the individual to lose confidence in his own perceptions, hypotheses, and judgments. A class, community, nation, or generation is held to have a collective privileged veto over the individual's rationality; its collective access to 'reality' is said to transcend scientific criteria. The 'revolutionary instinct' of the peasantry and proletariat, or the 'intuition' of the revolutionary youth, nation, or race are alleged to have a direct

[9] The 'twofold theory of truth' has a lineage in medieval thought. Cf. Andrew Halliday Douglas, *The Philosophy and Psychology of Pietro Pomponazzi*, Cambridge, 1910, pp. 245–6.

[10] Cf. Tilden G. Edelstein, *Strange Enthusiasms*, p. 55.

[11] F. H. Bradley, 'On Some Aspects of Truth', *Mind*, Vol. XX, July, 1911, p. 314.

knowledge of the essence of nature and history. Social circumpressures thus legislate the 'anti-truth', making it binding on the individual as the 'ideological truth', and forcing him to repress his spontaneous doubts and perceptions. Ideological officials are thus given a charter for controlling or supervising scientists, as has been the practice in Soviet Communist societies.

Linguistic usage in the Russian language curiously enabled Soviet ideologists to formulate their peculiar version of the twofold theory of truth. In Russian there are two words for 'truth',—'pravda' and 'istina'. The prisoners in Soviet camps and jails used to discuss the differences between these two words endlessly. For 'istina' signified the homely 'truth' of common sense, the correspondence between the proposition and objective fact, whereas 'pravda', 'a unique and specifically Russian concept', meant a 'higher concept of truth', the 'right truth', the 'party truth'. 'Pravda' was absolute, and overruled the humble 'istina', the truth-as-such. A trivial philological distinction, observed one prisoner, the former Secretary of the Palestine Communist Party,—'But in fact this small difference—this tyranny of *pravda* over *istina*—was the lever by which white was turned into black; no such dialectic had existed since the Inquisition. The notion of *pravda* was the basis of power.'[12] The agents of the secret police were not interested in a 'mass of petty istinas'. They wanted the 'ideological truth', the 'dialectical truth', as the Inquisition had insisted on the 'philosophical truth'. The 'Party truth' told you what you should be seeing, what Marxist ideology demanded that your perceptions should be if its 'truth' were to be verified.

Sometimes the ideologist holding to the 'higher truth' simply represses contravening 'lower-truths'. John Strachey, for instance, experienced 'strong inhibitions' at the thought of reading Arthur Koestler's novel *Darkness at Noon*. To describe his experience, he cited the words of another ideologist:

'Even if I had read such books, I should not have believed them
... I would have known that in the war between Capitalism and Communism, books are weapons, and like all serviceable weapons,

[12] *Shipwreck of a Generation: The Memoirs of Joseph Berger*, London, 1971, p. 53.

loaded ... ' When he read 'my first anti-Communist book', he ex-perienced a fever: 'I mean a fever quite literally; and furtiveness as if I was committing an unpardonable sin, as I was. For the fact that I had voluntarily opened the book could mean only one thing: I had begun to doubt.'[13]

Anatole France once said in *La Vie en Fleur* that dearer to man than truth are his illusions 'that encourage and console and set no limit to his hopes and aspirations'. Ideological misperception is born of the will to illusion, which explains the fierce nature of ideological tenacity. The Jewish editor, Abraham Cahan, went through a period of Bolshevik exhilaration; he chanced at that time to meet a noted Menshevik exile who tried to enlighten him concerning the Bol-shevik terror: 'Suddenly Cahan raised his hand, covered his ears, and shouted: "Don't destroy my illusions; I don't care to listen".'[14] Perhaps what Anatole France might have added was that no men are more cruel than those anxious lest their illusions be thwarted by reality.

Ideological perception is thus transmuted into ideological misper-ception. An ideology cannot allow itself to be tested in the manner of a scientific hypothesis. Contravening evidence is either barred, or so mixed with 'truth' that it is repressed, obliterated, distorted, or per-meated with obligatory auxiliary hypotheses.

4. ANTI-TRUTH AND MARGINAL INTELLECTUALS

The most recent ideology of anti-truth is that fashioned by Herbert Marcuse. It is inspired by an animus against the whole tradition of modern science, against the mathematical method of Galileo and Einstein, against the empirical verification of Bacon, against the analytic approach of Descartes. As an ideologist, Marcuse appeals to a primitivist longing to see the world restored to the pristine unity which people presumably enjoyed before tools of measurement and experimental apparatus wrought their violence. The principles of

[13] John Strachey, *The Strangled Cry and other unparliamentary papers*, London, 1962, pp. 12–13.
[14] Melech Epstein, *Profiles of Eleven*, p. 103.

modern science, Marcuse writes, are as a priori structures which, designed for dominating nature, falsified its character; the aim of Galilean science, he asserts, was to eliminate the 'individual, non-quantifiable qualities' which stand in the way of bourgeois exploitation of men and things. What is needed, according to Marcuse, is a new science based on a 'qualitatively new mode of "seeing"', on 'essentially different concepts of nature', born out of the new politics, 'that of a pacified world'. The new, Marcusean science will abrogate the mathematical conception of nature; it will reinstate the world of beauty, concrete, unanalyzed, 'seen, heard, smelled, touched, felt, comprehended', which positivistic analysis, subservient to defense and security, wishes to eliminate.

Therefore, as an ideologist, Marcuse condemns the logic and language of science. Einstein, with his operational analysis of the concepts of time and space, was the great innovator of modern science; but Herbert Marcuse denounces Einstein's method: 'operationalism, in theory and practice, becomes the theory and practice of containment'.[15] Somehow, from the standpoint of Marcusean ideology, there is an intrinsic logical bond between Einstein's theory of relativity and the foreign policy of President Dwight Eisenhower. And much the same applies to logic generally; 'the logic of thought remains the logic of domination', and 'the laws of thought' are formulated 'in protective accord with the laws of society'. Grammar itself, like scientific logic is designed to mutilate man: 'The noun governs the sentence in an authoritarian and totalitarian fashion . . .'[16]

To achieve 'the most radical and most complete revolution in history', what is required according to the ideological myth, is a dialectical logic' of 'explosions' (The latter is the most frequently used catchword of Marcuse).[17] Violent revolution, radical qualitative

[15] Herbert Marcuse, *One-Dimensional Man*, 1964, Boston, 1968, p. 17.

[16] Ibid., pp. 87, 139, 138. Cole too had a 'dislike for science, which grew until in his later years it became almost detestation, . . .' Margaret Cole, *The Life of G. D. H. Cole*, London, 1971, p. 34.

[17] Ibid., p. 44. Herbert Marcuse, *An Essay on Liberation*, Boston, 1969, pp. xiii, xv, 43, 89.

change, is held to be the law of existence; thus total reality is re-garded as isomorphic with the revolutionary's emotional longings. For the Kantian categorical imperative, Marcuse substitutes the com-pulsive imperative: 'explode all society', realize the 'exploding the social system' ... What matters it that 'revolutionary negation' is at odds with the criteria and standards of mathematical, operational science, or that the revolutionary myth contravenes the evidence, or borders on the nonsensical? For the revolutionary negation requires a new logic 'a different logic, a contradicting truth', 'non-operational' in its very structure, with a 'historical concreteness' which 'militates against quantification and mathematization ... '[18] Thus, contem-porary ideology restores a twofold theory of truth. Mathematical science makes voyages to the moon possible; Einstein's theory of relativity enables one to predict the deflection of light during the sun's eclipse; but these achievements are not 'true' in the Marcusean 'dialectical logic'; there is a more 'concrete' reality, never specified but closer to the wishes of 'critical theory'. The 'historical subject' is the name assigned to the new elite; the definition of the dramatic-logical term is simple: the new mythical hero will be the intellectual, indoctrinated with "critical theory", with ideology rather than science.[19]

Every ideology has sought some large class which would accept the leadership of the intellectuals, the ideologists. The Marcusean ideology is original in its special appeal among the intellectuals to those most misfitted, semi-educated, or obsolete in their capacities. Marcuse, wrote one writer in a New Left organ, became 'the cham-pion of all who do not wish to learn, of all the 'hangers-on' in the university'; in his 'dialectic' they found their theology.[20] Another sympathizer, discussing Marcuse's 'large influence on the noncon-fessional wing of the New Left', observes that the 'hip intellectuals' have 'been driven wild by a surfeit of rationalism', by 'the carefully

[18] Marcuse, *One-Dimensional Man*, pp. 141, 142.
[19] Ibid., p. 141.
[20] Julius Grey, 'The Paradox of Stanley Gray', *Canadian Dimension*, Vol. 6, No. 5, October–November, 1969, p. 6. Also cf. Burton H. Wolfe, *The Hippies*, New York, 1968, p. 91 ff.

manufactured chains of reason ... '; they seek for ideas not 'broken down into separate, analytical parts; subject and predicate, ... '[21] Another such ideologist, documenting the insurgence against reason and science among the New Left, observes that it differs from the Old in its 'remarkable interest in religion, magic, astrology and all the other "opiates" of traditional Left ideology'.[22] The poet, Allen Ginsberg, blending Marcusean multi-dimensional non-geometry with the vector of drugs, wrote: 'Now: the ancient "pre-scientific" ...("neolithic") gnostic/hermetic/hip understanding of identity (many-dimensional) (psychedelic) re-emerges, accompanied by resurrection of texts (modern spells, ...) and Gnostic (formerly heretical) understandings of universe complete with established Jehovaic interpretations, ... '[23] In the multifarious Youth Communes scattered through the United States, young neo-tribalists found an endorsement of their revolt against authoritarian grammar in Marcusean ideology. For among these marginal intellectuals, a retrogression in the speech pattern 'was under way', and 'a primitive tribal literacy' was the objective. 'Grunts, broken-off words, and moments of silence' were coming to 'comprise the language of the non- or demi-verbals, by far the larger majority of the commune hippies'. This will to illiteracy, this primitivist compulsion, was, said an observer, 'understandable in the context of a rejection of all values of the entrenched social structure'.[24] More particularly, however, it conveyed the resentment of the class of marginal intellectuals who still longing, despite their failure, to be society's elite, had perforce to look for social attention through regression into childhood patterns.

Thus Marcuse bears good tidings to the social stratum of young marginal intellectuals, a growing number who lack the discipline,

[21] Nicholas Von Hoffman, *We Are The People Our Parents Warned Us Against: A Close-up of the Whole Hippie Scene*, New York, 1969, p. 145.

[22] Arthur Waskow, 'The Religious Upwelling of the New Left', *Liberation*, Vol. 14, No. 4, July, 1969, p. 36.

[23] Ibid., p. 38.

[24] Roy Ald., *The Youth Communes*, New York, 1970, p. 17. Also cf. Harold Hurwitz, 'Germany's Student Revolt', *Survey*, No. 67, April 1968, pp. 93-4.

ability, or love for knowledge which are required today for the mastery of a science. In the German society in which he first conceived his notions, there was indeed a corps of displaced literary intellectuals; bred on Hegel, Fichte, and Schelling, they had lost status in the developing world of science; their metaphysical writing had a charlatanistic character compared to the achievements of Einstein or Bohr. They therefore longed to be reinstated as keepers of a shamanistic 'truth' higher than that of the sciences. Then the Hegelian philosopher, alienated and forlorn in the world of scientific advance, ridiculed by irreverent logical positivists as the purveyor of meaningless utterances would enjoy a restoration as philosopher-king. Old ideologists such as H. G. Wells and Thorstein Veblen had pictured the scientific elite, the corps of scientists, as guiding the new socialist society; Veblen, with a reverence for the machine process, thought that it would reinforce in society the impersonal, causal mode of thought, and render obsolescent the animistic, the anthropomorphic, the dialectical. But both Wells and Veblen reckoned not only without the wave-like and generational aspects of intellectual movements, but on the social consequences of a stratum of marginal intellectuals. Marcuse speaks for the corps of the lumpenintellectuals; they, not the scientists, will be the guilding elite in the new Mosaic myth, the new ideology.

The new ideologist, seeking a higher truth, an 'anti-truth' opposed to science, retreating from the confrontation with realities, regresses to more infantile modes of consciousness. Mathematical thinking, experimental work, require hours of consecutive devotion. To learn about time and space, one must choose to give one's self to years of study of physics. The new ideologist listens willingly therefore to the assurance that there is another 'method'. He can inbibe drugs, and be transported into other spaces, other-dimensions, without having to master non-Euclidean geometry. Here is the most magical labor-saving device, guaranteed by Ideology. Rather than painstaking work in statistical forecasting, he can turn to the readings of astrology,—rather than mathematical logic, 'dialectical logic', —rather than clear sentences which he fears would expose his inner emptiness, then childish sounds in regressive revolt. Many a child has felt rebellious against learning its arithmetic; now comes the Ideologist to give it in adolescence the sanction of his metaphysics: 'the logic of thought remains the logic of domination', and the law of $1 + 1 = 2$ is part of the logic of domination, that is, part of the horrid world of the adults.

Thus the regressive longings in the current generational revolt,—the assault against rationality and scientific truth found their Ideological Master in Marcuse.

5. THE INSURGENCE AGAINST VALUE-NEUTRALITY

At its inception, however, ideology placed its confidence unreservedly in science. Saint-Simon, had no doubt that the methods of science would confirm his vision concerning the direction of social evolution. Prophecy and prediction merged in the ideologist; as a prophet, his unconscious projected the mythical pattern on history with little concern for intervening causal lines; as a predictor, however, he affirmed boldly that the causal laws of social dynamics would lead to a final state which coincided with the content of the prophecy. As a consequence, the classical age of ideology shared with its contemporary science a basic assumption,—that a so-called value-free social science was possible. Charles Fourier, Karl Marx, John Stuart Mill, Herbert Spencer, Vilfredo Pareto, ideologists and social scientists alike all believed that the propositions of sociology could be confirmed as objective truths, and that there was an objective sociological truth, corresponding to social reality, which was independent of the wishes, values, or biases of the observer.

The new wave of ideology today, however, differs from the old, insofar as it challenges the very notion that an objective value-free social science is possible. The merger between myth and science, which was essential to the old ideology, has been in part disrupted; scientific method is increasingly discarded as an encumbrance. Behind this unusual development in the history of ideology lies an exceptional generational drama.

During the years from 1936 to 1956 there took place an unparalleled wave of de-ideologization. A generation of Marxists experienced what might be described as a recovery of their sense of reality. It differed in amplitude from previous waves of de-ideologization. Soviet reality contorted the Marxist myth; Stalin's murder of a generation of Marxists, the latters' masochist end in the 'Moscow trials', the pact with Naziism, the crushing of liberal socialism in Central and Eastern Europe after the war, the heightened anti-Semitism and intellectual repression, and the final revelations of Khrushchev, placed a tremendous strain on the union between mythology and science. In the de-ideologization which occurred during these years, former Marxists retaining their loyalty to science, proceeded to undermine myth.

The New Ideology, moved by a feeling of 'omnipotence of thought', believes that revolution can overcome the limits which realists find set by the nature of social reality itself. The development of the physical sciences, it should be recalled, has rested in large part physics might be defined as one who denies such impotence principles'. That perpetual motion machines are impossible, that engines cannot be driven by a flow of heat from a cold body to a warm, that the velocity of light *in vacuo* is an upper limit to attainable speeds,— such physical impotences have their counterpart in the most basic principles of physics, as, for instance, the law of the conservation of energy and the second law of thermodynamics.[25] An ideologist in physics might be defined as one who denies such impotence-principles. And in social science what took place indeed with the revival of ideology, with the New Wave, was indeed the determination to deny impotence principles in sociology: all was possible, the Revolutionary Utopia would not be denied, and if science denied it, so much the worse then for science; in that case, a value-free social science was impossible, and the very assertion of impotence principles in sociology must be a reflection of a concealed ideological bias; all were ideologists, none were scientists.

Certain 'impotence principles' indeed became during the era of de-ideologization the common platform of almost all social scientists: Michels' iron law of oligarchy, Pareto's law of the circulation of

[25] Sir Edmund Whittaker, *From Euclid to Eddington: A Study of Conceptions of the External World*, Cambridge, 1949, pp. 58 ff.

elites, Warner's law of the universality of class structure, Freud's law of the social repression of innate aggressive drives, all converged on a veto of sociological Utopias. In the sixties, however, the Utopian impulse revived strongly among the new generation of social scientists. They were little inclined to study the reality of actual Communist societies in the Soviet Union or China, for they realized the shock of fact might place a strain on their will to Utopia. They were also in revolt against the classics in social science which, written by men in their middle age, were largely de-ideologized works. For Marx was almost fifty years old when he published *Capital* in 1867, and had long put aside his youthful exuberances against alienation; Pareto, born in 1848, wrote his sociological treatise during the years from 1907 to 1912; Weber, born in 1864, was forty years old when he published the first section of his *Protestant Ethic*, and was still writing his major work when he died in 1920; Durkheim was fifty-four years old when his most influential book appeared; Freud was an old man when he wrote his sociological essays. The new wave of ideologists perceived that all these men, from left to right, had agreed that a value-free social science was possible; their scientific heritage was now plainly at odds with the new generational longings. A generational revolt which would express itself within the framework of scientific presuppositions seemed excluded, for the overwhelming weight of the evidence scientifically accumulated stood dead against one's rebellious Utopian impulses. Consequently, the New Ideology proposed to liberate social science, that is, to revive ideology expressive of their generational longings by an assault on the notion of an objective social science. Pamphlets of the Sociology Liberation Movement declared that behind the façade of value-neutrality were hidden the values that fitted the sociologists' class interests; 'the social scientist', declared a New Ideologist, 'is not and cannot be value-free and any attempt to achieve or increase the likelihood of value-free social science is doomed to failure'.[26] That this very statement was itself a sociological generalization concerning sociologists, and that it could be verified only if an objective know-

[26] Cf. A. K. Daniels, *et al.*, *Academics on the Line*, San Francisco, 1970, p. 98. Also, *Knowledge for Whom?*; *Sociology versus Society*,

ledge of social reality were possible, and that its truth was inconsis-
tent therefore with his standpoint, was of small concern to the New
Ideologist. The Liberators wished to liberate sociologists from 'their
"scientific" discipline, . . . to force it to recognize alternative values,
alternative systems of sociology, and alternative systems of society'.
How such alternative values and societies could be investigated apart
from the scientific methods of hypothesis, prediction, and observation was never specified. Indeed, a terrible sometimes unconscious
anxiety pervaded New Ideologists that their aims, judgments, and
proposals could never withstand the test of scientific method. They
therefore polemicized against the dualism between fact and value,
which the objective scientist took for granted. They cited an elder
fellow traveller who maintained that the dualism of value and fact
made for a 'moral indifference', that it warped reason with sadism.[27]
Actually the Nazi ideologists forty years ago had similarly proposed
to eradicate the dualism of value and fact, and to rid themselves of
objective social science. And the Nazis, with their value based social
science, had proved themselves the most sadistic of all. Evidently the
breakdown of the dualism inherent in the distinction between value
and fact, between the pleasure-principle and the reality-principle, can
lower the drawbridge to all varieties of irrationality. Nonetheless
every ideology, as its myth is contravened increasingly by its scientific component, is finally compelled to abrogate the principles of
scientific method. The Ideologist, in a sort of Fichtean voluntarism,
then posits his own 'facts' which have a higher Truth than the lower
order of scientific ones.

That human decisions and human actions can affect social realities, that the human will can affect the directions of social evolution,
in no way entails that an objective social science is impossible. Political activity does not invalidate the notion of a value-free sociology.
For if the choices of an individual, or group of individuals, can

Who Benefits?; Sociology Liberation Movement Proposal, pamphlets,
[Sociology Liberation Movement], 1970.
    [27] Alvin W. Gouldner, 'Anti-Minotaur: The Myth of a Value-Free
Sociology', in *Sociology on Trial*, ed. Maurice Stein and Arthur Vidich,
Englewood Cliffs, 1963, p. 51.

materially affect the direction or velocity of a sequence of events, it is because the sociological laws governing those sequences have regions of indeterminacy, which allow for the intervention of added individual variables. We might call a sociological law with such a region of indeterminacy a 'personalistic' one; such laws differ from those which are 'impersonalistic', as, for instance, the laws of supply and demand, according to which the actions of an indefinitely large number of individuals, under relatively perfect competitive conditions, are simply summated. The existence of personalistic laws, however, is a fact of objective social science; their existence underlies the possibility of alternative choices, made in accordance with differing values. A value-free sociological law allows us to affirm that a given situation is potential (within limits) with indeterminate, alternative outcomes. Without such objective laws, each activist or non-activist could subjectively legislate his own determinism or indeterminism; the social world would be a chaos with every Fichtean-like voluntarist 'positing' his own universe, and living in his own isolated make-believe. This indeed would be the practical metaphysical consequence of anarchist activist epistemology.

Of course, it is indeed the case that no social scientists have ever been perfectly objective, or value-free in their perceptions. Still, it is also the case that some have been far more objective than others. And so long as these relative differences in objectivity make sense, we can define as an ideal concept, as our guiding standard, that of the perfectly objective social scientist; in the theory of science, it is as useful as the notions of perfect gases, perfectly rigid bodies, perfect conductors, in their respective domains. If successive, increased approximations to truth are possible, then objective social science, ever diminishing the ingredient of ideology, is possible.

6. THE AUTHORITARIANISM OF THE MASTER IDEOLOGISTS

The rhetoric of ideology is always suffused with appeals to the historic mission of the chosen class, race, nation, generation, or people. Nevertheless, it is an astonishing fact in the history of ideology that the 'master-intellectuals', the masters of ideology, of every

I

generational wave have mostly agreed on one proposition—that the intellectuals should be the governing elite in society. Whether they are communists, socialists, anarchists, fascists, technocrats, or participatory democrats, the rule of the intellectual elite has been their common axiom. What is a master-intellectual? In any given period in the history of ideology, one or two ideologists stand preeminent; younger ideologists and student activists look to the master for an ideological blessing; the elder ideologist, like an Elijah, tells them his mantle is upon them, the company of Elishas. The innumerable articles and the reception on campuses devoted to Herbert Marcuse stamped him as a master-ideologist. Four generations ago H. G. Wells was the master-ideologist for young English intellectuals. As Margaret Cole recalled: 'I was just one of the many young who over three generations at least took their hope of the world from that vivid, many-gifted, generous, cantankerous personality,...'[28] During the mid-thirties, Harold J. Laski was a master-intellectual in Britain, and to a certain extent in America, so that upon his death in 1950, the distinguished political scientist, Max Beloff, wrote that 'the future historian may talk of the period between 1920 and 1950 as the "Age of Laski" '.[29] To the degree that a political party becomes the political instrumentality of the intellectuals, the role of the master-ideologist rises. In 1906, when the Labor Party first elected members to Parliament, none of them were university men. And at that time, the Bible was mentioned as the book that had shaped their thought more often than any author except John Ruskin. A half-century later, however, in 1961, close to half (45 per cent) of the

[28] Margaret Cole, *Growing up into Revolution*, London, 1950, p. 42.

[29] Max Beloff, 'The Age of Laski', *The Fortnightly*, Vol. CLXVII (New Series), 1950, p. 378. Also cf. Kingsley Martin, *Harold Laski (1893–1950): A Biographical Memoir*, London, 1953, pp. 256–7. John Strachey, 'Laski's Struggle for Certainty', *The New Statesman and Nation*, Vol. XXXIX, (1950), pp. 395–6. Freda Kirchwey, 'Harold Laski', *The Nation*, Vol. 170, 1 April 1950, pp. 291–2. Strachey alluded to Laski's 'hold over the minds of a whole generation of the British Labor Movement'. An 'unconfessed rivalry for the position of Oracle, Guide, Leader... of the Young' existed between Laski and Cole. Margaret Cole, *The Life of G. D. H. Cole*, p. 201.

Labor members of Parliament were persons with a University culture. A poll of their formative intellectual influences placed Shaw and Wells as the most popular,—32 and 26 mentions respectively among the 110 who responded. The Bible fell far down the list. Among the left wing of the members, 28 of them, not a single one mentioned Arthur Koestler or George Orwell as having exerted any influence; for the latter were critics of the intellectual elite.[30]

What characterizes the overwhelming majority of master-intellectuals is that they have been authoritarians, anti-democrats, advocates of the primacy of the 'mandarins'. Plato, from the time of Periclean Athens, has been the supreme master-intellectual not for his Theory of Ideas but rather because in his *Republic* he depicted the philosopher-kings as the guardian elite of the ideal society. The master-intellectuals in the history of ideology have been Platonists in this sense. The Fabians, led by Shaw and the Webbs, were very quickly disillusioned with democracy, when the people were slow to enroll under socialist leaders. 'It is a scientific fact', wrote Shaw, 'that the majority . . . is always wrong in its opinion of new developments, or rather is always unfit for them.'[31] 'The wage-earners are far more conventional, prejudiced, and "bourgeois" than the middle class . . . ' The chief obstruction to the advance of socialism, he declared, was 'the stupidity, the narrowness . . . of all classes, and especially of the class which suffers most by the existing system'. Shaw came to admire the 'strong men', the dictators, the Mussolinis, and the Hitlers who compel people to do what must be done; they were the harbingers of the Socialist Supermen. Toward the end of his life he blandly proposed the institution of a Socialist Inquisition as a supreme agency for planning: 'We need that institution badly . . . Its members should be selected from a panel of the highly qualified . . . Long ago I suggested that we should all be obliged to appear before a Board (virtually an inquisition) every five years, and justify

[30] K. W. J. Alexander and Alexander Hobbs, 'What Influences Labour M.P.s?', *New Society*, Vol. I, No. 11, 13 December 1962, pp. 11–14.
[31] Bernard Shaw, *The Quintessence of Ibsenism*, New York, 1917, p. 105. 'The Illusions of Socialism', in *Forecasts of the Coming Century*, ed. Edward Carpenter, Manchester, 1897, p. 160.

our existence to its satisfaction on pain of liquidation.'[32] That the Fabian leaders, Shaw and the Webbs, became such enthusiasts for the Soviet dictatorship was quite natural, for they had long endorsed Shaw's view that what socialism required was men 'qualified for more serious and disinterested work than "stoking up" election meetings to momentary and foolish excitements'.[33] Stalin shared the Fabians' view concerning democratic elections. Beatrice Webb saw the Soviet party dictatorship as the fulfillment of the Fabian conception of the rule by the intellectual elite: here was a society guided by 'specialists, with an agreed scale of values of what is right or what is wrong, and with sufficient knowledge of what has happened, and is happening, to be able to forecast . . .'[34] She cheered the rule of her fellow-ideologists, Stalin, Beria, and Zhdanov.

Authoritarianism has been an invariant trait among the master-intellectuals, the spiritual guides to generational rebels. H. G. Wells was at the height of his influence when he projected schemes for the rule of society by a scientific elite, a new samurai. Bertrand Russell fell from grace after his visit to the Soviet Union in 1920; his report compared the Communist Party to the Platonic guardians, and failed to evince the proper degree of enthusiasm for the Bolsheviks.[35] Laski

[32] Bernard Shaw, *Everybody's Political What's What?*, New York, 1944, p. 283.

[33] Edward R. Pease, *The History of the Fabian Society*, Revised Ed., New York, 1926, p. 283.

[34] Sidney and Beatrice Webb, *The Truth about Soviet Russia*, London, 1942, p. 42.

[35] 'most of my friends took the view that one ought not to say what one thought about Russia unless what one thought was favorable'. *The Autobiography of Bertrand Russell*, Vol. II, London, 1968, p. 124. Bertrand Russell, *Bolshevism: Practice and Theory*, New York, 1920, p. 29. Russell said in later years that Beatrice Webb's admiration for Soviet Russia was due to 'her own pleasure in bossing people. She, of course, conceived of herself as one of those who would give the orders in her ideal planned society. This was only natural, since, like John Strachey, J. B. S. Haldane, and other British Left Wingers who were admirers or defenders of Stalin's Russia, she belonged to the British governing class, and what is today called the Establishment.' Cf. Freda Utley, *Odyssey of a Liberal; Memoirs*, Washington, 1970, p. 153.

was at the height of his influence when he was defending in the mid-thirties the Marxist concept of the dictatorship of the proletariat, and its theory of the state; his influence was concentrated among the intellectuals of the Left Book Club and the activists in the constituency parties, not among the trade unionists.[36]

In the post-war period, Sartre's existentialism was most influential; he transformed the authenticity of the existentialist free choice into a recognition of the necessity for Marxist dictatorship. By contrast, Albert Camus, with his persistent effort for rationality failed to make a similar impress on 'progressive' French intellectuals. His refusal to overlook the massive repressions of Soviet rule rendered him unpopular with French ideologists. 'By 1952, therefore, Camus had achieved a splendid political isolation.'[37] Camus had been a Communist in his youth, and had put that experience behind him. Ideological intellectuals like Sartre, could maintain a life-long dalliance with Communism because they always avoided commitment, preferring Marxism as a mistress than as a wife. Camus, however, was a man who hoped to help people to surmount ideology. He refused to follow French ideologists in their masochist self-abnegation and condemnation of their own people: 'And it seems to me disgusting to proclaim one's sin by beating somebody else's breast, as our judge-penitents do, ...'[38] When he died in 1960, he was, as a man without ideology, virtually isolated.

Apart from Marx, Lenin, and Trotsky in the thirties, American ideologists turned among the classical writings to the works of Thorstein Veblen. For a brief period in the post-war years, David Riesman's concept of the 'inner-directed', autonomous man enjoyed an ideological vogue, to be followed later by the stronger attachment among the New Left to C. Wright Mills in the latter fifties and Marcuse in the sixties; such an ideologist as Georg Lukacs also enjoyed

[36] In the latter thirties, 'The Club became the greatest single force in England for the dissemination of left-wing thought.' Stuart Samuels, 'The Left Book Club', *The Journal of Contemporary History*, Vol. I, (1966), p. 84.

[37] Germaine Brée, *Camus*, New Brunswick, 1959, p. 55.

[38] Philip Tody, *Albert Camus 1913–1960*, London, 1961, p. 213.

a revival. Again, the uniformity of the elitist authoritarianism which surrounded these names is impressive. Veblen had already had a tremendous vogue among young ideologists in the first years of the twentieth century. Max Eastman, editor of *The Masses*, and the most brilliant editor in the annals of American Marxism, wrote in 1913: 'We have armed our critical judgment with Thorstein Veblen's "Theory of the Leisure Class"—perhaps the greatest book of our day, for it combines a new flavor in literature with a new and great truth in science. This theory has taught us how to see through "culture".'[39] Relatively forgotten during the period from 1914 to 1930, Veblen returned to favor as master-intellectual during the thirties. A writer in *The New York Herald Tribune* observed in 1934: 'The appreciation that was not accorded him in his lifetime has been growing in the five years since his death ... [I]f the revolution that he so subtly worked for is achieved, on the roll of its prophets the name of Thorstein Veblen should lead all the rest.'[40] Max Lerner, speaking for the new generation, wrote: 'If the middle road of the New Deal should prove impossible ..., in every one of Veblen's basic ideas there is dynamite that may burst asunder the whole fabric of institutions ... Veblen himself just before he died admitted that he saw no other way out than communism. The conclusion that he drew from his own thought can be drawn by others, but it will need a new generation of Veblenites to draw it.'[41] The plain fact, of course, was that Veblen was a spokesman for the rule of an intellectual elite. He never fully decided in which particular substratum to locate the chosen elite. Toward the end of his life he looked to a Soviet of Technicians to inaugurate the new society with a revolutionary general strike, what he called an 'act of disallowance'.[42] He had given up an earlier hope in the industrial working-

[39] Cited in Daniel Aaron, *Writers on the Left*, New York, 1961, reprinted 1965, p. 52.

[40] Babette Deutsch, 'Veblen-Freud and Darwin of Economics', *New York Herald Tribune Books*, 9 December 1934, p. 5.

[41] Max Lerner, 'What is Usable in Veblen?', *The New Republic*, Vol. LXXXIII, 15 May 1935, p. 10.

[42] Thorstein Veblen, *The Engineers and the Price System*, 1921, p. 159.

men. But he never took stock in democracy, anymore than did the Fabians, and he jubilated in 1921 that the Soviet system 'displaces democracy and representative government, and necessarily so, because democracy and representative government have proved to be incompetent and irrelevant for any other purpose than the security and profitable regulation of absentee ownership'.[43] Veblen opined that a Soviet session was analogous to a New England town meeting; the 'dispassionate' social scientist substituted fantasy for perception. A wave of generational rebels, however, found a sustaining ideology in Veblen's blend of myth and economics, seeing themselves as the agents of Veblen's discipline of the machine process ordaining the advent of the New Republic. It mattered little to the intellectuals that if Veblen had lived in the Soviet Union, he would have been put on trial, and purged with his fellow-technocrats of the Industrial Party.[44]

The vogue of David Riesman's *The Lonely Crowd* might seem an exception to the generalization that the master-intellectuals have been ideologists for the hegemony of the intellectual elite. A closer scrutiny, however, dispels this notion. During the post-war period many intellectuals became cultural critics of American society, deploring its mechanical and commercialized mass culture, its quality of life, its alienation of man.[45] A whole echelon of Marxist intellectuals,—many of them refugees from the Nazis, Fromm Horkheimer, Marcuse, others the editors of American leftist organs, specialized in the criticism of the masses and their culture. The intellectuals felt that the masses and history had betrayed them. When Moses saw the Hebrews dancing around the Golden Calf, he cursed them, and said they were not fit to receive the Law. It never seems to have occurred to him that there was a spontaneous joy in

[43] Thorstein Veblen, *Essays in our Changing Order*, ed. Leon Ardzrooni, New York, 1934, p. 441, Reprinted from 'Between Bolshevism and War', *The Freeman*, Vol. III, 25 May, 1921.

[44] Karl Radek, Preface, *A Blow at Intervention*, Moscow, 1931, p. 21.

[45] Edward Shils, 'Daydreams and Nightmares: Reflections on the Criticism of Mass Culture', *The Sewanee Review*, Vol. LXV, (1957), pp. 588–601.

their festival which perhaps had been lacking in the cold Yahvist cult which he was imposing. Moses, the first ideological revolutionary leader, was also the first to experience a feeling of rejection by the masses, at least temporarily. The intellectuals in the late forties till the mid-fifties felt indeed like rejected ideologists. In their own minds they still were the only ones fit to rule, the only autonomous men, but the masses, the lonely crowd not knowing how lonely and pathetic they were, rejecting the intellectuals in favor of Truman and Eisenhower, had evidently failed in their historic vocation. The intellectuals meanwhile could only retire into the role of cultural critics, until such time as the Lonely Crowd stopped worshipping the Golden Calf.[46]

7. THE MASOCHIST POLE IN THE IDEOLOGISTS' PSYCHE

The authoritarian sadistic traits of intellectuals are conjoined with an emotional obverse, a masochistic ingredient. The life-pattern of intellectuals has often been an oscillation between sadistic and masochistic ingredients. A young intellectual will go forth among peasants or proletarians in a self-abnegating back-to-the-people spirit hoping at the same time they will recognize his vocation for leadership. Rejected, he turns to terrorism against the established order, destroying rulers directly and physically, yet hoping to be brought to power in recognition of his moral purity; feeling, however, guilty for his deeds, he punishes himself. Revolutionary dictators finally exhibit a death-wish against themselves,—Danton wearying of the bloodshed, and longing for the guillotine himself,—(the most famed

[46] *Time* magazine in its sympathetic evaluation of Riesman noted that he was advising intellectuals to cultivate personal autonomy through the arts, thereby preparing themselves for a more fruitful return to politics: 'From such models, from men who respect and try to follow daydreams about their own lives, society may again learn to make social daydreams, those models called utopias.' Riesman, meanwhile, counselled his fellow intellectuals to stop worrying about their rejection by the citizenry, 'to cultivate "the nerve of failure" '. *Time*, Vol. LXIV, No. 13, 27 September 1954, p. 25.

playwright of the student movement, Georg Büchner, probed the masochist component lurking in Danton's revolutionary audacity); Nikolai Bukharin, led, as he said, 'to bend my knees before the Party', bent the spirit of a whole revolutionary generation, which lacerated itself as medieval monks, to prove their devotion to Revolution.[47] In moments of clarity when his reason penetrates the ideological fog, the intellectual will become aware of the self-destructive finale which he is preparing as the epilogue to the scenes of self-aggrandizement. Heinrich Heine, poet of a revolutionary generation, the only man in *Capital* whom Marx called 'my friend', depicted the new antagonist who would arise with the turn of 'the terrible wheel'. With Communism, 'the sombre hero' of the "modern tragedy" would emerge; the tragedy would have to be played to the end; he foresaw in 1854, 'these monsters, to whom the future belongs', who resembled 'the most terrifying crocodiles which ever crawled from out the mud'. Heine's ideological imagery took on a pathological unconscious hue. He wrote, in 1855, his vision of the intellectual under Communism:

'I made this admission, that the future belongs to Communism, in an agony and fear which, alas, was not feigned. I think with horror of the time when these gloomy iconoclasts will arrive in power. Their horny hands will mercilessly smash the marble statues of beauty . . . my *Book of Songs* will be used by the grocer to make paper-bags to hold coffee or snuff for the old women of the future. I foresee all this, and, alas, I am seized with the unutterable thought of the ruin with which the conquering proletariat threatens my poems which will surely perish together with all the romantic world. And yet I frankly admit that this same Communism, so hostile to my interests and to my inclinations, exercises a charm before which I am powerless. A terrible syllogism holds me in its grip, and, if I am unable to refute the premise (that every man has the right to eat,) then I am forced to submit to its consequences. From much thinking about it I am like to lose my reason; I see all

[47] People's Commissariat of Justice of the U.S.S.R., *Report of Court Proceedings in the Case of the Anti-Soviet Bloc of Rights and Trotskyites*, Moscow, 1938, p. 777.

the demons of truth dancing triumphantly around me, and at length the generosity of despair takes possession of my heart and I cry: . . . blessed be the grocer who shall one day use the pages of my poems as paper-bags for the coffee and snuff of poor old women, . . .'[48]

This 'terrible syllogism' which held Heine in its grasp,—was it a syllogism or an invalid argument whose lacunae were emotion-filled with untruthful premises? Ideology, encasing its myth in a carapace of presumable logic and science, seems to itself transformed into an irresistible syllogism. How to demonstrate that the notion that every man has the right to eat entails a totalitarian, anti-intellectual society? Did men indeed eat less in free societies than in totalitarian ones? No empirical, comparative evidence was ever sought to answer these questions. Instead masochist feelings took possession of the intellectual. Somehow because he was a writer of poems he was *prima facie* guilty, and his punishment would be well-deserved when his poems were used as paper-bags. And what was his guilt? The revolutionary myth assigned the intellectual a 'mission'; only if he fulfilled it would the guilt-feelings he already experienced be assuaged. He had espoused the rebel's life,—in religion,—in sexuality, in politics. But the generational rebel stood with a schism in himself which only death would end.[49]

Historical materialism indeed under the sway of ideological myth becomes historical masochism. 'History is the cruellest of all god-desses', wrote Friedrich Engels before his death, 'and she drives her triumphal car over heaps of corpses, not only in war, but also in

[48] Antonina Vallentin, *Poet in Exile: The Life of Heinrich Heine*, tr. Harrison Brown, London, 1934, pp. 240, 241, 247.

[49] How Heine thought in generational terms is shown by the letter of introduction he wrote for Ferdinand Lassalle: 'Lassalle is emphatically a son of the new age and will have nothing to do with that renunciation and humility with which *we* in our time more or less hypocritically bungled our way and drivelled our way through life. This new genera-tion is determined to enjoy itself and make itself felt in the visible world; we older ones, bowing down humbly before the invisible world, chased after shadow kisses and the scent of blue flowers, renouncing and snivel-ling; . . .' This is the ideologist in his masochist phase. Cf. E. M. Butler, *Heinrich Heine: A Biography*, London, 1956, p. 192.

peaceful economic development'. He took a curious delight in serving the cruellest of goddesses, but partially reassured himself.[50] 'There is no great historical evil without a compensating historical progress', he added. 'Let fate be accomplished.' Yet greed and the lust for power, he insisted, were the levers of history; accordingly he awaited the 'last great war dance' confidently.[51] Thus the ideologist rose to an intellectual love of evil; it was pregnant with good, and the ideologist since Socrates' time, has fancied himself as history's capable midwife.[52]

The abiding lesson of the 'Moscow trials' and the revelations of Khrushchev concerning them was the self-abnegation of the ideologist. One Soviet Communist intellectual after another died with adulation of the party and Stalin on his lips.[53] And this masochist behavior is indeed typical of the ideologist in those moments when reality is threatening his mythological defences. The novelist Anatole France wrote a classical portrait of the French revolutionary type in the character of Evariste Gamelin in *The Gods are Athirst*. As he rides in the cart toward the guillotine, Gamelin muses:

[50] Gustav Mayer, *Friedrich Engels*, trans. Gilbert and Helen Highet, (New York, 1936), p. 284.

[51] Engels criticized Feuerbach for neglecting 'the historical role of moral evil'. '[I]t is precisely the wicked passions of man-greed and lust for power—which, since the emergence of class antagonisms, serve as levers of historical development . . .' *Ludwig Feuerbach*.

[52] Historical masochism was much in evidence in the discussions by intellectuals of the war in Vietnam. The novelist Mary McCarthy was prepared to concede that a victory of North Vietnam would advance the chances for the triumph of 'world Communism'. She then commented: 'Never mind. Some sort of life will continue as Pasternak, Solzhenitsyn, Sinyavski, Daniel have discovered, . . .' But the precarious, narrow tolerance meted to these writers, who were persecuted in various ways, depended primarily on the existence of a free Western public opinion, and its impact on Soviet society. Yet Mary McCarthy is prepared to settle for an existence in which that safeguard has been eradicated. Mary McCarthy, *Hanoi*, New York, 1968, p. xxv.

[53] Cf. Nikita Khrushchev, *The Crimes of the Stalin Era*, ed. Boris I. Nicolaevsky, New York, 1956, pp. 29, 52.

'"I die justly", he reflected. "It is just that we should receive these outrages cast at the Republic, for we should have safeguarded her against them. We have been weak; ... We have betrayed the Republic. We have earned our fate. Robespierre himself, the immaculate, the saint, has sinned from mildness, mercifulness; his faults are wiped out by his martyrdom ... Let me perish! I have deserved ..."'

Anatole France wrote still another novel of revolution *Les Désirs de Jean Servien* in which he actually depicted the innocent, *naïf* hero as executed in an obscene frenzy by a woman of a Communard mob. Curiously the novelist's misgivings concerning the revolutionary unconscious did not prevent him for a time toward the end of his life from embracing ideology.[54] The prospect of the historically missioned role, as guide, teacher, and Platonic guardian of mankind, overwhelms the sense of reality.

The authoritarianism of the ideologists and their self-abnegating humility define the poles of a psychological oscillation in their characters; it corresponds to the duality among ideologists—which has been noted by the ablest observers. Leon Trotsky, for instance, wrote: 'It would be perfectly legitimate to speak of the psychological type of the Bolshevik in contrast, for example, to that of the Menshevik. An eye sufficiently experienced could tell a Bolshevik from a Menshevik even by his outward appearance, with only a slight percentage of error.'[55] It corresponded to the distinction which was much in vogue between two groups, the 'hard' and the 'soft', 'a difference in point of view, in resoluteness and readiness to go on to the end'.[56] Beatrice and Sidney Webb used to make a similar distinction; they were 'fond of saying', reported G. D. H. Cole, 'that everyone who was active in politics was either an "A" or a "B"—an anarchist or a bureaucrat—and that they were "B's"; ...[57] When the Christian

[54] Max Nomad, 'Comrade Anatole: The Political Evolution of Anatole France', *Queen's Quarterly*, Vol. LXVI, (1959), pp. 437–40.

[55] Leon Trotsky, *My Life*, p. 503.

[56] Ibid., p. 151.

[57] G. D. H. Cole, 'What Next? Anarchists or Bureaucrats?', *Fabian Journal*, Vol. 12, (April 1954), p. 31.

Laborite, George Lansbury, found the Soviet Cheka, the secret police, to be under the Commissar Dzerzhinsky a model of efficiency, he commented sardonically: 'It would rejoice Sidney Webb.'[58]

Ideologists in their own lifetimes tend to oscillate in the sadomasochist continuum between the two poles. The angered masochist will turn authoritarian; the guilt-beset sadistic authoritarian will in the last act turn masochist. The two types will have a curious affinity for each other; the only comrade Lenin really respected and loved for his nobility of character until his dying days was the 'soft' Menshevik leader, Julius Martov, while the latter was at critical times evolving Marxist rationalizations for Menshevik support to the Bolsheviks on the latter's own terms.

Historical masochism permeates the unconscious of the ideologists who in alternating moods dream of their vocation to rule. Bernard Shaw reflects sadly that those like himself, the talkers, must be superseded by the strong men of action.[59] Lincoln Steffens was thrilled by the contempt with which Lenin and Mussolini trampled over the intellectuals, disregarded liberal democratic notions, and seized power. Literary scholars who were becoming ideologists confided to each other in private correspondence that it all made their 'heart sick at times', 'nothing but grime and stink and sweat and obscene noises and the language of the beasts. But surely this is what *history* is. It is just not made by gentlemen and scholars, . . .'[60] Years ago, in a discussion with a noted Marxist professor, I observed that if his program were realized, an independent thinker such as himself would not long survive under a Communist American regime. He replied fiercely: 'People like myself deserve to go; we deserve to be liquidated.' The comment took one suddenly to his unconscious feelings, revealing a self-destructive vein in the brilliant ideologist. Shortly afterwards he became the editor of an 'independent'

[58] Raymond Postgate, *The Life of George Lansbury*, London, 1951, p. 96.

[59] Cf. Bernard Shaw, *Too True to be Good, Village Wooing and On the Rocks: Three Plays*, London, 1934, p. 273.

[60] Granville Hicks, *Part of the Truth*, New York, 1965, p. 100.

socialist magazine. How 'independent' is the historical masochist in his subjugated unconscious?

8. THE TOTALIST PRESUPPOSITION

If ideologists tend toward a total authoritarianism in political practice, so likewise does ideology project its myth upon the totality of social realities. Ideology is never content with a partial view; it intends to encompass all. A partial myth might explicate a particular institution, some innovation in technology, or it might explain some particular sociological fact in the manner in which the story of the building of the tower of Babel accounts for the many languages in the human race. A total myth is one which embraces the whole historic evolution in time of a people. And ideologists pride themselves above all on what we might call their 'totalism'. Georg Lukács, for instance, regarded such totalism as the outstanding characteristic of Marxism: 'It is not the primacy of economic motives in historical explanation that constitutes the decisive difference between Marxism and bourgeois science, but the point of view of totality', writes Lukács. The achievement of Marxism was that it 'reinstated the category of totality in the central position'.[61]

Now 'totalism', as an ideological trait, should not be confused with the scientific aim to achieve as complete explanations of natural phenomena as possible. The scientist, if he hopes to achieve a cosmogony, sees it not as his initial standpoint; he does not begin with some cosmological evolutionary principle from which the stages in the development of the elements, galactic, stellar, and planetary systems will be derived. Rather his conception of evolutionary cosmology is derivative from a combination of many verifiable laws of physics, gas laws, sub-atomic laws, laws for reactions under high temperatures and pressures. The elementary laws for observable phenomena, the laws of gases and radioactive dissociation, were not discovered by the use of a 'totalistic' standpoint: the validity of Boyle's Law was independent of any cosmology. The cosmological

[61] Georg Lukács, *History and Class Consciousness*, pp. xx, 27.

extrapolations are indeed the most speculative and conjectural part of physics. To be sure, such truths as the law of conservation of energy are affirmed in their universality for all physical phenomena. Yet such laws in physics are consistent with an indefinite number of possible alternative elementary laws for observable events. They limit the possible states of physical reality without determining them.

Moreover, the scientist is prepared to entertain the alternative that 'totalism' is unworkable. Whether in mathematical logic, with such generalizations as Gödel's Theorem rendering a 'total' theory of mathematics impossible, or the banning from the logic of propositions and classes of 'illegitimate totalities' (in Russell's phrase), or Niel's Bohr's view that no single physical standpoint can provide a complete approach to reality, that complementary standpoints are required, the scientist does not feel bound by 'totalism' as a necessary presupposition.

But the ideologist, as a myth-maker, is a 'totalist'. His mode of thought arises from the generational unconscious expressive of the child's emotional longings; the 'discipline' of suspended judgment, the postponed accumulation of evidence, the weighing of alternative hypotheses, is felt as repressive. The elder generation is regarded as tyranically imposing such constraints on the free projection of wishes and emotions on the facts. The 'discipline' of scientific method,—the very word which is used, 'discipline', evokes a sense of the intrusions of the elders on the 'omnipotence of thought' which characterizes the infantile. And 'totalism', from this standpoint, must be regarded as akin to the neurotic regression to or state of arrestment in such 'omnipotence of thought'.

The 'totalist' furthermore as he projects his mythical pattern of evolution identifies unconsciously the whole existing system as a parental product; this creation of ancestors and parents must be superseded 'root and branch', extirpated. He who thinks that partial reforms are possible is regarded as naïve because he does not perceive that the 'total' system is corrupt. Whatever problem is raised, whether it involve the life and work of races, women, intellectuals, or laborers, its evils will be attributed to the capitalist system as a whole. The ideologist is supremely unmoved by homely facts: that the place of women in Communist systems is far less favorable than in capitalistic societies, that a socialized planned economy assigns its most menial tasks to women, that anti-Semitism is far more virulent in Soviet systems, that writers and teachers have almost no independence in a strictly censored and policed system, that a socialized system denies its greatest writers the means of publication, and that the workingmen are far more 'alienated' in their jobs than in 'bourgeois societies', all are of small import compared to the compulsion to negate the 'total' system. The 'totalist,' shaped by the myth that a revolutionary uprising against the Pharaoh will inaugurate a new era of freedom, perforce believes in the total interdependence of existing institutions,—in the absence within the system of degrees of freedom for alternatives. The 'revolutionary act' of generational revolt, if it is to be endowed with supreme liberative consequences, thus legislates a 'totalism' in its ideology. The 'totality' is a dialecticized Leviathan; having mutilated its citizens, they have banded together, a phalanx of Captain Ahabs, who would destroy the Totem Animal.

The ideologist is consequently averse to the comparative weighing of alternatives. In everyday life, when some action is proposed to achieve a given aim, the rational person weighs the consequences of that action, as well as he can, against the available alternatives. If a surgical operation is proposed, if a new enterprise is to be undertaken, the gains, losses, and risks are weighed against those of alternative courses. A compulsive surgeon, whose pleasure in using the scalpel was greater than his concern for his patients' welfare would be avoided. The essence of rationality is the comparative evaluation of alternatives. An ideologist, however, in examining any evil in the workings of some social institution, is constrained by his emotional a priori, apart from any consideration of alternatives, to demand 'total' abolition of the existing society. In fact, the so-called 'dialectical' method forbids asking comparative questions; it is forbidden to ask for details as to the workings of the proposed alternative. One must simply accept the deliverances of history, though only the ideologists have signed its promissory note. 'History is the

Judge; its executioner the proletarian', said Marx in 1856, and presumably he was qualifying as clerk of the court.[62]

The ideologist speaks in the name of an absolute prophetic ethics, to pronounce an ultimate judgment on his society. The distinguished historian, R. H. Tawney, for instance, condemned the materialistic aspects of contemporary society: 'This is the citadel which must be attacked—the immoral philosophy which underlies much of modern industry.'[63] Tawney, wishing for a society in which men would not use others only as means, experienced a moral vocation to call for the abolition of the 'acquisitive society'. Yet he felt little need to measure comparatively the extent to which alternative societies have used peoples as means rather than ends. Every human relationship falls in a continuum of the relative degrees to which it involves regarding people as means or as ends in themselves. Presumably an absolute relationship in which people are regarded only as ends is not an actual one. And the rational imperative would simply be: Act to maximize the relative extent to which men in society are treated as ends in themselves rather than means. But this would constitute a comparative imperative; and the extent to which 'acquisitive society' uses people as means would have to be weighed against the extent to which a planned, bureaucratic society does so.

The comparative sense, however, is abhorrent to the absolutist and mythological ingredients in the ideologist. For the inarticulate premise of the ideologists is that in the next society they and their like will be the governing elite; they find it hard to question either the purity of their motives or the beauty of the society which will be their outcome.[64] Scientific doubts seem to them pettifogging. The

[62] Marx and Engels, *Correspondence 1846–1895*, p. 91.

[63] Cited in J. M. Winter, 'R. H. Tawney's Early Political Thought', *Past and Present*, number 47, May 1970, p. 87. According to J. D. Chambers, 'Few writings have done more to undermine the moral authority of capitalist society than *The Acquisitive Society* and *Equality*.' Cf., 'The Tawney Tradition', *The Economic History Review*, Vol. XXIV Second Series, (1971), p. 363.

[64] Maxim Gorky, in November 1917, during the Bolshevik Revolu-

K

Bourbons are not the only ones who are unable to learn from history.

Finally, in their obliteration of their comparative sense, ideologists hold to what we might call a political law of the excluded middle; they regard contraries as contradictories. To the ideologist, it is always an either—or, with only two alternatives, two extreme choices. The Italian Communist ideologist Antonio Gramsci, for instance, asserted in 1920 that for his country there were only two possibilities,—either proletarian conquest of power or fascist re-action.[65] The alternative of cooperating with liberals and socialists to preserve parliamentary government against the fascists was something which the ideologist tended compulsively to exclude. For the ideological mentality, looking at the world under the aspect of a myth, seeks the catharsis of the revolutionary experience. He looks to liberate himself from the Pharaonic oppressor-father, or to be a David conquering his Goliath, and achieving masculinity. Therefore, he has a compulsion to regard every problem-situation as a 'revolutionary situation'. And a 'revolutionary situation' is one in which all alternatives have vanished except the two extremist ones.

Ideologists thus tend to 'irrationalize' all political life. This pattern of 'irrationalization' is perhaps their most important effect on social existence. Suppose, for instance, that a small ideological group insists compulsively that in the American democratic society they are 'really' living under a fascist dictatorship, and that the only way to undermine the fascist rulers is by a campaign of terrorism and assassination which will 'unmask' its character as a police state.

tion, and before he capitulated morally to Stalin's regime, dared to appraise Lenin as an ideologist prepared to use people as his means: Lenin, he wrote, 'possesses all the qualities of a "leader" and also the lack of morality necessary for this role, ... Lenin is a "leader" and a Russian nobleman, not without certain psychological traits of this extinct class, and therefore considers himself justified in performing with the Russian people a cruel experiment which is doomed to failure before-hand'. Maxim Gorky, *Untimely Thoughts: Essays on Revolution, Culture and the Bolsheviks 1917-1918*, tr. Herman Ermolaev, New York, 1968, p. 88.

[65] Antonio Gramsci, *The Modern Prince and other Writings*, tr. Louis Marks, New York, 1959, p. 14.

What are the underlying unconscious processes in the psyches of such ideologists? They are aware that advocating assassinations and terrorism in a liberal democratic society stamps them as 'irrational', that is, as people whose choice of means is disproportionate to their avowed end because neurotic compulsions have dominated those choices. But the ideologists also sense that through assassinations and terrorism even the most liberal democratic society can be forced to adopt authoritarian measures in self-defence; police surveillance will be heightened, meetings watched and photographed, public officials guarded, the entry to governmental buildings controlled. To the extent that society is forced into a more authoritarian stance, to that extent the ideologist will find that his insistence on terrorism takes on more of a 'rational' character; his responses then seem more appropriate to the objective situation. This ideologically guided 'strategy' is known as 'polarizing' the situation, and 'radicalizing' the masses. The unconscious aim of the ideologist is to diffuse his neurosis through society by creating and inducing states of anxiety, such that the actions of irrational persons such as himself will have the appearance of rationality. The Ideologist in action thus tries to convert the abnormal into the norm by 'irrationalizing' the surrounding society with fears and anxiety. We might call this the law of ideological irrationalization.

The political universe is often an open one bounded by an amorphous domain, with indeterminate possibilities. The ideological unconscious projects itself on that universe,—abbreviating human freedom by curtailing its possibilities.

9. CATCHWORDS

Every generational wave in ideology tends to be associated with some distinctive catchword which dramatizes its principal unconscious impulse. As a parade has its slogans, so an ideological movement, thinkers in a collective march, has its catchwords; they 'think' to the emotional beat of their reiteration. The word 'alienation' served this purpose during the decade of the sixties. Its diffusion can be traced in the growing number of times it appeared in titles in reputable journals. It had no vogue in the fifties. During the three years from April 1952 to March 1955 there were no entries in the *International Index to Periodicals* under 'Alienation' (apart from one under its legal meaning with respect to the transfer of property). The next three years, from April 1955 to March 1958, 'Alienation' received only one item, not under its own classification, but under 'Social Isolation'. The following years brought a remarkable turn in the fortunes of 'alienation': 1958–60 produced 5 items; 1960–62 jumped to 11 titles; 1962–64 had 12. A retreat intervened in the year 1964–65 which showed only 3 items, but in 1965–66, 'Alienation', appearing for the first time in its independent right as a classificatory term, received 12 mentions. The next year, 1967–68, showed the highest number reached,—16 titles; it fell back to 6 in 1968–69 but recovered in 1969–70 with 12 items.

'Alienation' became the master-word in discussions of race, workingmen, literature, the problems of intellectuals, students, workers, the Ghetto, Park Avenue, and Scarsdale, the actor, the writer, the homosexual, man and God, father, son, man and woman. It was like such catchwords an 'ideological word' like 'historic mission'; one could always define for it a modicum of scientific sense, but superimposed on that meaningful kernel was its function as a cue in the ideological drama. In the Mosaic myth, the Hebrew slaves, severed from their land and God, were brought to a consciousness of their alienation when Moses and Aaron, intellectuals, came to lead them. 'Alienation' is no simple descriptive term such as 'frustration' or 'pain'; it links states of consciousness to the mandatory stages for action in the social drama which the intellectuals are writing; the alienators will be overcome, the expropriators will be expropriated, the sons will overthrow the fathers. The 'ideological word' is a call to action; it is an activist word rather than a scientific one; it assigns historical roles. Each time it is used the intellectual perceives himself above all as one who has been denied his just place in political power; this sense of 'alienation' from what he would truly be he projects into the experience of all people in all relations, especially so for that class or group whose 'mission' it is to bring him to power. In time, the word becomes tedious; all are using it, from the alienated of the left to the alienated of the right; the cycle is then complete, and the next generational wave will bring its new master-word.

'Ideological words' are later forgotten, but during their vogue they exert powerful emotional attractions. 'Solidarity', for instance, was the master-word at the end of the nineteenth century. It diffused from socialists to moderates and conservatives so that there were left solidarists and right, proletarian solidarists and bourgeois, syndicalist solidarists and royalist. 'Solidarity became the skeleton-key to all social problems.'[66] To mitigate the strains and insecurities of competitive existence, the anonymities of urban life and the anomies of a society in flux, came the ideological mandate of the will to solidarity: the strife of the labor market and the bureaucratic echelons would be supplanted by the solidarity of comrades. Leroux and Proudhon were ideologists of solidarity during the hectic years that preceded 1848. The Year of Revolution failed to achieve proletarian solidarity. But by the end of the century the liberal middle class had made 'solidarity' the aim of its social reforms; Léon Bourgeois, Prime Minister in 1895, published in 1896 a book *Solidarity*, two years after Emile Durkheim's treatise on the subject. 'The word "solidarity"', wrote Bourgeois, 'today appears all the time in political speeches and writings . . .; and the meaning that writers, orators, and public opinion in turn give to it seems, from day to day, more full, more profound, and more comprehensive.'[67] The sardonic Vilfredo Pareto tried to show 'solidarity' was vague and elusive in meaning, and possibly meaningless, but his criticism exerted no force in impeding solidarity's vogue.[68] In America, Walt Whitman echoed: 'The great word Solidarity has arisen.'[69] The smaller corps of American ideologists too had their time for the preachment of

---

[66] J. E. S. Hayward, 'Solidarity: The Social History of an Idea in Nineteenth Century France', *International Review of Social History*, Vol. IV, (1959), pp. 262–3.

[67] Léon Bourgeois, *Solidarité*, Troisième Ed., Paris, 1902, pp. 5–7.

[68] Vilfredo Pareto, 'Solidarité Sociale', *Journal des Economistes*, 5e serie, Tome XXXIII, (1898), pp. 161–71.

[69] Walt Whitman, *Democratic Vistas*, London, 1888, p. 27.

solidarity, and then the master-word receded into the antiquarian realm of ideological songs.[70] Its career is being recapitulated by 'alienation'.

When an ideological master-word, tenet or principle becomes stale and cliché-like, the revolt against it in the next generational wave often begins with the charge that the old doctrine is 'formalist', sterile, lifeless. Ralph Waldo Emerson set the note for his life's work when in his address at the Harvard Divinity School in 1838 he characterized the prevailing Unitarian creed as 'formalist'; Emerson, filled with the new Kantian idealism was longing for the quickening of the Oversoul; nearly thirty years passed before Harvard forgave Emerson for that rebellious manifesto. John Dewey in turn attacked the Kantian idealism as a species of 'formalism', as repressive of life's practical efforts and values.[71] And a later generation found pragmatism, or empiricism, too 'formalist' in its application of a criterion of verifiability which seemed to repress the significance of so much human religious and ethical thinking. Each successive generation tends to experience its predecessors' doctrine as repressive. Therefore, revolts against formalism are a recurrent feature in the history of ideology. But 'formalism', whatever its manifest meanings, has a more abiding, invariant, and latent meaning: it denotes the inevitable experience of the doctrine received from the elders and fathers as repressive.

10. GEMEINSCHAFT AND ANTI-SEMITISM

Ideology, in its generational myth, not only regresses to pre-rational modes of thought; it also expresses the longing for community, *gemeinschaft*, which is indeed today regarded as the antithesis of alienation. Community seems indeed a noble ideal; it evokes, as

[70] Austin Lewis, 'The Basis of Solidarity', *New Review*, 15 August 1915, pp. 185–8. 'Solidarity and Scabbing', *New Review*, Vol. III, 15 May 1915, pp. 34–6. 'Solidarity—Merely a Word?', ibid., 15 July 1915, pp. 125–8.

[71] Lewis S. Feuer, 'John Dewey and the Back to the People Movement in American Thought', *Journal of the History of Ideas*, Vol. XX, (1959), p. 563.

Ferdinand Tönnies explained, the world of warm intimacy and familial comfort, the security of the relationships between mother and child.[72] The family indeed is the primal model of community; physical ties, shared memories and experiences of the deepest sort, bind its members. The adolescent trauma is in large part the sundering of communal existence which takes place as the child moves from the personal community to impersonal society, from *gemeinschaft* to *gesellschaft*. The world wherein one was valued for one's self, as an end in himself is superseded by one of exchange relations, wherein one is regarded as a means. In the ideological myth, the juvenocratic elite overthrows that society, and restores the community; the enslaved become comrades and brothers, reborn in a new movement.

The guardian and guiding elite of *gemeinschaft* naturally hates any group which chooses to stand outside the community. Such voluntary ex-communicates are surd members; they are embodiments of doubt, objective presences whose existence is a latent questioning of the ideological myth. Such persons are the Jews, these mysterious strangers, unclubbable, elusive. The stranger in the family reawakens childhood fears. Then too the Jews, despite their partial separatism, are rival contenders for elite leadership themselves; they are an elite people, observed Charles de Gaulle. They challenged the Roman elite in ancient times; they challenged the supremacy of the clerical elite in Imperial Spain; they contested, even from positions of weakness, the Czarist bureaucratic elite. As Karl Marx's father said, as he tried to avoid conversion to Christianity, despite the measures aimed to degrade them, they bore the unmistakable stamp of a noble humanity.[73] To the intellectual elite, however, vying for political power under the charter of its ideology, the existence of the Jews constitutes the existence of a competitive elite; the intellectual, seeking after power, wishes to discredit and eradicate his rivals. Lastly, the neo-tribal, communalist society, is

[72] Ferdinand Tönnies, *Community and Society*, tr. Charles P. Loomis, East Lansing, 1957, p. 37.

[73] Lewis S. Feuer, 'The Conversion of Karl Marx's Father', *The Jewish Journal of Sociology*, Vol XIV, 1972, p. 155.

helped toward its equilibrium of *gemeinschaft* if it can direct its uneliminable hatreds toward some non-communalized outsider. What threatens every communal society from commune to Soviet, is the presence of free-floating, drifting, uncontrolled and unharnessed aggressive energies. The frustrations of communal, neo-tribal, and Soviet societies, fed by envies, jealousies, indifferences, hatreds, are an ever-present storehouse of threatening powers. They portend break-up, fission, fraction and faction, secession and schism,—the centrifugal forces which will burst through the centripetal communal ones. The ideological community therefore seeks to stabilize itself by directing these disruptive energies against an external enemy, or an internal 'externalized' one; the Jews, as an example of the latter, are a convenient drain for the non-communizing aggressive energies. The 'revolutionary instincts' of the masses have been thus channelized by the ruling elite, under the Soviet Security organs as under the Spanish Inquisition.

Hence, we can explain that most unusual fact in the history of ideology,—that the overwhelming majority of the most famous ideologists in the nineteenth and twentieth centuries have been anti-Semites. We may omit from our inventory Nazi, fascist, nationalist, and racial ideologists, since their anti-Semitism is usually blatant. More significant of the underlying ideological unconscious in the inventory of the socialist ideologists. The central names, according to the histories of socialism, were Saint-Simon, Robert Owen, Charles Fourier, Proudhon, Louis Auguste Blanqui, Michael Bakunin, Karl Marx, Friedrich Engels. Their feelings concerning the Jews were in most cases filled with active hostility; we may provide a few citations.

Charles Fourier, ideological founder of the phalansteries, the communes of 'passional attraction', said the Jews should have been excluded from society 'as a social plague'; he bewailed the 'monstrous' outcome of 'liberal preconceptions', namely the granting of citizenship to the Jews; this was the 'most shameful' of all the 'recent vices': 'And are not the Jews ... the leprosy and the ruin of the body politic? ... If time could improve them would they not have been cured in London, where they have been living for such a

long time and where they walk along the streets, inciting gentlemen's sons to steal, etc.?' Fourier resented especially the Jews'
separatism with regard to their foods (their rejection of the most
primitive gastronomical communion) their 'refusal to eat food prepared by other sects.'[74] His younger contemporary, Pierre Leroux,
is believed to have invented the word 'socialism'; though nurtured
by Jewish Saint-Simonians, he did not extend the blessed community to the Jews. His essay, *Les Juifs, rois de l'Epoque*,
condemned 'the Jewish spirit, the spirit of profit, of lucre, of gain,
the spirit of commerce, of speculation, in a word, the banker spirit'.
They were the rejected ones of the Christian version of the Mosaic
myth: 'A terrible predestination,' he wrote, lay upon the Jews, for
they had failed to recognize the Messiah;[75] they were at war with all
mankind.

The famed Proudhon, master libertarian of French ideology,
expressed too a terrible wrath against the Jews; by their obstinacy
with regard to the Messiah, they had placed themselves, he wrote,
'beyond the conscience of the human race'. The Jews, he charged,
had since ancient times considered themselves an elite, distinguished
by their monotheism, and destined to rule the world. Proudhon, the
chief of a rival elite, denounced the Jewish competitor: the Jew was
the principle of evil in history: 'The Jew is by temperament an anti-
producer, ... He is an intermediary, always fraudulent and parasitic, ... His policy in economics has always been entirely
negative, ...; it is the evil principle, Satan, Ahriman, incarnated in
the race of Sem, and which has already been twice exterminated by
the Greeks and Romans, the first time at Tyre, the second time at
Carthage.' It was in his notebooks in 1847, on the eve of the
Revolution, that Proudhon's hatred for the Jews was most ruthless
and sanguinary:

'Call for its expulsion [this race] from France, ... abolish the
synagogues; ...

[74] Edmund Silberner, 'Charles Fourier on the Jewish Question',
Jewish Social Studies, Vol. VIII, (1946), pp. 250–1.
[75] Edmund Silberner, 'Pierre Leroux's Ideas on the Jewish People',
Jewish Social Studies, Vol. XII (1950), pp. 368–71.

'It is not for nothing that the Christians have called them God-killers. The Jew is the enemy of humankind. It is necessary to send this race back to Asia, or exterminate it.

'What the people of the Middle Ages hated by instinct, I hate by reflection, and irrevocably.'[76] In calmer moments, Proudhon complained that 'the Jews dominated the press and controlled the government. Under the Republic, as under Louis Philippe, and as under Louis XIV we have always been at the mercy of the Jews.' One was either 'an apostle of human brotherhood' or 'a Jew'.[77]

The intransigeant Louis Auguste Blanqui, the exalted chieftain of many generations of activists of the Left Bank and Sorbonne, conspirator, happiest in the comradely elitism of secret societies, alternating insurrections with imprisonment, was in solidarity with Proudhon as far as their hatred for Jews was concerned. The Jews, wrote Blanqui in the secrecy of his manuscripts, were 'the type, and ideal, and the incarnation of swindling, usury, and rapacity. They are the horror of the nations because of their pitiless cupidity, as they had once been because of their hostility and war to the death against the human race.'[78]

What anxiety motivated such men as Proudhon and Blanqui so that they frantically condemned the Jews as enemies of the human race? The ideologists saw themselves as the new elite; that was an essential latent aim of their revolutionary activity; they were the inheritors of the Mosaic myth, the new redeemers. And here were

[76] *Carnets de P. J. Proudhon*, ed. Pierre Haubtmann, Deuxieme Volume, Paris, 1961, p. 338.

[77] The kindly historian of anarchism, George Woodcock, charitably omits this aspect of Proudhon's thought from his accounts. How Proudhon's radicalism, in a meeting of extremes, merged with fascist ideology was first shown by J. Salwyn Schapiro, *Liberalism and the Challenge of Fascism*, New York, 1949, pp. 332 ff. George Woodcock, *Pierre-Joseph Proudhon*, London, 1956. Schapiro, pp. 358–9.

[78] Alan B. Spitzer, *The Revolutionary Theories of Louis Auguste Blanqui*, New York, 1957, p. 82. The subject of Blanqui's anti-Semitism is omitted in the recent biography by a Jewish orthodox Marxist. Cf. Samuel Bernstein, *Auguste Blanqui and the Art of Insurrection*, London, 1971.

the Jews, who with emancipation were emerging as a new intellectual elite, who might deny their claims to leadership as they once
had denied those of Jesus. So, though young Jewish intellectuals gave
themselves to the Revolution, many Ideologists claimed they could
detect a community of interest between a Rothschild and a Marx,—
the bond of the Jewish elite. The towering anarchist of the nineteenth century, Michael Alexandrovich Bakunin, articulated most
clearly the antagonism of the community-seeking elite to the Jews:

'Now the whole Jewish world which constitutes one exploiting
sect, one people of leeches, one single devouring parasite closely and
intimately bound together not only across national boundaries, but
also across all divergences of political opinion—this Jewish world
today stands in large part at the disposal of Marx on the one hand,
and of Rothschild on the other. I am sure that the Rothschilds, on
the one side, value the merits of Marx, and that Marx, on the other
side, feels an instinctive attraction towards, and great respect for the
Rothschilds.'

'This may seem strange. What common ground can there be
between Communism and the big bank? Oh! but the Communism
of Marx wants powerful governmental centralization, and where
this exists, . . . the parasitic Jewish nation, which speculates in the
labor of the people, will always find means to exist.'

Whether Society was Communist or Bourgeois, the Jews, according to Bakunin, were candidates for the governing elite; and he was
a candidate too. He assailed Marx; the latter, he said, was surrounded by 'a crowd of little Jews who are more or less clever,
scheming, nimble, and speculating, as Jews everywhere are, commercial or banking agents, literati, politicians, correspondents for
newspapers of all shades of opinion, . . .' The language was almost
a model for Pareto's metaphor in the struggle of rival elites, the
speculators against the rentiers, the foxes against the lions. Bakunin,
as Proudhon and Blanqui, invoked the powers of *Gemeinschaft*,
what Pareto would have called the residue of 'the persistence of
aggregates'.[79]

[79] Edmund Silberner, 'Two Studies of Modern Anti-Semitism; Part 2,
the Jew Hatred of Mihail Alexandrovich Bakunin', *Historia Judaica*,

Robert Owen, the idealistic manufacturer and founder of British socialism, was a rare exception,—a socialist thinker genuinely without hostility to the Jews. His formation, one must notice, however, was not that of an intellectual; he was a successful business man and plant organizer, not a journalist, not a professor.[80] On the other hand, the intellectuals who led the Chartist movement generally regarded the Jews as exploiters of the British people; the Government was even reproached for having adopted the 'Jewish theory of Mr. Ricardo'. *The Northern Star*, the Chartist organ, declared: 'Woe to the Jews and jobbers, oppressors and murderers ... who trample upon the oppressed.'[81]

In short, socialist ideologists, of all countries, peoples, and places were drawn, in their pursuit of *Gemeinschaft* to anti-Semitism. The leader of the first avowedly ideological socialist organization in Britain, Henry M. Hyndman, of the Social Democratic Federation, Beatrice Webb, first among the Fabian women, Robert Blatchford, the most popular of the socialist propagandists, were all regarded as anti-Semites. The Webbs especially felt that the Polish Jewish immigrants were 'a constant influence for degradation' among the British working class, and unfit for trade unionism.[82] The Fabian *Gemeinschaft* was rendered ill at ease by the Jews. George Bernard Shaw was so indifferent to Hitler's treatment of the Jews that his friend Lawrence Langner, director of the Theatre Guild, refused to produce the play *Geneva* even after its anti-Semitic speeches were omitted. As an admirer of total community planning, the Hitlerite model included, Shaw from the outset was undisturbed by Nazi

Vol. XIV, (1952), p. 101. Cited from Bakunin, *Gesammelte Werke*, III, pp. 208-9.

[80] As G. D. H. Cole observed: 'Owen, however, differed from most writers in that he was not at all an "intellectual", or a student in any ordinary sense.' *The Life of Robert Owen*, London, 1930, p. 315.

[81] Edmund Silberner, 'British Socialism and the Jews', *Historia Judaica*, Vol. XIII, (1951), pp. 32-4.

[82] Ibid., pp. 37, 40. Sidney and Beatrice Webb, *Industrial Democracy*, New Ed., London, 1902, pp. 687, 744. Beatrice Webb, *My Apprenticeship*, Vol. II, Middlesex, 1938, pp. 488-9. Melech Epstein, *Profiles of Eleven*, Detroit, 1965, p. 34.

anti-Semitism: 'The extirpation of the Jew as such figured for a few mad moments in the program of the Nazi party in Germany,' he wrote beamingly in 1933.[83] J. A. Hobson, author of the influential book *Imperialism*, viewed the 'Jew-Imperialist' as the exemplar of the phenomenon. 'The Jews are *par excellence* the international financiers... They fastened on the Rand... as they are prepared to fasten upon any other spot on the globe...'[84] They were alleged to be using British arms to make themselves the political rulers of South Africa. This mysterious alien elite aroused neo-tribal anxieties in the socialistic intellectual akin to those of the politically illiterate Afrikaners.

Alone among the ideological schools for its lack of anti-Semitism was the Saint-Simonian. This, the first of the socialistic movements was notable for the high proportion of brilliant young Jews who were attracted to its ranks. Aspirants for the highest intellectual elite, their Jewish descent had set obstacles to their careers in Restoration France. The Saint-Simonian ideology brought the promise of a society redeemed for rationality by a new industrial-scientific elite; directing its message unequivocally toward such an elite, this first scientific version of the Mosaic myth won the loyalty of young Jews; they revelled in its grandiose blend of myth and science. Gustave d'Eichthal, who later tried hard to convert his young friend John Stuart Mill, remembered the pain the word 'Jew' had brought him in his childhood. Olinde Rodrigues, whose father had been secretary of the Napoleonic Sanhedrin, was denied admission to the Ecole Normale because of his Jewish descent; thereupon he shifted to the Ecole Polytechnique, where he met Saint-Simon.[85] He supported

[83] Lawrence Langner, *G. B. S. and the Lunatic*, New York, 1963, pp. 161, 170. Bernard Shaw, *Too True to be Good, Village Wooing and On the Rocks: Three Plays*, London, 1934, p. 145.

[84] Harvey Mitchell, 'Hobson Revisited', *Journal of the History of Ideas*, Vol. XXVI, (1965), pp. 397–416. Also R. Koebner and H. D. Schmidt, *Imperialism: The Story and Significance of a Political Word, 1840–1960*, Cambridge, 1964, pp. 250–6.

[85] Zosa Szajkowski, 'The Jewish Saint-Simonians and Socialist Antisemites in France', *Jewish Social Studies*, Vol. X, (1947), p. 35.

Saint-Simon both morally and financially after the latter, discouraged and penurious, had tried to commit suicide in 1823.[86] Then too there were the brothers Pereire, Jacob Emile and Isaac, also students at the Polytechnique.[87] The Saint-Simonians became known as the 'new Jews'. The Fourierist school, was naturally hostile to the Saint-Simonian competitive elite, and perforce extremely anti-Semitic.[88] The Saint-Simonians engaged in a series of Messianic acts and manoeuvres; they even searched for a Mother for the movement expecting her to be a Jewish woman from Turkey; later, however, they were de-ideologized. The brothers Pereire became the pioneers in railway construction during the reign of Napoleon III.[89] The Jewish Saint-Simonians always recognized in an oblique way the continuity between their ideology and the Mosaic myth. Once, on the Jewish holiday of Rosh Hashanah, d'Eichthal and four other Saint-Simonians went to the Paris synagogue dressed in their Saint-Simonian costume 'to show their respect for the religion of Moses'. And when the sect organized 'a society for welcoming the Mother', they published an appeal to Jewish women to participate.[90] Léon Halevy wrote a book which delineated the common mission which animated Judaism, Christianity, and Saint-Simonianism.[91] All this was forgotten as Saint-Simonians became the de-ideologized organizing industrialists of the Second Empire. George Sand, famed as a Saint-Simonian novelist, still feared in 1857, that the Jew aspired to become the king of the world, and to destroy the ideal Jesus.[92] The conflict of socialist sects was indeed a rivalry of would-be elites. The rupture of the Jewish Saint-Simonians with the sect began when, under the leadership of 'Father' Enfantin, it made its turn towards free love. Olinde Rodrigues, for instance, an ardent

[86] Georges Weill, 'Les Juifs et le Saint-Simonisme', *Revue des Etudes Juives*, XXXI (1895), p. 261.

[87] Ibid., p. 37. Also cf. Silberner, 'Pierre Leroux's Ideas on the Jewish People', p. 375.

[88] Zosa Szajkowski, 'The Jewish Saint-Simonians and Socialist Anti-semites in France', *Jewish Social Studies*, Vol. IX, (1947), p. 46.

[89] Ibid., p. 44.

[90] Ibid., p. 39 Georges Weill, op. cit., p. 267.

[91] Szajkowski, op. cit., p. 43.   [92] Szajkowski, op. cit., p. 41.

disciple, nonetheless loved his wife and child; he was angered when the chief of the sect proclaimed that in the future society the children would no longer know their father.[93] De-ideologization begins when generational revolt has run its course.

The anti-Semitism of Karl Marx has been so often documented that we need not dwell upon it. Author of the anti-Jewish essay *On the Jewish Question*, contributor of anti-Semitic articles to *The New York Tribune*, interspersing his correspondence with anti-Semitic jibes at Lassalle, Marx wrote in *Capital* of the capitalist knowing that all commodities, 'however badly they may smell', were 'in truth money, inwardly circumcised Jews, . . .'[94]

Friedrich Engels, his closest friend, co-worker, and benefactor for many years, shared Marx's anti-Semitism. He was enthusiastic in 1845 over Marx's essay on the Jewish question, and similarly admiring in 1846 of a pamphlet circulating in Paris entitled *Rothschild I. King of the Jews*; he thought its success in twenty editions showed it was 'an attack in the right direction'. He vied with Marx in the invention of anti-Semitic epithets for the abuse of Lassalle. After 1878, however, Engels largely scrapped his anti-Semitism. In Germany, Marx's intellectual leadership of the socialists was being challenged by a scholar Eugen Dühring, who harped continually upon Marx's Jewish origins. Meanwhile the ablest of the new generation of socialists were often Jews, as Victor Adler in Austria, Eduard Bernstein and Paul Singer; Adler and Bernstein, the latter especially, were Engels' closest associates in later years. Then, too, Marx's youngest and favorite daughter, Eleanor, became deeply attached to her Jewish origins. She went frequently to the Jewish Socialist Club in London, reportedly began to learn Yiddish, and told the delegate to the International from the United States, Abraham Cahan: 'We Jews have a special duty to work for the working class.'[95] Evidently she told Engels much about the life of

[93] Georges Weill, op. cit., p. 246.

[94] Karl Marx, *Capital: A Critique of Political Economy*, trans. Samuel Moore and Eduard Aveling, Chicago, 1906, p. 172.

[95] Cf. Edmund Silberner, 'Friedrich Engels and the Jews', *Jewish Social Studies*, Vol. XI, (1949), pp. 325, 326, 330, 332–5.

the Jewish working class in London. And Eleanor Marx ('Tussy') was very dear to Engels.

Gradually then Engels adopted a strongly critical attitude toward the new wave of anti-Semitism. He published an eloquent letter condemning it in 1890:

'Antisemitism is thus nothing but a reaction of the medieval, perishing strata of society against modern society, which essentially consists of capitalists and wage-earners; under the cloak of apparent socialism it, therefore, only serves reactionary ends; it is a variety of feudal socialism . . .' It was 'the distinctive sign of a backward civilization . . .'

What evidence could Engels, however, adduce that anti-Semitism was a medieval survival? If part of the motivation of socialist ideology was to restore the Gemeinschaft (Community) of pre-capitalist societies, then a reawakening of anti-Semitism was altogether likely. And if different elites were contending for the leadership of the socialist society, what would be more natural than that one elite should try to disqualify its competitor by reason of its Jewishness? Anti-Semitism would then be a distinctive sign of an 'advanced ideology'. Moreover, despite his affection for his Jewish friends, Engels finally found himself in 1892 sympathetically comprehending of the French anti-Semites: 'I begin to understand French anti-Semitism when I see how many Jews of Polish origin and with German names intrude themselves everywhere, arrogate everything to themselves and push themselves forward to the point of creating public opinion in the ville lumière, of which the Paris philistine is so proud and which he believes to be the supreme power in the universe.'[96] One might imagine from Engels' remarks that France was being inundated by an avalanche of Polish Jews. Yet the Jewish population in all France in 1899 was only 75,000. Of these 45,000 lived in Paris; 20,000 of their number were workers.[97] One can understand why French socialism was riven within the next

[96] Fredericks Engels, Paul and Laura Lafargue, *Correspondence*, tr. Yvonne Kapp, Vol. 3, Moscow, n.d. p. 184.

[97] Edmund Silberner, 'French Socialism and the Jewish Question 1865–1914', *Historia Judaica*, Vol. XVI, (1954), p. 37.

five years by the Dreyfus Case. The Marxist wing explained their indifference to the fate of a Jewish captain on ideological grounds. But it was the fact that until 1898 in France 'Socialists, generally speaking, flirted with anti-Semitism because they considered it a useful, though aggressive, auxiliary'.[98] It was above all the non-Marxist, Jean Jaurès, who refused to allow ideology to warp his humanity, and helped liberate his party from ideological trammels.

The unusually high proportion of anti-Semites among ideologists clearly points to a relationship of causation. That the phenomenon has occurred among ideologists in countries both advanced and backward, industrial as well as agricultural, indicates a common origin in the motivation and emotion. That the New Left in the United States, with its revival of ideology, very quickly took on an anti-Semitic guise was something foreseeable. Perhaps of all the ideologists the one who was most bewildered by the phenomenon of socialist anti-Semitism was Leon Trotsky. He recognized that the Stalinist elite had without compunction availed itself of anti-Semitism in order to isolate and destroy his own faction: 'The struggle against the opposition was for the ruling clique a question of life and death ... These people stop at nothing in order to guard their privileges and power.' Throwing aside principles and program, the Stalinist elite proceeded, wrote Trotsky, 'to emphasize my Jewish origin', and doing likewise with 'the names of Jewish members of casual and secondary importance'. In accordance with their Marxist creed, as early as 1925, 'the Opposition saw in this situation the unmistakable symptom of the decay of the ruling clique'. Was it however a 'decay' so much as a reappearance of a universal trait in the ideological search for *Gemeinschaft*? The Stalinist elite, as their predecessors, Bakuninist, Proudhonist, Blanquist, and Fourierist, resented and hated their Jewish competitor. Trotsky challenged the gentle Nikolai Bukharin to investigate an example of anti-Semitic methods in one factory. 'Bukharin agreed, but Stalin categorically forbade him to do so.' Bukharin, the future right-wing deviationist, was helpless against the authentic spokesman for the bureaucratic elite. 'The slogan, "Beat the Opposition", often took on the complexion of the old

[98] Ibid., pp. 35–6.

L

slogan "Beat the Jews and save Russia".' Trotsky was rendered confused and uncertain: 'I have always worked in the Russian workers'
movement. My native tongue is Russian. Unfortunately I have not
even learned to read Jewish. The Jewish question therefore has never
occupied the center of my attention.'[99] Yet here the Bolshevik
Marxist party was acting like the Black Hundreds. He reasoned that
the Stalinist bureaucratic cadre was striving to divert the indignation
of the masses from itself to the Jews. But he could not face squarely
the fact that the Bolshevik leaders fully shared this anti-Semitism,
and that this was why they adopted it so readily. Trotsky and his
fellow Jewish intellectuals, who occupied places not only in the
highest bureaucracy but especially so 'in its lowest and middle levels'
were almost all eradicated during the thirties. They were surd elements in the Ideological Community.

The strain of anti-Semitism is moreover inherent in the ideological
process itself; it is not solely a fact concerning the temperaments of
ideologists and their surrounding society. Edmund Silberner has,
indeed, argued that 'Socialist anti-Semitism' was 'nothing but a
name for anti-Semitism professed by people who happen to be
Socialists'[100] It was not unlike ' "bourgeois" anti-Semitism', he
wrote, and arose from the same variety of causes, but it did not per-
tain to the essence of socialist ideology. Another scholar believes that
socialist anti-Semitism was a transient fact of Europe in the nineteenth century which has vanished from the Socialist movement, and
is scarcely likely to recur.[101] Meanwhile, anti-Semitism has been pursued most vigorously by the most ruthlessly socialist elements in
Poland and Czechoslovakia; Jews who were in the forefront of the

[99] Cf. Leon Trotsky, 'Thermidor and Anti-Semitism', *The New
International*, Vol. VII, No. 5, May 1941, pp. 91–4; written on 22
February 1937. Joseph Nedava, *Trotsky and the Jews*, Philadelphia, 1972,
p. 168. Lenin recorded the anti-Semitism of Plekhanov, the founder of
Russian Marxism. Ibid., p. 51.

[100] Edmund Silberner, *The Anti-Semitic Tradition in Modern Socialism*, Jerusalem, 1953, p. 18.

[101] George Lichtheim, 'Socialism and the Jews', *Dissent*, Jan.–Feb.
1968, pp. 314–42.

Bolshevik Revolution are virtually absent from Soviet ruling echelons; and anti-Semitism is a tenet of the American New Left.[102]

The commercial and industrial leaders of Britain and Holland beginning in the seventeenth century, whatever their personal religious views, took the liberation of the Jews as a natural corollary of their new society. Each person became a free citizen by virtue of his free participation in a free competitive market. There was no demand for consolidation or absorption into an embracing community; the bourgeois society liberated energies as no other system had precisely because it liberated them from coercive communities, whether feudal ties, guilds, or estates. Aggressive energies and individualistic striving were channelized into the constructive competition of the market-place. A socialist community, on the other hand, perceives individual differences, however, as an incipient challenge to the shared scheme of values. Virtually every American socialist colony that has ever been founded became an oasis of intolerance, which subsequently disintegrated amidst schisms and secessions; the few that survived were religious dictatorships. The socialist intellectual elite, moreover, as we have seen, anxious for its access to power, scarcely wishes to see prizes taken by the Jewish elite. The sense of community lastly is enhanced when aggressive energies are drained by direction toward the outsider. Community is stabilized by anti-Semitism because it lacks the natural outlets for aggression which a competitive capitalism possesses. For such reasons, the psychological dynamic of socialist ideologists engenders a propensity for anti-Semitism.

11. REGRESSION TO PRIMITIVISM

'Cultural primitivism', wrote Arthur O. Lovejoy, 'is the discontent of the civilized with civilization, ... the belief of men living in a relatively highly evolved and complex cultural condition that a life

[102] French Communist ideologists unreservedly accepted Stalin's charges in the so-called 'Jewish Doctors'' plot in 1953. David Caute, *Communism and the French Intellectuals 1914–1960*, London, 1964, p. 202.

far simpler . . . is a more desirable life'.[103] Cultural primitivism, an enduring theme of human nature ever since the civilizing process began, probably began, as Lovejoy conjectured, when early men sought out the refinements of cave-dwellings, and brought down upon themselves the first primitivist protest. The author of the myth of Adam, an early ideologist, bewailed the advance through knowledge from the food-gathering economy to the agricultural. Now it is a universal law that every ideology tends towards a revival of primitivism. Even those ideologies, like Marx's, which exalt the role of technology finally introduce the theme of man's overcoming the class divisions of society, and recapturing the primitive classlessness. Engels thought that under communism men and women would regain the sexual freedom they had enjoyed in primitive times. Kropotkin was enthralled by the primitive tribes in Siberia, and later even interpreted the wildly competitive practice of potlatch among the Kwakiutl as a sign of mutual aid.[104] The current Leftist ideology is preeminently one of cultural primitivism, more frankly so than any since the Nazis. Young ideologists emphasize the restoration of the tribal community and its drug rituals, and they aspire toward a restoration of magic, astrology, and primitive dress.

The roots of primitivism in the ideological mode of thought are related to its mythological component. Ideology as we have seen is always an unstable union of myth and logic and science. The scientific, the civilizing ingredient, always imposes some strain on the growing child. He finds himself compelled to de-personalize his thinking, to de-anthropomorphizing his basic categories. The very notion of a 'law of nature', founded as it is on the analogy of law in society constraining all human beings according to its decree, is one that smacks of authoritarianism, of discipline, of the Father's rule.

[103] Arthur O. Lovejoy, George Boas, *Primitivism and Related Ideas in Antiquity*, Baltimore, 1935, p. 7.

[104] Peter Kropotkin, *Memoirs of a Revolutionist*, New York, 1930, p. 216. Prince Kropotkin, *Ethics: Origin and Development*, tr. Louis S. Friedland and Joseph R. Piroshnikoff, New Ed., New York, 1936, p. 75. Peter Kropotkin, *Mutual Aid: A Factor of Evolution*, New York, 1925, pp. 78, 83.

Thus, one wing of youth, in generational rebellion, has always been moved to challenge the primacy of scientific method on behalf of myth. But only in recent years has this mode of thought really acquired a considerable number of followers among Western youth.

The insurgence against science today is founded on three facts: (1) whereas the advancement of science until 1945 was associated with invention which generally enhanced the prospects of the human race, the discovery of atomic energy brought doubts as to the consequences for human survival, (2) whereas the emotions of generational rebellion previously associated themselves with novel conceptions of science such as evolution and relativity, which overthrew those aspects of the universe which made it more humanly congenial to traditionalist fathers, the wave of these Copernican revolutions was now complete; the traditional world-view was dismembered, and within the orbit of some new 'scientific revolution', there was no new tenet which could foreseeably undermine or discredit the old world-view any more than it already was; revolt therefore tended to move toward some doctrine of anti-science, towards anti-Copernican revolutions; (3) the huge increase in the numbers of semi-intellectuals, sharing in some of the fruits of the intellectual advancement, but never really among its participants; resentful toward a scientific discipline which exceeded their powers, this new corps of marginal and sub-marginal intellectuals, were ready to hate science as the displaced Luddite workingmen hated technology, and were ready to become the 'machine wreckers'.

The self-hatred of the intellect, was once confined to a few individuals such as Rousseau, who was then promptly ridiculed by Voltaire as proposing that we should walk upon all fours. Now, however, it is part of the 'collective regression' of a whole group. This regression can take two directions, a Utopian-maternal one, or a Nietzschean-aggressive one. The Utopian intellectuals were such as went into colonies in the fields or forests, the Brook Farmers, and their many brethren and sisters. They sought to return to a pristine, womb-like quietude: 'The good place is a lovely green hollow', they could say with Virgil, with expressive maternal imagery; the machine was an intruder, crude, masculine, aggressive, invading the tender, disrupting 'the peace of an enclosed space'.[105] The Nietz-schean primitivists, on the other hand, looked forward to a comrade-ship of warriors, enjoying the brute aggression, the stalking of the enemy, the pleasures of destruction, and insofar as love was con-cerned, making the bond of a homosexual collective of young warriors their norm. The 'charismatic' names in recent ideologies have all been the chiefs of guerrilla warriors who led their comrades in marches through Chinese, Cuban, or Bolivian fastnesses,—Mao, Castro, Che Guevara. Lenin, the bookworm in the libraries of Zürich, Berne, and London, never would have qualified for 'charis-matic' anointing today, nor would Trotsky the townsman, contemp-tuous of primitivist cults.[106] The French existentialist *co-guerrillero* with Guevara, Régis Debray, declared that in Latin America 'there is a close tie between biology and ideology'; the elderly men could never endure the ordeals of mountain guerrillas; thus, 'rejuvenation' takes place among the ideologists; the primitivists in action accom-plish a tactical parricide; nature itself is invoked to purge the party ranks rather than the staged scenarios of Moscow trials. The *guerrilleros* are neo-primitivist tribesmen: 'The first law of guerilla life is that no one survives it alone ... Petty bourgeois psychology melts like snow under the summer sun, undermining the ideology of the same stratum. Where else could such an encounter, such an alliance, take place?' The Oedipal ties and feminizing corruptions of civilization are severed,—these umbilical cords of running water, a house, a roof, electricity: 'Nothing like getting out to realize to what extent these lukewarm incubators make one infantile and bourgeois.' The primitivist guerrilla can 'erase the marks left on his body by the incubator—his weakness'.[107] No manual of ideology has

---

[105] Leo Marx, *The Machine in the Garden: Technology and the Pastoral Ideal in America*, New York, 1964, pp. 22–9. Lovejoy similarly distinguished between a 'soft' and 'hard' primitivism. Cf. Lovejoy, op. cit., p. 10.

[106] Leon Trotsky, *Literature and Revolution*, reprinted, New York, 1957, pp. 131 ff., 179, 51.

[107] Régis Debray, 'Revolution in the Revolution?', *Monthly Review*, Vol. 19, No. 3, 1967, pp. 71, 102, 110–11.

ever been so explicit about the generational source of ideology as this manual of primitivism in which the incubator becomes the primary symbol.

Ideological primitivism oscillates between the Utopian and Nietzschean varieties, with various combinations of the two strands. Common to both is a hatred for reason and science. The distrust of analytic thinking, the faith in obscurer faculties of the soul, in unanalysable, subconscious intuitions, the apotheosis of free, creative action, the pursuit of an indefinable infinite, the zeal in berating the bourgeois, the philistine, the 'square',—all these typical traits of romantic ideology have recurred in the most exaggerated form in current neo-primitivism.

At the beginning of the century, Herbert Spencer, Victorian philosopher of evolution, expressed his fear that industrial society might be confronted with a wave of 're-barbarization'.[108] The possibility disturbed the simple linear optimism of his philosophy, so that he feared the signs of a 'recrudescence of barbaric ambitions, ideas and sentiments and an unceasing culture of blood-thirst'. It is possible that the great civilizing waves alternate with anti-civilizing ones. Certainly the thousand years of Greco-Roman civilization saw in their last centuries the rise of a group of ideologists, often Christians, who identified themselves with the primitivism of the barbarian invaders, and desired the collapse of the Roman civilization of which they were part. The historian Priscus, who, in A.D. 448, accompanied a Roman mission to the court of Attila, the commander of the Huns and their allies, met at the headquarters with a Greek who had cast his lot with the barbarians: 'He considered his new life among the Scythians better than his old life among the Romans, and the reasons he gave were as follows: After war the Scythians live in inactivity, enjoying what they have got, and not at all, or very little, harassed. The Romans, on the other hand, are in the first place very liable to perish in war, as they have to rest their hopes of safety on others, and are not allowed on account of their *tyrants*, to use arms. And those who use them are injured by the cowardice of their generals, who cannot support the conduct of war. But the conditions

[108] Herbert Spencer, *Facts and Comments*, New York, 1902, p. 188.

of the subjects in time of peace is far more grievous than the evils of war, for the exaction of the taxes is very severe, and unprincipled men inflict injuries on others, because the laws are practically not valid against all classes . . . The climax of the misery is to have to pay in order to obtain justice.' The Roman historian defended the Empire: 'The Romans treat their servants better than the king of the Scythians treats his subjects . . . They are not allowed, like the Scythians, to inflict death on them. They have numerous ways of conferring freedom; . . .'[109] The Greek defector 'shed tears', but remained barbarized.

Christian spokesmen enlarged on the theme of the inferiority of Roman civilization to primitive barbarism. Salvian, a priest of Marseilles, wrote between A.D. 439 and 451 a treatise *On the Governance of God* in which he declared: 'in the districts taken over by the barbarians, there is one desire among all the Romans, that they should never again find it necessary to pass under Roman jurisdiction'. Unlike the Romans, 'The Franks are ignorant of this crime of injustice. The Huns are immune to these crimes. There are no wrongs among the Vandals, and none among the Goths.' The Vandals conquered the African provinces, but they remained chaste: 'In so great abundance and luxury, none of them became effeminate . . . Certainly, the Roman families, even those of noble birth, were in general effeminate . . . None of the Vandals was stained by the incest of the effeminate Romans in that country. Certainly, effeminacy had been long considered a virtue rather than a vice by the Romans.' But the Vandals 'repressed impurity with the sword of the law, . . .' Thus too the Franks were 'generous', and the Saxons and Goths 'chaste'. Men everywhere, he claimed, were migrating to the Goths, the revolting Bagaudae, 'or to other barbarians . . . They prefer to live as freemen under an outward form of captivity than as captives under an appearance of liberty.' ' [T]he name of Roman citizens, . . . is now repudiated and fled from, . . .'[110] Much the same were the

---

[109] J. B. Bury, *History of the Later Roman Empire from the Death of Theodosius I to the Death of Justinian*, Vol. I, London, 1923, pp. 283–5.

[110] *The Writings of Salvian, the Presbyter*, tr. Jeremiah F. O'Sullivan, New York, 1947, pp. 215, 219, 207, 136.

judgments of the Spanish priest, Orosius, who in A.D. 418 at the be-
hest of Augustine surveyed all human history to confute those who
criticized Christian primitivism. God's punishment was just, and
people 'should enjoy the barbarians themselves as mercenaries,
helpers, and defenders'. The barbarians, he claimed, 'now cherish
the Romans as comrades and friends, so that now there may be
found among them certain Romans who prefer poverty with freedom among the barbarians than paying tribute with anxiety among
the Romans'.[111]

The ideologists of the Roman world had their own conception of
a Third World,—like the intellectual today who condemns the white
race as the cancer of the human race, or those who call for a repudia-
tion of civilization, or a masochist union of spirit with the peoples of
the 'underdeveloped' areas, Asia, Africa, and Latin America. 'I had
no longer any belief whatsoever in what I had more or less consciously believed before—that anything good could come from
Europe', writes one such. 'We are not the bearers of consciousness.
We are the whores of reason.'[112] The mood of primitivism has such
deep roots that Lucretius, on the eve of the great expansion of
Roman civilization, yielded for a time to its spirit in *De Rerum
Natura*. The primitivist emotion tends to become especially strong in
a time of ideology, and for two reasons. Ideologies tend to elevate
some group as chosen by history,—the peasantry, proletariat, backward peoples or races, or the marginal intellectuals; the ideology
locates 'truth' as the privilege of some group whose prejudices are
already against science and the intellect. Second, as bearers of a doctrine of twofold truth or anti-truth, the ideologists are driven to
praising the deliverances of primitivist intuition and feeling. Thus
primitivism is a natural consequence of the ideological frame of
mind.[113] To recover 'Nature's simple plan', the manhood and clear

[111] Paulus Orosius, *The Seven Books of History against the Pagans*,
tr. Roy J. Deferrari, Washington, D.C., 1964, p. 358.

[112] Jan Myrdal, *Confessions of a Disloyal European*, New York, 1968,
pp. 199–200.

[113] As Lovejoy writes: 'Equalitarians, communists, philosophical anarchists, insurgents against existing moral codes, including those of

perception of the primitive man,—and thus to undo one's education, and the laws, categories and method of the elder generation,—
this primitivist call to a neo-tribal community, reinstated by a new
revolt of the brethren, is the recurrent myth of countless semi-intellectuals who feel themselves enfeebled, bereft of energy.

Sharing in this primitivist strain, the fantasies which ideologists
have projected of their idyllic communities have a remarkable resemblance. Marx, Engels, Lenin, Trotsky, the American ideologist in
the pre-World War I era, the transcendentalists, the New Left today,
all projected similar dreams. The American ideologists of 1912, in
Walter Lippmann's recollection, could have joined spirits with the
Commune dwellers of 1970: 'we had, I think, vague notions that
mankind, liberated from want and drudgery, would spend its energies writing poetry, painting pictures, exploring the stellar spaces,
singing folk songs, dancing with Isadora Duncan in public squares,
and producing Ibsen in little theaters'.[114] Only the exploration of
stellar space would be omitted from today's New Leftist platform.
Marx and Engels in their youth in 1844 contemplated erecting a
Community on the model of the plans of Owen and Fourier, and
engaged in steps for the drafting of 'a plan of organization and
regulations'.[115] And in old age, Engels still spoke with admiration of
the Harmony Hall Colony, 'whose communism left nothing to be
desired in definiteness', led by Robert Owen, whom Engels praised
as having practised as well as preached 'clear-cut communism'.[116]
Trotsky recalled that he and Lenin 'more than once discussed the
possibility of allotting to the anarchists certain territories where, with
the consent of the local population, they would carry out their state-

sexual relations, vegetarians, . . . all these have sought and, as they
believed, found a sanction for their preachments and programs in the
supposed example of primeval men or of living savages.' Lovejoy, op. cit.,
pp. 16–17.

[114] Wellborn, *Twentieth Century Pilgrimage: Walter Lippmann and
the Public Philosophy*, pp. 20–1.

[115] Lewis S. Feuer, *Marx and the Intellectuals*, pp. 165–6.

[116] Frederick Engels, *Herr Eugen Dühring's Revolution in Science*,
tr. Emile Burns, New York, n.d., pp. 297–8.

less experiment. But civil war, blockade, and hunger left no room for such plans.'[117]

Such then are the visions of the primitivist in his Utopian phase. The same ideologists, however, feeling resentment towards a recalcitrant and resisting people, and resolved then to impose forcefully their Utopia, become the Nietzschean primitivists, organizing the recalcitrant, and proclaiming the curative, functional virtues of violence.

[117] Leon Trotsky, *Stalinism and Bolshevism*, New York, 1937, pp. 22-3.

CHAPTER V

Ideology and Society

I. THE INDIFFERENCE OF THE WORKING CLASSES TO IDEOLOGY

Ideology, as we have seen, is a mode of thought characteristic of young intellectuals. From this standpoint, the phrases 'proletarian ideology' and 'bourgeois ideology' must themselves be regarded as symptoms of ideological projection; the ideologists wish to see themselves as spokesmen not for their own restlessness and ambitions but for some class which ratifies their role, and undertakes to provide the foot-soldiers for the ideologist-commanders. Marx, of course, never regarded his own work as ideology; the proletariat, he felt, had no need for ideology but wanted only science; the bourgeoisie, in his view had, however, deserted science for ideology. Lenin did nonetheless advocate socialism as the 'proletarian ideology', and his usage, as against Marx's, became prevalent; such writers as Karl Mannheim regard ideology as a class-based phenomenon.

Yet ideology has had little part in the intellectual life of the working classes. Today in the United States, the working classes stand apart from the ideological movement which has swept the intellectuals. Such ideologists as C. Wright Mills and Herbert Marcuse have turned with some fury against the workingmen: Mills decided it was time to give up the 'labor metaphysic', and Marcuse said the workers were corrupted by 'administered comforts'.[1] The workingmen paid no heed to the ideologists' mandate to elevate the intellectuals into the ruling elite. Even during the years of the depression, the workingmen tended to ignore the mythology of historic missions. So-called proletarian literature, that is, novels depicting the working class in ideological hues, were not read by them at all. One radical writer reported sadly in 1934, 'the overwhelming majority' of the

[1] C. Wright Mills, 'On the New Left', *Studies on the Left*, Vol II, No. 1, (1961), pp. 70–1

working class 'hardly reads anything apart from the local Sunday and daily newspapers and an occasional copy of Liberty, True Romances, Wild West Tales or Screen Romances'. A leading English Communist author observed: 'The authentic proletarian literature of every day consists of the thriller, the love stories, the cowboy stories, the popular movies, jazz and the yellow press.'[2] These leftish writers were perhaps unduly chagrined that the workingmen were not among their readers. For there were indications that a stratum of workers was drawn to great literature which transcended ideology. In the public libraries of St. Louis, for instance, it was found that Mark Twain was the most widely read author, and that his 3,289 adult readers were almost entirely drawn from the working class.[3] The radical ideologist, however, lamented that among the workers, in mines and mill towns, he 'found almost no awareness of the fact that among the intellectuals in Manhattan, Chicago, and Hollywood there was a considerable excitement about a thing called proletarian literature'.[4]

2. VARIATIONS OF SOCIETIES AS 'IDEOLOGY-PRONE'

What then determined whether a society was 'ideology-prone'? If we take as a measure the degree of a country's reception of Marxism in the latter part of the nineteenth century, then the country which was most 'ideology-prone' was Russia, followed by Germany, and then France, while Britain was the least ideology-prone. Karl Marx observed in 1868 that the young Russian intellectuals in Germany and Paris 'always run after the most extreme that the West can offer', and that his books 'had a greater sale in Russia than anywhere else. And the first foreign nation to translate Kapital is the

[2] Cf. Christopher Caudwell, cited in Renati Poggioli, The Spirit of the letter; essays in European literature, Cambridge, Mass., 1965, p. 339.

[3] Robert Cantwell, 'What the Working Class Reads', The New Republic, Vol. LXXXIII, (17 July 1935), pp. 274-6.

[4] Louis Adamic, 'What the Proletariat Reads: Conclusions Based on a Year's Study Among Hundreds of Workers throughout the United States', The Saturday Review of Literature, Vol. XI, No. 20, 1 Dec. 1934, pp. 321-2.

Russian.'⁵ The leaders of German socialism, in both its Lassallean and Marxist wings, were heavily affected with Marxist–Hegelian ideology; it was a German workers' representative in the International Workingmen's Association who formally moved the resolution in 1868 at Brussels commending Marx's *Capital* to the socialists of all countries as 'the Bible of the working class.'⁶ At the same time the kind of phenomenon which developed among the Russian intellectuals, who were possessed of an ideological passion, was not characteristic of the Germans. For one, whereas Russian intellectuals were from their student days at the universities partisans of the left and revolution, this was scarcely the case among German university students. The German socialist intellectuals were more often either self-taught workingmen or Jews like Eduard Bernstein, Kurt Eisner, Robert Michels, or Rosa Luxemburg. The Russian intellectuals, wrote Engels in 1893, unable to do anything effective were prey to 'an overactive mental speculation, an attempt at discovering or inventing new and almost miraculous means of action'. They engaged in disputations over fine points in the interpretation of the Marxian myth: 'passages from Marx's writings and correspondence have been interpreted in the most contradictory ways, exactly as if they had been texts from the classics or from the New Testament, by various sections of Russian emigrants'.⁷ The German debate over the revisionism of Bernstein scarcely attained any such virulence; Bernstein was not expelled from the party, nor was there a division into irreconcilable factions. The French socialists had a lively Marxist section, but its ideologists, such as Paul Lafargue, Marx's son-in-law, never acquired the commanding stature of Jean Jaurès, who based his socialism on universal human ideals, rather than ideology; it was Jaurès who persuaded French workers that justice to a single bourgeois, French Jewish captain Dreyfus, had a human significance which affected all; the Marxist ideologists vehemently opposed him. Britain was the least concerned with Marxist ideology. Bernard

---

⁵ Karl Marx, *Letters to Dr. Kugelmann*, New York, 1934, pp. 77–8.
⁶ *Reminiscences of Marx and Engels*, Moscow, n.d., p. 85.
⁷ Marx and Engels, *Basic Writings in Politics and Philosophy*, p. 442.

Shaw engaged in some personal philosophizing about the Life-Force, but the Fabian Society advocated its socialist reforms on the basis of their practical contribution to health and well-being; there was no mythology of a chosen heroic class in the historical drama. The British Labor Party had little ideology; religious socialists and Fabians joined in its leadership. Only the small sectarian Social Democratic Federation, led by H. M. Hyndman, tried to inculcate a Marxist, ideological standpoint.

3. BRITAIN AND THE UNITED STATES AS RELATIVELY NON-IDEOLOGICAL

What then accounts for these variations in the propensity to ideology? Wherever one has gotten a class of intellectuals, in the sense of persons either educated by themselves or in schools, who feel themselves 'alienated', and who then judge that the existing social order denies them the power and status which they deem warranted by their intellectual qualities, then the receptive base for ideology will exist; such a class of intellectuals, quite apart from the degree of technological development of the country, will have a high propensity for ideology. Britain was less prone to ideology because it was relatively lacking in a class of intellectuals: 'The British educational system, unlike the German, did not encourage the production of any large surplus of free, institutionally unattached intellectuals. In a sense it was, at the highest levels especially, severely vocational.'[8] There was also little rift between the generations among the British educated class, and consequently, little of a sense of 'alienation'. An English educated class, composed of civil servants, editors, scientists, began to differentiate itself within the middle class at the beginning of the nineteenth century. They became critics of the aristocratic ruling class, but they never became estranged from the middle class to which they belonged. They had a 'stability', notes an English historian, that one does not associate with an intelligentsia, 'a term which, Russian in origin, suggests the shifting, shiftless members of revolutionary or literary cliques who have cut themselves adrift from

[8] Philip Abrams, *The Origins of British Sociology: 1834-1914*, Chicago, 1968, p. 101.

the moorings of family'.[9] There was not in Britain that sense on the part of an intellectual class of the de-authoritization of their elders which is essential to the genesis of the ideological passion, the propensity to fashion myths which confer a messianic role upon the young. Hence, there were less ideologists in Britain. An educated person can choose to be an ideologist, on the one hand, or to orient himself toward his profession, science or skill. In Russia, thousands of students chose to be ideologists. First they would study philosophy, then they would become revolutionary plotters. At Oxford they studied philosophy, and then became churchmen of England. In Britain, the waves of generational revolt were of low amplitude,— from absolute idealism, for instance, to the Bloomsbury belief in an intuition of the 'good', never to be defined in naturalistic terms, and the reality of the sensory world. Ideological passion is a concomitant of generational waves of high amplitude.

And for similar reasons, America has been a country singularly lacking in ideology. De Tocqueville observed that 'in America the family, in the Roman and aristocratic signification of the word, does not exist. All that remains of it are a few vestiges in the first years of childhood, ... But as soon as the young American approaches manhood, the ties of filial obedience are relaxed day by day; master of his thoughts, he is soon master of his conduct. In America there is, strictly speaking, no adolescence; ...'[10] A young lad like Abraham Lincoln, resentful of his father's ignorance and heartlessness, went further West on his own. True, his intellectual companions were sceptics and materialists, but one's generational revolt was directly diverted into independent life on the frontier.[11] The language of American politics was far more experimental than ideological. The Gettysburg Address, the most cited and memorized American docu-

---

[9] N. G. Annan, 'The Intellectual Aristocracy', in *Studies in Social History: A Tribute to G. M. Trevelyan*, ed. J. H. Plumb, London, 1955, pp. 243–4.

[10] Alexis de Tocqueville, *Democracy in America*, tr. Henry Reeve, ed. Phillips Bradley, New York, 1954, Vol. II, p. 202.

[11] *Herndon's Life of Lincoln*, ed. Paul M. Angle, New York, 1936, pp. 227–8, 355.

ment, did not set forth a myth of historical destiny; it invoked the notion of an experiment to test the power of a democratic society to survive: 'now we are engaged in a civil war testing whether this nation, or any other so conceived, can long endure'. The whole notion of testing, with all its uncertainties, is foreign to ideology.

This language of experiment was deeply involved in American education and civilization. The most widely used children's school-books, the McGuffey readers, inculcated the experimental approach. The Eclectic Fourth Reader of 1838, for instance, said: 'The great experiment is now making, and from its extent and rapid filling up, is making in the West, whether the perpetuity of our republican institutions can be reconciled with universal suffrage.'[12] The McGuffey readers taught, as Benjamin Franklin's *Poor Richard's Almanac* had, the virtues of thrift, industry, honesty, and good will, And very often it is said that herein we have the middle-class virtues, the ideology of capitalist society, the 'bourgeois' values. Also it is argued that we are altogether wrong in affirming that America has been a country relatively less affected with ideology than the major European ones; rather, it is said, America has had its own ideology, and that every society has its ideology in equal proportions to every other; for every society, it is said, requires ideology to instill in its members those values which are essential to its maintenance; it is said that whereas 'revolutionary ideology' challenges the social system, the existing society has equally its counterpart of ideology, unconscious of it though we may be since it has always been part of our social environment.

More is at issue here than arbitrary definitions of words. For if the laws and patterns of the ideological mode of thought are to be explored, we cannot obliterate the distinction between it and the scientific mode of thought. We do distinguish, as Marx and Engels did, between scientists and ideologists. The standpoints of ideologists, with their elaborate mythological structures of the totality of world-history, with their mandate upon an elite, differ basically from statements such as those of Franklin: 'Early to bed, and early to rise,

[12] Richard M. Mosier, *Making the American Mind: Social and Moral ideas in the McGuffey Readers*, New York, 1947, p. 18.

M

makes a man healthy, wealthy, and wise.' The ideological stand-point fixated in attitudes of generational revolt, condemns such statements as 'bourgeois'. Actually such proverbs have been uni-versal, cross-societal, trans-systematic; they have been common to all societies, primitive, ancient, Greek, Roman, feudal, African, Asian, bourgeois, and socialist. For they are propositions concerning the conditions for men's survival and prosperity under all social settings in their confrontation with nature and fellow-men. They involve no dramatic myth of the universe; very rarely indeed do the peoples' proverbs refer to any supernatural power. There is no unconscious compulsion which expresses itself in proverbs as they enunciate their virtues; they are hard-earned empirical generalizations of common experience: 'If you want to be secure, then the best way is to work diligently (no matter in what society you live).' No proverb claims that the elect are either bourgeois, aristocrats, proletarians, or peasants. Their standpoint is classless. The overwhelming univer-sality of proverbs confutes the notion that they are ideological, class projections. 'Once or twice though you should fail, Try, try again; . . .' Was the virtue of perseverance, valued by human beings in all societies, an invention of 'bourgeois' ideology?

Only where one has a movement for a 'Revolution of the Intellec-tuals', as Lewis Namier called that of 1848, does one have an efflorescence of ideology. More precisely, a movement of young in-tellectuals. So-called 'bourgeois' revolutions have been remarkably devoid of ideology. Karl Marx himself referred to the intellectual spokesmen of the rising middle classes not as ideologists, but as economists,—men such as Adam Smith and David Ricardo.[13] These men wrote books of clearly stated propositions which could be verified or falsified by empirical facts; there was no Smithian or Ricardian myth. Adam Smith did once speak of the 'invisible hand' as guiding the interaction of individual economic decisions to pro-mote the general welfare; thus persons directing their industry 'in

[13] 'Just as the *economists* are the scientific representatives of the bour-geois class, so the *Socialists* and the Communists are the theoreticians of the proletarian class.' Karl Marx, *The Poverty of Philosophy*, Moscow, n.d., p. 125.

such a manner as its produce may be of the greatest value', and intending only their own gain, are 'led by an invisible hand to promote an end which was no part of his intention'.[14] Academic sociologists later spoke similarly of the 'unintended consequences' of actions. But there was no mythological element in Smith's analysis. He traced the verifiable, observable components in the causal chains of economic decisions and their consequences, and in his pleasure that the processes culminated in a higher well-being, he used the metaphor of an eighteenth-century optimist, the 'invisible hand'. The latter, however, never intervened for any moment in any economic causal sequence. There are no 'ideological leaps' in Ricardo as in Marx to such a super-extrapolation as the advent of a classless society of the most advanced culture, with the free development of each,—no assignments of historic missions to classes, vanguards, or elites. If an 'ideological scale' were formulated to measure the relative propensity to ideology on the part of the so-called bourgeois thinkers, the economists as compared to that of the Communists, whom Marx called 'the theoreticians of the proletarian class', the thinkers of the bourgeois revolution would scarcely rank among the ideologists.

4. IDEOLOGY AND RELIGION: THE DIVERGENCE OF INTELLECTUALS AND WORKERS

Ideology, it has often been said, is a substitute for religion, that it is indeed a secular religion. Invariably, indeed, when ideologists have written autobiographical accounts, they have described their search for ideological experience as a replacement for the religious. Georg Lukács writes of 'my intellectual passion for revolutionary messianism'.[15] Lewis Corey, founder of the American Communist Party,

[14] Adam Smith, *An Inquiry into the Nature and Causes of the Wealth of Nations*, Book IV, Chapter 2, Modern Library reprint, New York, 1937, p. 423. Thus Thorstein Veblen acknowledged that Smith's optimistic philosophy was not an integral feature of his economic theory, nor that Smith fell back on a 'meddling Providence'. *The Place of Science in Modern Civilisation*, New York, 1919, pp. 115–18.

[15] Georg Lukács, *History and Class Consciousness*, p. XIV.

wrote how at the age of sixteen, 'I had already cast off my religion —much too easily, I now suspect. I felt that the moral human values of early Christianity were embodied in Socialism...'[16] Max Eastman, editor of *The Masses*, described his fellow intellectual rebels as coming into sympathy with the labor struggle 'not by the road of theory or plan of action, but by the road of Christian sentiment bereft of Deity yet carried to a bellicose extreme'. '[Z]ealots of universal brotherhood among the children of God and of arrant individualism in dealings with the Father', they tried 'to recapture that early extremism without the belief in God upon which it rested'.[17] To Eastman himself Marxism brought a sense of release: 'I need no longer extinguish my dreams with my knowledge. I need never again cry out: "I wish I believed in the Son of God and his second coming." '[18] An important Communist functionary, reviewing his life's evolution, wrote: 'Looking back over the twenty-five years I was a member of the party, I can now see what the "dialectic" had concealed: that I, too, was groping for a new spiritual center, for a new God to replace the Jehovah that had failed, for a new absolute, for a new faith.'[19]

Beneath his academic manner and vocabulary, Harold J. Laski, the leading intellectual of the British Labor Party, and in 1945 its chairman, was filled with a passion which had turned a religious vacuum into an ideological plenum. His first book, *The Chosen People*, written at the age of nineteen, was never published. It revealed the psychological sources of ideology. Laski wrote of the conflicts within himself, the 'super-rational' ingredient of his Jewish outlook; for all his saturation in European culture, he still repudiated whatsoever contravened Jewish dogmas. Estranged, as a Jew, within himself, he wrote: 'the Jew is by nature a man who desires always, because he has been so separated from his fellow-men to declare him-

---

[16] Esther Corey, 'Lewis Corey (Louis C. Fraina), 1892–1953: A Bibliography with Autobiographical Notes', *Labor History*, Vol. 4, No. 3, Spring, 1963, p. 106.

[17] Max Eastman, *Enjoyment of Living*, New York, 1948. p. 424.

[18] Cited in Daniel Aaron, *Writers on the Left*, p. 50.

[19] George Charney, *A Long Journey*, Chicago, 1968, pp. 28–9.

self one of them . . .' To overcome the exclusiveness of Judaism, Laski welcomed, in a universal spirit, the ideas of Darwin and Marx. He depicted his hero's conflict with his father, and his own loyalty abiding after the agnostic immersion: 'I cherish love for the Jewish nation because I believe its continuance is necessary to the existence of civilization.'[20] Within a few years the proletariat was to be substituted for the Jews, and a Marxist ideological equivalent for Judaism; the structural pattern was much the same.

To regard ideology as simply a replacement for an outmoded religion would be, however, to overlook a most essential point. Ideology is the activity especially of intellectuals, and what it provides them is the equivalent of the role of priests and prophets in traditional religions. It offers a redemptive sketch of history in which they, the intellectuals, will supplant the traditional elites, and become the new governing elite. It is not simply a new philosophy to live by; it is an assignment of particular roles, of both the rights and privileges of intellectuals (as well as responsibilities) which are set forth by the new ideological 'scenario'. The religious vacuum is most keenly felt by intellectuals because they require a charter that will validate their new messianism. This is what ideology provides.

Therefore, when the working classes shed traditional loyalties, unlike the intellectuals, they do not show that phenomenon of craving for an ideological substitute. In Britain, for instance, Laborites of the upper and upper-middle class were, unlike their Tory counterparts, hardly likely to believe in life after death; among the working classes, however, the differences between Laborites and Tories were found to 'all but vanish', with about half as believers.[21] One's being a Laborite, among the working class, did not involve the thoroughgoing ideological rupture which characterized the intellectual. The Bible was replaced as the leading influence among Labor members of Parliament only when they were replaced with intellectuals. To be sure, working-class people were much more likely than those of the

[20] Kingsley Martin, *Harold Laski (1893–1950): A Biographical Memoir*, New York, 1953, pp. 14–18.

[21] Charles Y. Glock and Rodney Stark, *Religion and Society in Tension*, Chicago, 1965, p. 199.

upper classes to regard politics as more important than religion, and to be lax in church attendance, the more so when they were Laborites.[22] But the conception of the universe which the workingman had was nonetheless not the politicized conception which is the heart of ideology. Workingmen are Laborites because they hope thereby to achieve specific improvements in their conditions of life. They almost never speak of their 'mission' in world-history. In every country where a labor party has existed, from Canada to Britain to Australia, from the time Karl Marx was an officer in the International Workingmen's Association and workers tried to expel him as an intellectual to the resentment they have felt against all manners of socialist intellectual leagues, the workingmen have been at odds or uneasy with ideologists.

The French worker is probably the most non-religious in Western Europe. 'The French working class today is an advanced stage of dechristianization', was one conclusion of a remarkable study.[23] French workers, with the heritage of the anticlericalism of the Revolution of 1789, and with traditions of 1848 and 1871, tended to regard the Church as an instrument of the ruling class. The percentages of observing Catholics among workers became minuscule; among the dockers in Rouen in 1952 it approached zero.[24] The French workingman after the Second World War tended to vote for Communist candidates. Nonetheless, it can hardly be said that ideology was his substitute for religion. 'Rarely' did 'serious argument or extensive reading' precede his decision to vote for Communists.[25] He had no concern for Marxist ideology. 'Voting behavior' is far less an indication of intellectual commitment than attendance at church, for instance. Issues of economic immediacy, the belief that more Communists in the National Assembly might help bring about higher wages, for example, determine a workingman's vote rather than any doctrine of historical inevitability or mission. 'Voting behavior' is usually ideologically neutral for the working

[22] Ibid., pp. 194–5.
[23] Joseph N. Moody, 'The Dechristianization of the French Working Class', *The Review of Politics*, Vol. XX, (1958), p. 50.
[24] Ibid., p. 51.   [25] Ibid., p. 63.

class. The French Communist Party strove after the War 'to rescue the masses from the influence of Hollywood' yet its numerous publications 'tended to pass over the heads of the great public'.[26] The ideologists fulminated against the heretics Camus and Koestler, but the peasants, who were approximately 30 per cent of the Party's membership, didn't know either from Beelzebub.[27]

In short, decline in religion is experienced as a vacuum most acutely on the part of the intellectuals. For the intellectual suffers from two modes of guilt. The first is that of the man who, exempted from physical labor, does work akin to the play of the spirit. The workingman feels no compulsion to 'justify' himself; his job speaks for itself, and he is not haunted by the awareness that affects the intellectual that he lives on the fruits of others' labor, especially so during his student years when he has enjoyed leisure, books, and science. Secondly, the intellectual, aiming for his intellectual independence through a generational uprising against those who have nurtured him, experiences a burden of guilt. The workingman's revolt ends when he gets his own job and becomes self-supporting. Since the religious vocation can no longer assuage the intellectual's feeling, he turns to the ideological.

The therapeutic function of ideology is secondary to its endorsement of the mission of intellectuals to guide and rule. Ideology provides more than a Magna Carta for intellectuals; it confers on them the especial privileges inherent in the heroes of Mosaic myths. If one's place in the religious scheme of salvation is removed, one substitutes a place in historical salvation. The working classes have never been able to nominate themselves, as the intellectuals do, as an ideological elite.

The great ideologists have been keenly aware that where a religious vacuum existed among intellectuals, there the emotional soil was best prepared for the planting of ideological seeds. Marx when young, and Lenin too, both perceived that where religious belief was shattered, the intellectuals would be most prone to become ideologists

[26] David Caute, *Communism and the French Intellectuals 1914–1960*, London, 1964, p. 52.

[27] Ibid., p. 367.

in an endeavor to cope with the misery of atheist vacuity and meaninglessness. The Young Hegelian movement, in which Karl Marx was nurtured, had its inception in a concern with mythology and myth-making, especially, as the process was exemplified in the story of Jesus.[28] Not out of the sciences, not out of economics, did this left Hegelian movement arise, but from studies in mythology. The student of comparative religion is frequently the person with an unsatisfied religious need. And similarly with the Young Hegelians. They delved into mythology because they longed for a new myth to supersede the old religious ones; Marx and Engels wrote the new myth for them in the economic language of Ricardo.

Marx was definitely aware that his theory fulfilled the function of a religious myth. He compared the similarities in psychological consequence of his theory with those of the Christian myth,—writing in 1881:

'The dream that the end of the world was at hand inspired the early Christians in their struggle with the Roman Empire and gave them confidence in victory. Scientific insight into the inevitable disintegration of the dominant order of society continually proceeding before our eyes ... all this is a sufficient guarantee that with the moment of the outbreak of a real proletarian revolution there will also be given the conditions ... of its next immediate *modus operandi*.'[29]

Though Marx had for many years taken it for granted that the development of science and technology would render obsolescent and extinct the mythological propensity, in the last part of his life he came to recognize that myth might enjoy a widespread recrudescence in modern society. The advancement of technology, in other words, did not determine society's mode of thought; ideology and myth rather than science might flourish. 'Up till now it has been thought', he wrote in 1871, 'that the growth of the Christian myths during the Roman Empire was possible only because printing was not yet

[28] Cf. David Friedrich Strauss, *The Life of Jesus*, tr. George Eliot, London, 1846, Vol. I, p. ix.

[29] Karl Marx and Friedrich Engels, *Correspondence 1846–1895*, tr. Dona Torr, London, 1934, p. 387.

invented. Precisely the contrary. The daily press and the telegraph, which in a moment spreads inventions over the whole earth, fabricate more myths (and the bourgeois cattle believe and enlarge upon them) in one day than could have formerly been done in a century.'[30] Far from an 'end to ideology' taking place of the sort which Engels envisaged, technological advance was consistent with renewed cyclical waves of ideology, the amalgams of myth and science. The existence of the ideological mode of thought is far more dependent on the extent to which a class of 'intellectuals' has come into existence, characterized by a high degree of generational disequilibrium.

5. THE WOMEN'S MOVEMENT AND FEMINIST IDEOLOGY

The ideology of feminism, founded on sexual tensions and struggles which cut across all classes, nations, races, peoples, and generations, naturally exhibits peculiarities of its own. Nevertheless, its basic traits exemplify the classical traits of ideology from the Mosaic myth to 'isomorphic projection'. Like every ideology, feminism commingles mythlology with science. That women have been economically exploited, that sexual relations have for countless men been opportunities for sadistic, aggressive behavior, that modern literature is imbued with imagery, language, and detail of sexual cruelty, that women have been regarded perhaps especially in leftist circles as sexual means only, has been documented beyond reasonable doubt. There is the usual 'ideological leap', however, from these scientific propositions to the ideological ones.

Feminist movements were conceived in the setting of Leftist ideologists. Whether in the Abolitionist movement in pre-Civil War days, or the Bolshevik movement, or the New Left of 1966, women discovered that Left ideologists prated of equality but were actually filled with contempt and callousness toward women. Attitudes of sexual sadism and exploitation, as Lewis Corey long ago showed, were endemic among ideologists. From Rousseau and Robespierre, to Byron and the Utopian Socialists, to the Fascists and Communists alike, sexual inequality and masculine domination were emotional

[30] Karl Marx, *Letters to Dr. Kugelmann*, p. 128.

axioms, no matter what the ideological phraseology: 'A theory of "elites" comes naturally to people with a twisted sexuality.' Totalitarian despotism often began with sexual despotism.[31] At any rate in 1833, when the leading abolitionists convened to establish the American Anti-Slavery Society, they would not allow the few women present to join their Society or sign its declaration. As a consequence, women founded the Philadelphia Anti-Slavery Society. Then in 1840, the World Anti-Slavery Convention refused to seat women delegates. Two of the latter, Lucretia Mott and Elizabeth Cady Stanton returned to the United States to agitate for women's rights.[32] The story became part of the lore of the women's movement. In 1848, the year of dreams and ideology, their Seneca Falls Convention took place. A similar experience of disenchantment with male ideologists took place more than a hundred years later in the mid-sixties. Women in the New Left organizations encountered strongly entrenched attitudes of 'male supremacy'. What they were discovering was the latent totalitarianism in Leftist ideology which manifested itself in a spontaneous contempt for women, and a readiness to dictate to them. In 1966, at the convention of Students for a Democratic Society, 'women demanded that the subject of women's liberation be dealt with in a resolution. The response was a barrage of insults and tomatoes.'[33] Not since the Nazis had student ideologists

[31] Cf. Lewis Corey, 'Marquis de Sade—the Cult of Despotism', *Antioch Review*, Vol. XXVI, (1966), pp. 17–31. Corey's essay was written in 1952 shortly before he died, though its publication was long delayed.

[32] Alma Lutz, *Susan B. Anthony: Rebel, Crusader, Humanitarian*, Boston, 1959, p. 27. Vivian Gornick, 'The Next Great Moment of History is Ours', in *Liberation Now! Writings from the Women's Liberation Movement*, ed. Deborah Babcox and Madeline Belkin, New York, 1971, p. 28.

[33] *Liberation Now!*, p. 3. '[T]he Women's Liberation Movement started out from the Civil Rights Freedom Movement, Student Movement, and Anti-War Movement. Women got the notion working in these movements that the idea of freedom should apply to women too. But the males in these movements never intended the freedom struggle to extend to women . . . So many women who got the freedom bug too bad left to

been so brazen in their exhibition of sexual sadism toward their would-be women adherents.[34] Women activists drew their conclusion: 'The male Left has absolutely no interest in a female revolution. Rather, the male Left has a direct interest in perpetuating the status quo, i.e., male privileges, and preventing any real threats to male supremacy from both within the Left and without it.'[35] Thus the new feminist ideology had its birth when women Leftists discovered the authoritarian personality of the male Left.

It was a rediscovery made periodically. In America in the nineteenth century Victoria Woodhull had been a leading practitioner of the free sexual morality which Marx, Engels, and the Young Hegelians had advocated. In the course of time in 1871, she and her sister organized the famous Section Twelve of the International Workingman's Association, and in their *Weekly* were the first American editors to publish an English version of the *Communist Manifesto*. But Victoria Woodhull and Tennessee Claflin were soon expelled on a motion by Citizen Karl Marx from the International. The minutes of the General Council on 28 May 1872 recorded Citizen Marx's view that the proceedings in the United States to nominate Victoria Woodhull for the presidency and Frederick Douglass for the vice-presidency 'had become the laughing-stock of America'. Citizen Engels later said that Mrs. Woodhull and her associates were 'a lot of middle-class humbugs'. In an essay 'American Split', Marx freely expended his invective against Victoria Woodhull: 'In October 1871 was published in the journal of Woodhull (a banker's woman, free-lover, and general humbug) and Claflin (her sister in the same line) an Appeal of Section No. 12 (founded by Woodhull, and almost exclusively consisting of middle-class humbugs and worn-out Yankee swindlers in the Reform business...)' The Appeal affirmed that 'the object of the International was simply to emancipate the laborer, male and female', and to achieve a social freedom

relate to women in a Female Movement.' Barbara Burris *et. al.*, 'The Fourth World Manifesto', *Notes from the Third Year: Women's Liberation*, New York, 1971, p. 104.

[34] Marlene Dixon, 'Why Women's Liberation?', ibid., p. 15.

[35] Ibid., p. 105.

for men and women alike which would extend to 'the sexual relation, habits of dress, etc.' This Appeal wrote Marx in German–
English, 'Dieser Appeal—und die Formation daraufhin of all sorts
of middle-class humbug sections, free-lovers, spiritists, spiritist
Shakers, etc.—gab den Anlasz zum split, . . .' He quoted disapprov-
ingly the demand for 'the extension of equal citizenship to women,
the world over', as a condition precedent for the change in the relations of capital and labor. He cited the charge that Victoria Woodhull was ' "using the organization . . . as a sort of adjunct to the free-
love branch of the women's rights' party . . ." ' On the basis of
Marx's report, the General Council placed Section Twelve out of the
purview of the International.[36]

Years later in the midst of the Bolshevik Revolution Alexandra
Kollontai, whose theories and practices were akin to those of Victoria
Woodhull, encountered similar vulgar attitudes on the part of her
comrades, especially Stalin. And Lenin's wife, Krupskaya, was
insulted by Stalin in such terms that the dying Lenin dictated a letter
breaking 'all personal and comradely relations' with him. But it was
Stalinism which triumphed.[37]

Every ideology tends to engender its counter-ideology; and ideological feminism had its countervailing propositions to male authoritarianism. From its inception it had the tendency to see women as
history's elite. In the pages of their journal *The Revolution* in 1868,
Elizabeth Cady Stanton and Susan B. Anthony proclaimed: 'Let
woman fulfil her God-like mission. She is nobler, purer, better
than man . . . Let her vote and the reformation begins. Women would

---

[36] *The General Council of the First International, 1871–1872 Minutes*,
Moscow, n.d., pp. 210, 251, 323–4, 330, 332, 555, 568. Engels then
wrote a whole article 'Die Internationale in Amerika' directed against
Victoria Woodhull and Tennessee Claflin, 'the two sisters, millionaires,
preacher's of women's emancipation and especially "free-love".' Cf. Karl
Marx, Friederich Engels, *Werke*, Band 18, Berlin, 1962, pp. 97–103. An
American Internationalist attacked the sisters for 'this nonsense which
they talk of, female suffrage and free-love, . . .' cf. Samuel Bernstein, *The
First International in America*, New York, 1965, pp. 117–18.

[37] Cf. Leon Trotsky, *Stalin*, tr. Charles Malamuth, London, 1947,
pp. 243–4, 374–5. Leon Trotsky, *My Life*, New York, 1930, p. 485.

purify the polls . . .'[38] The most brilliant of American women, their first herald, Margaret Fuller, 'the organizer and executive force of the first thoroughly American enterprise', in Higginson's words, experienced this sense of calling in a messianic way: 'There are also in every age a few in whose lot the meaning of that age is concentrated. I feel that I am one of those persons in my age and sex. I feel chosen among women.'[39]

In the current ideology, the 'ideological leap' beyond the scientific to the mythological has had an unprecedented daring. Shulamith Firestone is impatient with women's ordinary demands: 'Day-care centers' for children, she writes, 'buy women off'. Her faith as a neo-Marxist is in a technological revolution in the mode of reproduction. 'Pregnancy is barbaric.' What the feminist revolution seeks is 'the full development of artificial reproduction'. Then, the biological family would be abolished,—the universal incest taboo would finally be repealed,—a new androgynous culture would arise, reintegrating the male with the female, the technological mode with the aesthetic, like a matter-antimatter explosion. For culture, she affirms, develops not out of an underlying economic dialectic, but a deeper sexual dialectic. 'The essential mission' of the feminist movement is to create the conditions necessary for the new ecological balance; cultural lag and sexual bias are impeding, in her view, the kind of research into the mode of reproduction which will make possible 'qualitative change in humanity's basic relationships'.[40] This was perhaps the most complete ideological myth of the new feminism. But the longing for myth is affirmed even by its more moderate advocates. Germaine Greer, for instance, looks to 'inventing a new

[38] 'Woman the True Reformer', *The Revolution*, Vol. I, No. 3, 22 January 1968.

[39] *Love Letters of Margaret Fuller 1845–1846*, London, 1903, p. 20. Higginson, *Margaret Fuller Ossoli*, p. 130. She wrote Emerson how she longed to be a ruler of men, a Pericles rather than an Anaxagoras. Ibid., p. 310.

[40] Shulamith Firestone, *The Dialectic of Sex: The Case for Feminist Revolution*, New York, (Bantam Ed.), 1961, pp. 206, 198, 202, 60, 190, 189, 201, 197.

mythology', which will blend Lao-Tse, Whitehead, Norman O. Brown, and Herbert Marcuse,—the advocates of a strange new science which will transcend the allegedly bourgeois, mathematical, operational kind.[41] Though the revolt against patriarchy is the avowed theme of the feminist myth, relatively little animus is shown against the fathers; rather the resentment is directed against the mothers who indoctrinated the daughters in submissiveness, and who imposed the so-called female sex roles on them.[42]

Every ideology specifies the highest elite, those who will see the direction, as Marx put it, of the movement as a whole. Within the feminist movement this place has been frequently assumed by the Lesbian section. 'What is a lesbian? A lesbian is the rage of all women condensed to the point of explosion.'[43] The aim of radical feminism, it is said, is the total elimination of sexual roles,—the demonstration that biology does not determine them. Given this aim, it follows that 'lesbians are the vanguard of the women's movement', for they were the pioneers in the eradication of sexual roles, and in dispensing with men.[44] Moreover, the feminist ideologist has elaborated her own variety of 'isomorphic projection'; as Marx and Kropotkin tried to find in biology the structural analogues of their sociological theories, so the feminist projects an ideological physiology. The notion of a vaginal orgasm is alleged to be an anatomical myth which Freudians perpetrated in order to fit female anatomy and physiology to their basic male bias. The Freudians, as psycho-ideologists of male supremacy, followed their master's dictum: Anatomy is destiny. Therefore, according to the feminist ideologists, they repressed the orgasmic functioning of the clitoris in favor of the

[41] Germaine Greer, *The Female Eunuch*, 1970, London, 1971, p. 113.

[42] 'Your fury focuses on the select group of individuals who have done you the most damage. You are furious at your parents for having wanted a boy instead; at your mother (and this fury is mixed with compassion) for having let herself be stifled and having failed to show you another model of female behavior; at your father for having gotten a cheap bolster to his ego . . .' Susie Kaplow, 'Getting Angry', ibid., p. 16.

[43] Radicalesbians, 'The Woman Identified Woman', *Notes from the Third Year: Women's Liberation*, p. 81.

[44] Anne Koedt, 'Lesbianism and Feminism', ibid., p. 86.

vagina. For, it is said 'the establishment of clitoral orgasm as fact would threaten the heterosexual institution';[45] for if women can fulfill each other with clitoral orgasms, men are rendered redundant from the clitoral standpoint, and heterosexuality is demoted from an absolute necessity to an optional choice. The predetermined system of male–female roles is replaced by an improvised one; in fact, improvisation rather than predetermination is the culminating goal of feminist ideology as the leap to the kingdom of freedom from the realm of necessity was of the Marxist.

Thus, the classical traits of the ideological mode of thought repeat themselves in the feminist variant. The consequences of the myth, or the realization of some of its desiderata, are never scientifically explored. What, for instance, might be the consequences for society if artificial reproduction became a reality? Would the abrogation of motherhood tend to extend the domain and intensity of aggression on the part of persons toward each other? Would people hate each other more in such a society? Or, would society decline toward a vapidity of the kind H. G. Wells used to foresee? Meanwhile, quite apart from revolutions in biological technology, the increase in homosexuality which the new ideology has tended to elevate as a new sexual norm will have its own social consequences. In the Roman Empire, the increase in homosexuality went hand in hand with the decline of population; the first signs of the phenomena which Juvenal described helped bring about in several centuries the collapse of the powerful Roman organization. Was the survival of the Chinese empire, by contrast, related to its maintenance of the integrity of the family? Little is known about such matters, but the ideologist is content to fill ignorance with ideology. That its latent consequences are possibly those of a retrogression of civilization toward a barbarian torpor is conveniently repressed by the ideological unconscious.

Naturally a contest has arisen within the women's movement, between its scientifically-minded and its ideologists. Betty Friedan, the chief 'spokesperson' of the former, thus decried those whom she

[45] Anne Koedt, 'The Myth of the Vaginal Orgasm', *Liberation Now!*, pp. 319–20.

called the 'female Chauvinists', that is, the ideologists: 'Those who would make an *abstract ideology* out of sex, aping the old fashioned rhetoric of class warfare or the separatist extremists of race warfare, paradoxically deny the concrete reality of women's sexuality, . . .'[46] The first wave of the women's movement in America, she noted, had begun as a struggle for equality but had ended (perverted) 'with the notion that women as a class were purer, morally superior and . . . would clean up America'. Today, 'the most spirited women', defining the oppressing class in sexual terms, regarded women as one class oppressed by another, the men; consequently, they were repudiating 'marriage, motherhood, children, even their own sexuality'. Classical traits of ideology repeated themselves isomorphically in the feminist interpretation. In the 'consciousness-raising groups', the 'new mystique of specialness', with its call for 'special privilege', was being inculcated;[47] 'consciousness-raising', we might say, was a conditioning of the woman's thinking and perception so that all reality would be regarded under the aspect of the emotional a priori categories of the ideology. In secluded groups, the ideological collective representation could wax for a while 'without even touching the test of reality'. To withstand the shock of realities, ideological feminism invoked its own twofold theory of truth, and insisted that all men were in a conspiracy for the economic and social exploitation of women. A kind of 'fantasy playacting' ensued.[48] Hostility between men and women was exacerbated so that the chances for eradicating unfairness were sacrificed for indulgence in ideological invective,—the 'backlash', as it was called. Ideology was under a compulsion to magnify every difference into an irreconcilable antagonism, and every antagonism into a manifestation of the system's contradictions; people's emotions and ideas were aligned into mutual opposition. To the ideologist, the ideological experience of dramatic confrontation and denouement is the supreme end in itself. The revolutionary experience itself is the goal of the revolutionist; no one feels less at home in the post-revolutionary world than the ideologist.

[46] Bety Friedan, 'Beyond Women's Liberation', *McCall's*, Vol. XCIX, No. 11, August 1972, p. 83.

[47] Ibid., p. 83, 134.   [48] Ibid., p. 134.

CHAPTER VI

Ideologists, Prophets, and Intellectuals

The term 'ideology' is naturally precious to the ideologist; always ready to 'unmask' in others their unconscious motivations and material interests, he develops extraordinary resistances to the scientist who would probe the unconscious motives and material interests of ideologists themselves. 'Do not unto us what we would do to others', is the imperative which issues from the ideologists' unconscious.

The term 'ideology' has itself thus been put to an extensive ideological use. Let us, therefore, distinguish between the scientific and ideological uses of 'ideology'. The chief characteristic of the scientific use is that it preserves the distinction between science and ideology; the chief trait of the ideological use of 'ideology' is that it tends to obliterate this distinction, and to regard every set of ideas as an ideology. The scientific usage maintains that some ideas are more truthful than others, that other ideas are more the sheer projection of the unconscious, of the pleasure-principle; according to the ideological usage, on the other hand, since all ideas have an originative source in interests, avowed or unavowed, all are equally ideology; objective truth does not exist; to each generation and class its ideology; everyman his own ideologist.

The Marxist usage of 'ideology' was a thoroughly scientific one. 'Ideology is a process accomplished by the so-called thinker consciously, it is true, but with a false consciousness. The real motive forces impelling him remain unknown to him; otherwise it simply would not be an ideological process. Hence he imagines false or seeming motives,' wrote Engels in 1893.[1] He included under the rubric of ideology such departments as law, theology, politics, and philo-

---

[1] Marx and Engels, *Basic Writings on Politics and Philosophy*, p. 408.
N

sophy; furthermore, Engels held there was a gradation in the ideological character of these respective departments, an 'ideological scale', one might say. Thus religion and philosophy 'soar still higher in the air' than legal principles, which 'reflect' more closely the causal basis of economic relations; in other words, there are less intervening variables between economic factors and jurisprudence than there are between the economic foundation and theology. The more ideological departments, according to Engels, 'have a prehistoric stock, found already in existence and taken over in the historical period, of what we should call today bunk'. As opposed to these ideological notions, grounded in a primitive past, science is the progressively anti-ideological force: 'the history of science is the history of the gradual clearing away of this nonsense, or rather of its replacement by fresh but always less absurd nonsense'.[2]

Now one is at once troubled by Engels' conception of science. For in the history of science, strong unconscious motives have often affected the thinking of scientists. Werner Heisenberg was affected by the romantic philosophy of his circle in the youth movement in opposition to materialism and determinism; Einstein moved in a student circle which was marked by hostility to every form of absolutism, political, moral, and scientific. Then it is not the mere presence of unconscious factors in the thought-processes which separates the ideologist from the scientist. Rather something more is involved,— namely, the power of scientific method to transcend the unconscious motives through its reliance on prediction, experiment, verification, falsification. The ideologist, as a myth-maker, remains unanswerable to the confirmations or infirmations of predicted consequences. Without the impelling force of unconscious motives, science too would languish; but without the work of experiment and verification, it would regress toward myth.

Again, religion is scarcely today regarded as ideology. For increasingly, the religious thinker rarely tries to 'prove', or demonstrate the truth of his ideas. He holds them as a matter frankly of faith, or tradition, or as a stand toward the unknown based on his personal hopes or longings. The ideologist, as Engels observed, does try to

[2] Ibid., p. 405.

prove the truth of his ideas, but deceives himself as to his impelling motives. Religious thinkers today rarely deceive themselves as to their underlying motives, and also rarely try to 'prove' them. And in jurisprudence, today, the realistic recognition of the social, political, and economic influences operating on judges and lawyers is so widespread that its character is far more that of a legal science than an ideology. In short, it is only in the field of political thinking, among the intellectual constructions which urge and justify the messianic aims of a would-be political elite, that one finds ideology; there we have that specific mixture of Mosaic myth, with argument and purported evidence which is characteristic of ideology.

The ideological usage of 'ideology' is most notably found in Soviet writings, and forms also part of the theory advocated by the sociologist Karl Mannheim. A leading historian of Soviet ideology, Gustav Wetter, writes: 'Ideologies, in historical materialist parlance, are the various forms of "social consciousness", as manifested primarily in law, morals, art, science, philosophy, and religion.'[3] It follows from this definition that any form of thinking whatsoever is ideological, for one cannot imagine any human reflection which wouldn't fall under one of the sub-classes of ideology. If so, it follows next that all societies are equally ideological, and since each has its conception of truth, each regards its consciousness as truthful and the other false, and it makes no sense to say that one can objectively gainsay the other. The Soviet usage corresponds to what Mannheim calls the 'total conception of ideology', by which he means the 'fundamentally divergent thought-systems', peculiar to different historical eras or social strata, the 'total structure' of the mind of an age, class, or historical group; by contrast, the 'particular conception' regards as ideological only that part of an intellectual scheme in which the group's interests have given rise to lies, deceptions, or distortions.[4] The notion of 'total conception of ideology', as 'fundamentally

[3] Gustav Wetter, *Soviet Ideology Today: Dialectical and Historical Materialism*, tr. Peter Heath, London, 1966, p. 234.

[4] Karl Mannheim, *Ideology and Utopia: An Introduction to the Sociology of Knowledge*, tr. Louis Wirth and Edward Shils, New York, pp. 56–8.

divergent thought-systems', leads, however to some confusion. For the fact is that thought-systems neither fundamentally diverge nor converge; the patterns of thought in all societies are a mixture of scientific generalization, empirical facts, mythological and religious notions, political and ethical ideas; no society could survive unless its pattern of thought had a considerable scientific ingredient, and to this extent, all human thinking converges; it is in the realm of myth, religion, and politics that divergences ensue. The intellectual history of any group is, in large part, the story of the conflict of these convergent and divergent aspects. But if we begin to restrict the 'total conception' of ideology to the divergent aspects, we are back at Engels' distinction between science and ideology. And if we hold on to an even looser usage, then 'ideology' means any thinking whatsoever, and calling it ideology adds nothing consciously to its connotation, (though unconsciously suggesting that all thinking is 'ideologically tainted').[5] To this extent, the 'total conception' of ideology subserves the relativism, the negation of objective truths, to which all ideologists, in their common opposition to science, are drawn.

What, however, happens when a revolutionary ideology becomes the official ideology, the official creed of a government, or nation? If ideology is essentially a mode of thought which expresses the generational unconscious of young intellectuals, what happens to this mode of thought when it is congealed into the official doctrine? The social process in an ideology's later career we might call the 'institutionalization' of an ideology. The ideological myths are taught in schools; its history, the sacrifices of the founding ideologists, the battles of their partisans, are narrated; its slogans and phrases are on posters in the streets, and recited on the radio; novels, motion pictures, and plays tell its stories; Lenin's life for instance is told in films from his youth in Siberia through the October Revolution; the last chapter closes with the advent of a glorious present.

A contradiction confronts a revolutionary ideology which has come to power. The victorious young ideologists in time grow older; inevitably as middle-aged and old men they look with disfavor on any tendency on the part of a fresh generation of ideologists to sup-

[5] Ibid., p. 61.

plant them. Consequently a process of limited de-ideologization ensues. It differs, however, from the kind of de-ideologization which takes place in free movements, as, for instance, in the revisionist trends beginning with Eduard Bernstein. For the official regime must preserve its status as the bearer of the ideological mantle; it wishes no matter what happens to keep its prestige as the historic vehicle for ideological realization. Therefore the de-ideologization is directed to tenets which might be seized upon by the younger generation, and turned against the highest governing echelon. Some tenets are repealed; others are rendered recessive. Thus Stalin in 1950 announced the abrogation of a law of the dialectic, the 'transformation of quantity into quality'. Some 'comrades', he said, had an 'infatuation' for 'sudden explosions' in transitions 'from an old quality to a new' in social development. But, said Stalin, though this law 'is compulsory for a society divided into hostile classes, . . . it is not at all compulsory for a society which has no hostile classes'.[6] In the Soviet society, according to Stalin, revolutions henceforth would take place 'from above, . . . on the initiative of the existing power; therefore revolutions would no longer take place by means of an explosion'. Thus, too, the official Soviet ideologists announced that unconscious psychological processes had no place in the Soviet psyche. Engels' definition of ideology had emphasized that it was impelled by unconscious motives. The Soviet leaders could ill afford however to have young intellectuals analyzing the decisions of the ruling elite and their writings and speeches in terms of their unconscious causal mechanisms. Imagine what a psychological analysis of Stalin's unconscious would have done, what a young Solzhenitsyn or Sinyavsky would have done with Stalin's anxieties, Stalin's hatred of able men, his suspiciousness, his role in his wife's suicide, his murder of the Old Bolshevik generation, his sadism toward his daughter,—Soviet ideology would have been revealed as Soviet psychopathology. And imagine what young Soviet writers could do with the monotonous speeches of Brezhnev and Gromyko if they were allowed to explore their underlying motivations. The Soviet façade would totter.

[6] Joseph Stalin, *Marxism and Linguistics*, New York, 1951, p. 27.

Therefore the Soviet regime has strenuously assailed Freud's conception of the unconscious. In so doing they have divested themselves of Engels' notion of unconscious motives as well. Soviet ideology, they affirm, is the product of pure consciousness, pure rationality; they have no need to introduce unconscious processes.

If some tenets are repealed by the official ideology, others are allowed to grow recessive. Recessive tenets are familiar enough in the evolution of religions. The Calvinist dogma of original sin, for instance, has been allowed to become recessive in Presbyterian churches; it may still be recorded in theological texts, but one would scarcely find a churchgoer who knew it was part of his theology. The Roman Catholic tenet concerning the perdition of non-Catholics is now largely recessive. Similarly with the Marxist tenet of the 'withering away of the state'. The ideological texts mention it, but it rarely appears even in theoretical discussions, and never in practical considerations.

Yet the Soviet ruling elite cannot surrender Marxism–Leninism. For it can justify the continuance of its dictatorial rule only by claiming that it is still leading a revolution, that it is guiding the world's proletariat in a battle with the international, bourgeois, counter-revolutionary capitalist class. When bourgeois society came into existence, it did not require the notion of a 'world-historic mission'. The Soviet ruling elite does require it as an ideological device for securing the allegiance of citizens who would otherwise grow restive with the lack of both freedom and the goods of life. Periodically therefore the Mosaic myth has to be rekindled; the regime then engages in efforts at ideological revivalism. An international crisis or dispute may be provoked to lend credence to the anxieties of 'counter-revolution'. President Harry Truman was portrayed as the 'mad haberdasher' following in Hitler's footsteps. Roles of Zionist plotters have, in recent years, been favorites. The 'Maoist clique' has also shared the stage of villainy with American capitalists. Such revivalism, however, encounters its limits. When the divergence between 'ideological perception', or planned misperception, and the reality-principle becomes extreme, and when citizens have experienced many propagandistic reversals in doctrine, an unstable ideological

equilibrium arises. Such indeed is the situation in Soviet ideology today, as social forces grow which would work for 'de-ideologization',
or possibly, an anti-Marxist ideology.

2. THE DISTINCTION BETWEEN PHILOSOPHY AND IDEOLOGY

Ideology rises and declines; it might even end. Philosophy endures
in every society, but it indeed flourishes only when ideology declines. Russia, for instance, in the half-century before the Bolshevik
Revolution abounded in ideologists. Despite its advancement in
science and large cities, no such country in the world was as backward as far as original philosophic thought was concerned.[7] What
then is the distinction between philosophy and ideology. The distinction is readily seen when we consider the outstanding characteristics
in the relation between great philosophers and their social circumstances. No outstanding philosopher has ever fitted into any party;
some of his ideas, attitudes, and decisions have always been at
variance with those of the party which would have claimed him. No
philosopher has regarded his views as designed for the needs of some
political party or faction. In short, a philosophy is only regarded as
such when it is conceived as the genuine, un-counterfeit, un-imitative
expression of the person's experience in relation to the universe; a
philosophy is the fullest self-discovery of an individual and what he
stands for. A philosophy is one's own to the extent that the individual rids himself of the effects of clichés and catchwords, placards,
parades, slogans, and watchwords; disengaging himself from the
social circumpressures of ideological clubs, circles, peer and populist
groups, professional orthodoxies and associations, thereby surmount-
ing the laws of fashion, the individual can define for himself his own
individual standpoint. A philosophy is the fullest expression of an
individual temperament and experience. It is precisely that aspect of
intellectual reality which cannot be subsumed under general laws of
sociological fashion or alternation, and whose causation insofar as it

[7] Thomas Garrigue Masaryk, *The Spirit of Russia: Studies in History,
Literature, and Philosophy*, tr. Eden and Cedar Paul, Vol. One, London,
1919, pp. 199–201.

is determined, would be explained through the causal lines of the individual's psychological life. An ideology, on the other hand, is the outcome of social circumpressures; it takes philosophy, and reduces it to the lowest common social denominator. It is like the uniform of a party, or the dress of a particular faction; one wears the same ideas as one's comrades; the emphasis is on the being 'one of us', and the free, uncontrolled, venturing idea is suspect. An ideology is an 'ism', that is, a philosophical tenet which has been dissociated from the process of investigation and search, and has been affirmed as the axiom for a political group. Darwin's theory of natural selection becomes Darwinism, the doctrinal axiom of political groups; Newton's laws of motion and gravitation become Newtonianism, the alleged foundation for constitutional monarchies. Between the scientific tenet and the alleged political application there is a wholly spurious 'deduction'. But above all, the ideology closes the door to search and doubt; Darwin's patient, stubborn questioning, Newton's rules of philosophizing are forgotten; the ideology claims answers that are certainties; like the resolutions of a political conference, it closes questions; it records terminal collective decisions; it is not a franchise for the individual questioner.

Take the leading philosophers in modern times, and you will find that none were ideologists. None could regard himself or be regarded as the expression of some group seeking political power; every philosopher is a 'deviationist'. William James brought 'pragmatism' to the fore, yet the young imperialists, Theodore Rooseveltians, and business men who took up the word scarcely found either his anti-imperialism, or animus against 'bigness' congenial; James was not an ideological pragmatist. John Dewey inherited his mantle and was far more ideological in vocation; yet though ideologists liked his word 'practical', they were uncomfortable with the impractical man who talked unpredictably of children's cooperation, supported America's entry into the First World War, defended Leon Trotsky, and refused to join the young New Dealers in a vote for Franklin D. Roosevelt. Bertrand Russell found himself unwanted in both the Liberal and Labor Parties, and excoriated after 1921 by the Communists; the ideologists cast him into limbo, where for many years he attracted little attention, apart from stories of personal scandal in the newspapers; in 1940 when he was prevented from teaching at the City College of New York, the Communist ideologists refused to mount any public campaign for his appointment, because the Communists, partisans of the Stalin–Hitler pact, condemned Russell for supporting the war against the Nazis. Nor did the ideologists relish Russell's advocating after the Second World War an ultimatum to the Soviet Union with the threat to use the atomic bomb. Only toward the end of his life, when his Anti-Americanism became fierce did Russell become an idol of ideologists. The rejection of philosophers by ideologists is indeed an empirical law of intellectual history. Thomas Hobbes wrote a philosophical justification for absolutist rule, but none of the political factions, royalist or parliamentary, found his philosophy usable for their ideological purposes. Immanuel Kant was too revolutionary for the Prussian monarchists, and too Pietist for the revolutionaries. John Stuart Mill was, for the most part, an isolated presence in British politics, too radical and socialistic for the Liberals, too attached to individual liberties for the socialists. Philosophers and ideologists have always been at odds.

Ideologists, moreover, have drawn their recruits from young marginal intellectuals eager for political power but not unmindful for the chance to dominate as ideologists over superior thinkers and creative artists. Ideology has an especial attraction to the mediocrats, the intellectuals of mediocre abilities, who wish nonetheless to be the administrators of the new society. The Soviet ideologists, found their natural followers in such persons as the incompetent researcher who was enabled by the party apparatus to cross-examine and humiliate the scientist Vavilov;[8] the prophet of the marginal intellectual was the research-ideologist Lysenko. Similarly the Soviet literary ideologist, elevated as a bureaucrat of the Writers' Union, can threaten a creative poet that he will grind him to the dust.[9] In

[8] Zhores A. Medvedev, *The Rise and Fall of T. D. Lysenko*, tr. Michael Lerner, New York, 1969, pp. 56, 71, 260, 262.

[9] When the Soviet poet Andrei Voznesensky in 1967 protested the lies which were being published concerning him by the bureaucrats of

France, likewise, the mediocre Stalinist intellectuals, constituting 'a new breed, an army of scribes and literate sergeant-majors', could channelize their envy by barking their orders at their privates, namely the superior artists and scientists. 'Nonentities told Prenant what to think; Lefebvre was ostracized and humiliated by his own pupils; Picasso, Léger and Pignon kept silent while Fougeron laid down the law; ... Malraux, Koestler, Gide, Sartre and Camus were attacked not by men of their own calibre, in intellectual terms which might have commanded respect, but by "hatchetmen" resorting to personal slanders, aspersions, insults.'[10] Underlying the revival of ideology today is its role especially in the universities in providing many young semi-intellectuals and marginal intellectuals with a rationale for their hegemony over genuine scientists and scholars. The 'responsibility of the intellectual' then becomes the ideological slogan for the dictatorship of the mediocrat, the semi-intellectual.

A philosophy represents in the individual at least a partial transcendence of social circumpressures, his self-liberation from them; an ideology is the reduction of a philosophy by a kind of committee of the generation into a uniform credo; the inconsistencies, hesitations, and doubts banished, it becomes the generational, and then, perchance, the governmental dogma. When ideas are used as weapons, they are finally evaluated for their fire-power in psychological warfare, not for their truth. Unless, as a believer in the twofold theory, the ideologist defines 'truth' in terms of an idea's fire-power. An idea gains in fire-power to the extent that it can arouse aggressions, envies, hatreds, resentments. Truth as weaponry finally leads every

the Writer's Union, the editor-in-chief of the newspaper *Pravda* responded, as he described: 'I told him that he might get off with a reprimand the first time, but if he ever did it again, he would be ground to the dust. I myself would see to it that not a trace of him remained.' The trouble with Solzhenitsyn and Voznesensky, he complained, was they 'consider themselves geniuses', Cf. *Problems of Communism*, Vol. XVII, No. 5, Part II, (Sept.–Oct. 1968), p. 48.

[10] David Caute, *Communism and the French Intellectuals 1914–1960*, London, 1964, p. 366.

ideology to anti-intellectualism and assists in the irrationalization of political life.

3. THE BASIC CONSEQUENCE OF IDEOLOGY: THE IRRATIONALIZATION OF HUMAN LIFE

What then is the upshot? Granted that ideology is a blend of myth and science, that its doctrines vary with the wave-phases of philosophies, that it projects the longings of an elite,—is this not, however, a pattern by which man makes his fitful progress in the world? Moved by irrational stirrings, he is nonetheless moved; new ideas, new institutions, are born, and the 'cunning of history' trans-mutes the irrational motive into rational achievement. To which we must respond: history has too often lost its cunning to warrant our confidence.

For the trails that ideologists have blazed have led to the fires of the Nazi crematoria, and to the Arctic wastes of the Soviet labor camps. Men's visions have been warped by ideology; their hatreds have been exacerbated; and every anointed elite has felt itself anointed to misuse human beings. Ideological warfare within and among societies has superseded religious warfare; ideologists, like their religious predecessors, have a propensity to think in terms of St. Bartholomew's Days. Political movements which have been relatively free from ideology have contributed far more to human well-being and freedom than those which apotheosized it.

The wisdom of the matter was probably best stated by John Stuart Mill in 1872. At that time, the secretary of a branch of the International Workingmen's Association sent Mill a pamphlet of their aims, 'The Law of the Revolution', and invited him to join. Mill replied that he found much that he warmly approved in their program, and little from which he dissented. Nonetheless, he queried, why involve these principles in the notion and language of 'revolution'? 'What advantage is there in designating the doctrines of the Association by such a title as "the principles of the political and social Revolution"? ... There is no real thing called "the Revo-lution", nor "any principles of the Revolution".' The important thing was to discuss the program, not to treat 'abstractions as if they were realities which have a will and exert active power'. 'When instead of this men range themselves under banners as friends and enemies of "the Revolution"', the important question, said Mill, was kept out of sight.[11]

Mill was pleading indeed for the abrogation of ideology. Central to ideology is the notion of the revolutionary myth. As Romain Rolland said, 'the word revolution always exercises a prestige "over" the younger generation'.[12] And this perhaps was what Mill did not sufficiently recognize. The irrational and unconscious side of man longs for ideology to the extent that it longs for revolutionary experience; and ideology, is the mode of thought which, issuing most often from the generational unconscious, speaks the language of 'Revolution'; more than the social changes themselves it seeks the experience of the violent expression of energies and the exhilaration of mastery over and humiliation of the traditional authority. 'Revolution' was a therapy of violence which Marx and Engels wanted for its own sake. Quite apart from any political considerations, 'revolution is necessary', they wrote, for producing a 'communist consciousness' on a mass scale, 'because the class overthrowing it (the bourgeois society) can only in a revolution succeed in ridding itself of all the muck of ages and become fitted to found society anew'.[13] They never considered how much 'muck' the revolutionary process would add anew compared to methods of social reform. Revolution has often been personified as a goddess demanding her sacrifices; in her blood and womb the ideologists feel union with and birth again from that Mother.

Ideology exacerbates political fanaticism; for the ideologist presumes that he has the warrant of a world-destiny; the ideological myth has exalted him as a hero, and an alleged science provided the

[11] *The Letters of John Stuart Mill*, ed. Hugh S. R. Elliot, Vol. II, London, 1910, pp. 346–8.

[12] Romain Rolland, *I Will Not Rest*, tr. K. S. Shelvankar, New York, 1937, p. 315.

[13] Karl Marx and Friedrich Engels, *The German Ideology, Parts I and III*, ed. R. Pascal, New York, 1939, p. 69.

credentials. The ideologist mistakes the proddings of neurosis for the law of history, the ordinance of class or race.[14] But ideology envelops him in intellectual ramparts which make him immune to criticism. He has a complete world-system with prefabricated answers to every question, and he is impervious to disconfirming evidence. Above all, ideology, by dividing people into two classes, one elected, the other rejected, sets the stage for untrammelled violence and warfare. No one is so ruthless as those who believe themselves denominated by history as the children of light. The consequence is that where ideologies flourish, the society is disrupted. Finally, the society, concerned in desperation with the minimum requirements of personal safety and security, invokes or surrenders to totalitarian rule. To the degree that ideologies flourish in people's minds, the advent of totalitarian rule becomes more likely.

It is usually forgotten how it was that the most distinguished liberals and men of good will found themselves driven into the support of the fascist regime of Mussolini. Pareto, whom Bertrand Russell admired for his opposition to the First World War, thought the democratic, decentralized Swiss cantons were close to the ideal form of government; yet Pareto welcomed Mussolini's rise to power. The *New Republic* in the United States declared that fascism 'came into existence to meet an imperative practical and psychological need', that it was the response of the Italian people to 'a condition of political and social disorder which compromised their future as a nation . . .' Charles A. Beard, America's greatest historian, felt that Fascism had created 'the most competent and unified organization of capitalists and laborers' that the world had ever seen, and that its criticism of democracy coincided with the ideas of Hamilton, Madison, and John Adams.[15] Ideological fanaticism and warfare

---

[14] Thomas Wentworth Higginson observed that if reformers were 'put in one common harness, they turn and eat each other up'. *Margaret Fuller Ossoli*, p. 140.

[15] Liberalism vs. Fascism', *The New Republic*, Vol. L, 2 March 1927, p. 35. Charles A. Beard, 'Making the Fascist State', Vol. LVII, 23 January 1929, pp. 277–8. John P. Diggins, *Mussolini and Fascism: The View from America*, Princeton, 1972, pp. 228 ff.

indeed had so riven Italian society that people longed for a powerful authority to restore the elementary functions of government. The Marxist ideology has depicted fascism as a last stand of monopoly capitalism. Actually, the question of socialism had little to do with Fascism's coming to power. There have been industrially developed societies which have brought large segments of their economy into the socialist sector; their economic reforms have not evoked any counter-revolution of the middle or capitalist class.

For Fascism has been a reaction not to an economic program but to a declared policy of ideological violence. The one great truth which Thomas Hobbes seized upon and reiterated was that the most ultimate purpose of government is physical security for its people. If that is threatened, any people will be prepared to give dictatorial powers, if necessary, to suppress those who endanger them. Liberal societies can advance to goals beyond security only because a general agreement exists to maintain the public peace. Where that consensus is cancelled, personal security will be a goal more highly prized than civil liberties. That is why liberal constitutions provide for the decreeing of martial law in times of crisis.

Fascism indeed was a Hobbesian reaction to the continued practice and threats of violence by Leftist ideologists. The great Italian liberal Gaetano Salvemini noted how a kind of 'post-war neurasthenia' spread in Italy in 1919–20:[16] 'Trials for political crimes were postponed by the magistrates who lacked the courage to pronounce sentence. Strikes on the most trivial pretexts were frequent, many of them exasperating, especially those which occurred in the essential services, such as the railways, tramways, postal and telegraph facilities, and the light and food supplies of the large towns.' Socialist ideologists propagandized the notion that only through an intensified class struggle could the working class make a qualitative revolutionary leap to a higher society; the master-word in Leftist ideology was always 'Revolution'. Socialist ideologists never seem to have asked Mill's question: what would be the consequences of urging continually 'Revolution' and the Dictatorship (allegedly) of

[16] Gaetano Salvemini, *The Fascist Dictatorship in Italy*, New York, 1927, pp. 8–9, 25.

the Proletariat? When the Left justified violence and ideologically condoned political murders, the Fascist counter-ideology proceeded to do likewise. As Salvemini wrote: 'It is undoubtedly the case that in those years riots and threats of violence were frequent and often exasperating. Unless we take these brutalities into account we shall not be able to understand the ferocity of the Fascist reaction.'[16] The Fascists, who had numbered less than 10,000 in 1919, grew as the Ideological Left pursued relentlessly its ideological mission of class struggle. Leftists never seem seriously to have questioned the consequences of their ideological direction: what would many persons of the lower middle classes, teachers, storekeepers, peasants, feel when told that their historical destiny was to be discarded as significant personalities, that they would be deprived of their liberties in the forthcoming 'dictatorship of the proletariat', and if they resisted 'liquidated'? The words were put into partial practice with the occupation of the factories. As Joseph Schumpeter wrote: people like Pareto 'witnessed with something like horror the social disorganization in Italy which it is necessary to have seen in order to believe'.[17] A few years later, the world was horrified when Mussolini's gangsters murdered the brave idealistic socialist deputy Matteotti. But Socialist ideology had broken ground for the model; on 21 November 1920, Leftist gangsters assassinated the Deputy Giulio Giordani, causing 'a flare of horror and indignation throughout the Po valley and the whole country'.[18] All this had nothing to do with the economic content of socialist proposals. Ideology created fears and anxieties which rendered the ideologists still more irrational, and eventuated in actions and words which irrationalized people generally. Perhaps the anxieties were excessive, and there was no genuine likelihood that the Communists would essay a seizure of power. Yet as Herman Finer wrote: 'The agitation and the occupation had been sufficiently frightening, and caused the rich and the

---

[16] Ibid., p. 25.

[17] Joseph Alois Schumpeter, *Ten Great Economists from Marx to Keynes*, New York, 1951, p. 117.

[18] Herbert L. Matthews, *The Fruits of Fascism*, p. 69.

middle classes to look to *any* savior.'[19] The distinguished philosopher Benedetto Croce until 1924 staunchly supported Fascism, and expected from it 'the renovation of the country'.[20] The Italian Jewish community, repelled by the incessant political violence, looked welcomingly to the advent of Fascism. As Angelica Balabanoff, the first Secretary of the Communist International, wrote: 'Jews figured prominently even among the "Fascists of the First Hour".' Jewish youth were during the first years of Fascist rule 'entirely swallowed up in the world of Fascist ideals'.[21] In short, the Hobbist anxiety made the people at large as well as the circles of liberals and Jews ready to accede to Fascism.[22]

The working classes were still prepared to vote for the Marxists of all sorts, but 'voting behavior' is, under ideological constraints, a small factor of 'political behavior'. The workingmen themselves grew tired of the violence, and ceased to rally to defend their trade union and cooperative headquarters when they were attacked by Fascist bands. Their 'political behavior' grew passive; they withdrew from the political 'activism' which ideology demands. When Communism spread, it produced, as Salvemini said, 'a remarkable strengthening of the Fascist party'; by 1927, he wrote, 'The majority, if offered no other choice but that between the Fascists

[19] Herman Finer, *Mussolini's Italy*, London, 1935, p. 127. In Germany, as Ruth Fischer observed, the 'fury of the Nazis' after 1929 fed on the 'real and not at all imaginary danger of Germany's russification'. Ruth Fischer, *Stalin and German Communism: A Study in the Origins of the State Party*, Harvard University Press, Cambridge, 1948, p. 644.

[20] G. A. Borgese, *Goliath: The March of Fascism*, New York, 1937, p. 296.

[21] Angelica Balabanoff, 'Anti-Semitism in Italy', *Socialist Review*, Vol. 6, No. 8, Sept.–Oct. 1938, p. 18. Also cf. Guido Bedarida, 'The Jews under Mussolini', *The Reflex*, Vol. I, No. 4, Oct. 1927, p. 56.

[22] As Elie Halevy wrote: 'In 1920, the year of the occupation of the factories, there was anarchy. . . . What carried him (Mussolini) forward was the memory of the fear felt in 1920 . . .' Elie Halevy, *The Era of Tyrannies; essays on socialism and war*, tr. R. K. Webb, New York, 1966, p. 278.

and Communists, would leave the field free for the Fascists.'[23] The achievement of ideology is to polarize the society into two ideological extremes. Thus it achieves a projection upon society of its own neurosis, that of the all-or-none principle, or the law of the excluded political middle. The world's problems are difficult enough so that one wonders whether the powers of human reason are sufficient to solve them. The contribution of ideology is to imperil human reason, and by so doing, to render men's problems insoluble.

4. PROPHETS AS IDEOLOGISTS: THE PROPHETIC MASOCHISTS

Ideologists in modern times have often been depicted as the successors of the Hebrew prophets, and as filled with the same moral passion and vision. Ideology itself is seen as prophecy in a modern guise. Enveloped in the prophetic mantle, ideologists are candidates, as neo-prophetic personalities, for the reverence and awe traditionally associated with the names of Isaiah, Jeremiah, Amos and Hosea.[24]

The linkage indeed of ideologist with prophet is a real one. What, perhaps, is not realized, however, is that the prophetic personalities were a blight on the life of the ancient Hebrews; they misled their countrymen into a foreign policy that was suicidal; they carried on an endless polemic, anti-intellectual in character, against the advancement of the civilization of the towns; they were fanatics who revelled in the idea of the destruction of their own society, and with their endless imprecations upon the sins of the Hebrews, and the punishment (in their view) justly meted out to them, they left the imprint of masochism on their consciousness. If the Jews managed to survive for two thousand years as a people, it was by resolutely shelving the prophetic tradition, and declaring that the age of prophecy was over. In a sense, Judaism put an end to ideology, an end to prophecy.

Two modes of thought contested for hegemony among the Hebrews, wisdom and prophecy. Wisdom was similar to what we call

[23] Gaetano Salvemini, 'Who Opposes Mussolini?' *The New Republic*, Vol. XLIX, 9 February 1927, p. 324.

[24] Jack Newfield, *The Prophetic Minority*, introd. Michael Harrington, 1966, New York, 1967, p. 9.

O

today the scientific spirit. It was associated in Hebraic antiquity with Solomon the king, and his policies. For Solomon pursued a policy of promoting trade, and developing the cities. He established an alliance with Egypt, and friendship with the Phoenician merchant-city of Tyre. He extended freedom of worship to foreign religions. He avowed himself a seeker after wisdom, the sciences of 'the children of the East'; he was an internationalist, a cosmopolitan. All this was anathema to the prophets.

By contrast, the latter, as J. M. Powis Smith has written, were prophets of woe; 'the unbroken tradition of prophecy was the preaching of disaster'. Even if the times were prosperous and hopeful, an Amos was at hand to conjure up images of doom and destruction for all. Ahab was portrayed as villainy in kingship, and Jezebel his queen, a Phoenician woman, as femininity in evil essence. Ahab was a statesman 'whose policy of alliance with his neighbors was doubtless well thought out and had large ends in view'; he was unwilling to embark on the persecution of local religious tutelary cults. Ahab, recognizing the peril from Assyria, gave a 'sympathetic tolerance' to the gods of Israel's allies.[25] A friendship with the Phoenician trading towns was 'not to be lightly broken upon the word of a mere long-haired "prophet" from the desert'. The Jewish kingdoms, surrounded by Egypt, Babylonia and Assyria, could hope to survive only if they made alliance with one strong power, or at least with the Phoenician neighbors. But such realistic wisdom filled the prophets, as Renan said, with 'a sort of paroxysm. The hatred of Tyre and Sidon quite blinded them.'[26] Ezekiel too was vindictive against the Phoenician mercantile towns. The prophetic cry was one to abstain from any alliance, and rely only on the might of Jehovah. Isaiah inveighed against the natural alternative, alliance with Egypt. To drive home the warning against Egypt, Isaiah walked 'naked and barefoot' for three years among his countrymen; the Lord, he said, had commanded him to engage in this form of protest.

[25] J. M. Powis Smith, *The Prophets and Their Times*, sec. ed., Chicago, 1941, pp. 51, 57, 66, 185.

[26] Ernest Renan, *History of the People of Israel from the Reign of David up to the Capture of Samaria*, Boston, 1892, p. 39.

Jeremiah in turn prophesied the downfall of the kingdom of Judah as punishment for the people's lack of faith in Jehovah; resistance and Egyptian aid, he said, would be futile. The prophets, as ideologists, claimed to know the plan of God in history, and His long-term purposes; they modestly enunciated the stage-directions to the actors.[27] It was never made clear why the Hebrews had a guilt to expiate from which the Assyrians and Babylonians were free. Only Habakkuk, a solitary dissenter, dared suggest that Judah was 'more righteous' than the Chaldeans.[28] If Israel fell to the invading imperial armies, it was not, according to the prophets, because the latter had more divisions, but because Jehovah in the scheme of history had to chastise His people. And since the Hebrews dared not question God, they had to accuse themselves. The prophetic achievement was to introduce self-hatred, masochism, into the Jewish ethic. The Jews, like a later proletariat, were assailed for not having fulfilled their 'historic mission'. But where Moses imposed a forty years' sentence in the wilderness, the prophets' sweep extended to eons and eras; as ideologists, their myths embraced the totality of history. Far from being agents of historic progress, prophets, as opponents of the Solomonic policy, were a regressive force, 'hostile to the advance of civilization, and culture'.[29]

The great French scholar, Ernest Renan, first perceived the identity of the ideologist with the prophet. Renan had felt the prophetic impulse himself during the Revolution of 1848, when, under socialistic influences, he wrote a book depicting the future society as ruled by an intellectual elite.[30] When he wrote the history of the Hebrews, the prophets suddenly loomed as contemporaries of 1848; the prophet of the eighth century B.C. was 'an open-air

[27] J. M. Powis Smith, *The Prophets and Their Times*, pp. 116, 170, 175. Also cf. Abraham J. Heschel, *The Prophets*, New York, 1962, p. 68 ff.

[28] Adolphe Lods, *The Prophets and the Rise of Judaism*, tr. S. H. Hooke, New York, 1937, p. 235.   [29] Smith, op. cit., pp. 51, 37.

[30] H. W. Wardman, *Ernest Renan: A Critical Biography*, London, 1964, pp. 36 ff. Also cf. Ahad Ha'am, 'Priest and Prophet', in *Selected Essays*, tr. Leon Simon, Philadelphia, 1912, p. 130; also p. 312.

journalist'; wallowing in 'doctrines of despair, such as the Russian nihilism of the present day'; a fanatic allegedly on behalf of social justice, he 'proclaimed that if the world was not just, or capable of becoming so, it had better be destroyed'; the socialists were unwittingly 'the disciples of the prophets'.[31] The ideologist was a recurrent type in social intellectual history.

For a brief period, during the reigns of Josiah and Zedekiah, the prophetic party attained a virtual hegemony over Judah. A juncture of generational rebellion with peasant and proletarian discontent helped in a great revival of ideology. The priest Hilkiah reported finding the 'Book of the Law'; a scribe negotiated better wage conditions for the temple workmen; his son later saved Jeremiah from death, and criticizing the elder generation, said: 'Our fathers have not harkened unto the words of this book.'[32] Josiah, who began his reign at the youthful age of eight, destroyed the places which Solomon had built for the foreign religions; complying with the wishes of the prophetic party, he went to war with Egypt. In so doing, however, he met his death in battle, belying the prophecy which assured him of a peaceful end.

Jeremiah reminded Ernest Renan of a Paris Communard of 1871, Felix Pyat, fanatical, Utopian, destructive, and as Marx said, devoid of common sense.[33] The ancient prophet took on the character of a journalist in beleaguered Paris, marching around its boulevards, preaching debacle and predicting defeat at the hands of God's instruments in history, the Prussians.[34] He and his fellow-ideologists 'preferred seeing their country annihilated to its being less saintly', and at a time when a strong state was a necessity for survival, they would not brook the formation of a real army.[35] With a 'terrible joy', Jeremiah enumerated the devastation and extermination of the

---

[31] Ernest Renan, *History of the People of Israel till the Time of King David*, Boston, 1892, pp. viii, ix. *History of the People of Israel from the Reign of David to the Capture of Samaria*, Boston, 1892, pp. 356, 454, 453, 414, 415, 91, 394.   [32] *Second Kings*, 22:13.

[33] Renan, *History of the People of Israel from the Time of Hezekiah*, p. 285.

[34] Ibid., pp. 273, 238.   [35] Ibid., p. 230.

towns and peoples adjacent to Judah. His 'god of armies' persists for later generations of ideologists through Attila, Tamerlane, Genghis Khan, Adolf Hitler—the conquerors who have hated science and civilization and its works.[36] The ideologist, always experiencing rejection by his people, who never fulfill their mythical assignment, reacts like a lover spurned and maddened; he invariably decrees that the judgment of history will be against them; ideology then becomes a litany of destruction.

An 'end to prophecy' movement developed among the Jews shortly after their return from Babylonian exile. The *Book of Jonah* dared to satirize the destructive self-righteousness of the prophets; Jonah, the *reductio ad absurdum* of a prophet, would prefer to see the city of Nineveh destroyed rather than damage his reputation as an ideologist. God wonders at the end about the motivation of the prophet: how much love was there really in his heart? *Proverbs* advised the young man to eschew the seekers of political power. *Ruth* was a parable of a love which outreached tribalism. Ecclesiastes, the sceptical epistemologist, rebutted the prophetic claim to know the purpose of God, and Job challenged His justice in history and society. The Wisdom Books are not manuals of political activism; their ideal of man is not the prophet but the sage, the man who has passed beyond ideology, beyond mythology. 'From this time henceforth', from the time of Ezra on, said the Rabbis, the era of prophecy was over.[37] To prevent the advent of ideologists, of alienated intellectuals, they insisted that nobody should make his living from the Law, that everyone should have an occupation.

The Jews survived as a people because they cultivated wisdom rather than prophecy; they became rationalists because they lived on the precipice of an irrational world, and dared not act on illusions, fantasies, and unrealities; to do so meant extinction. The revival of ideology among intellectuals today has revived as well all those traits which characterized the prophets,—the propensity to condemn, in the name of an allegedly higher morality, to speak for history, and

[36] Ibid., p. 236.

[37] Robert Gordis, *The Book of God and Man: A Study of Job*, Chicago, 1965, pp. 347–8.

to claim to guide and rule on its behalf; the compulsion to political unrealism, the apocalyptic defeat of their own people, and the destruction of their own liberties, are the renewed characteristics of the prophet as ideologist.

5. INTELLECTUALS ARE IDEOLOGISTS

The noun 'intellectual' in the course of its seventy years' usage has really come to have two basic variants in meaning. On the one hand, the word denotes anyone whose ideas range beyond his profession or vocation; endowed with an enduring concern with the questions of existence, he ventures on the basis of his own experience to have opinions on the unanswerable questions of ultimate reality. On the other hand, the word refers to those persons who have a compulsive commitment to the criticism of the social order; ideologists rather than philosophers, their 'ideas' are much more the by-products of the laws of intellectual fashion; their concern is less with the truth of things than with ideas as weapons; their 'thoughts' are usually predictable because they conform to the impersonal laws of ideological fashion; their categories are akin to a modish vocabulary, attachments to the transient vogue rather than the product of individual experience and reflection. The second usage embraces the intellectuals in politics, the new class which vies for political power and privilege, and whose avenue to power is ideology.

Each elite in the world's history has used some instrumentality peculiar to itself for the attainment of power. The warriors used sheer physical force and prowess, and ruled society as its military elite; the ancient Hebrew judges and kings, Samson, Saul, David, were men of this kind, and the American frontiersman, Andrew Jackson, was in their tradition. A commercial elite of merchant princes ruled in the Italian and Dutch trading towns for several hundred years from the time of the end of the Middle Ages; their money brought economic power. Medieval churchmen and Protestant parsons rose as a clerical elite to govern men through the power of religious anxieties concerning the hereafter. Lawyers became a political elite in the United States because their skills in negotiation

and debate, and their capacity to be intermediaries between contending classes in legislative chambers, lent themselves to a representative democracy. The intellectuals, on the other hand, have no instrumentality for rising to power or 'legitimizing' its acquirement but
ideology. When economists were first enlisted by Franklin D. Roosevelt to serve as his 'Brain Trust', their function was to provide the
technical means to achieve the ends which Roosevelt defined; their
role was that of technicians, not ideologists, and they scarcely constituted a distinct political group. The role, however, of intellectuals
today in politics is not that of technicians; they are more than experts
in economics or city planning, or foreign areas; their role is as ideologists, with a conception of their world mission and design for
society, seeking power for themselves in the name of that ideology.
Ideology will last as long as intellectuals are claimants to political
power who must compulsively define the social order as in virtual
collapse, and nominate themselves as the trustees duly certified by
history itself.

The history of the political intellectuals, the ideologists, has gone
through three stages. At first, they were unattached intellectuals,
few in numbers, 'free-floating' journalists, writers, and marginals,
feeling misplaced in society, denied a place in its councils, searching
for an ideology. In this stage, the intellectuals wrote Utopias, works
of political fantasy, which projected nonetheless the unconscious
wish of the small intellectual elite; for from Plato to Campanella,
Thomas More, Edward Bellamy and H. G. Wells, the Utopias have
almost always shared one trait—they have been described as ruled by
an elite of intellectuals. Utopias are a pre-ideology; they express the
longings and presumable interests of an incipient elite.[38] Then came
the second stage, when the intellectuals found their class ally, their
'mass base,' their social carrier force; the peasantry, proletariat,
nation or Third World was assigned the historical role for providing
the physical force which would bring the intellectuals to the status
of the governing elite. This second stage is that of classical ideology;
in this stage, the effort to unite science with mythology is the primary

[38] Mannheim's view that Utopias are not ideological in character, nor
bound to interests, seems to me, therefore, mistaken.

characteristic; the scientific, rationalistic method is still, however, regarded as central. In the third stage, the intellectual corps, predominantly of the young, and greatly augmented in numbers, tends to reject the notion of a historical class, the 'progressive proletariat', or what C. Wright Mills called the 'labor metaphysic'. Ideology becomes more self-consciously irrational, anti-scientific, mythological, and juvenocratic,—the straightforward claim of the intellectuals to rule.

No doubt, if rule comes to the intellectual corps, it will be as short-lived as was that of their Soviet counterparts. But, whereas, the Zamyatins could escape to a free West, and the Solzhenitsyns were sustained in their isolation by their consciousness of free Western opinion, one wonders at the depths of masochism which will be excavated by a future intellectual *rejeté*.

Intellectuals, then, as a sociological species, are the bearers of ideology. Scientists and scholars are not as such 'intellectuals'; nor can one define 'intellectuals' as the purveyors of symbolic culture; a mathematician, lecturing on the differential calculus or symbolic logic, is not necessarily an 'intellectual'. Nor are intellectuals coextensive with educated persons; most engineers, chemists, accountants and physicians would not be regarded as 'intellectuals'.[39] Are they persons concerned with social reforms? Many persons, lawyers, economists, who have advocated various reforms on the basis of their professional experience have not been regarded as 'intellectuals'.

[39] Max Weber defined 'intellectuals' as a group of men who have a 'special access to certain achievements considered to be "culture values", and who, therefore, usurp the leadership of a "culture community" '. But there is a big gap between the scientist or musician, with his cultural values, and the endeavor to secure the leadership of a 'culture community'; and there is an even bigger gap in trying to move beyond the association of scientists or artists to leadership in the community as a whole. Many scientists do not regard themselves as specially qualified to exercise the political leadership of society. It is precisely the role of ideology, not 'cultural values', which converts the educated person into an 'intellectual', that is, an ideologist. Cf. *From Max Weber: Essays in Sociology*, ed. H. H. Gerth and C. Wright Mills, New York, 1946, p. 176.

Then what constitutes the defining characteristic of the intellectual: Clearly, he is then a person, with at least some knowledge of contemporary ideas, who is under an emotional compulsion to challenge the social world in which he lives; he is a generational rebel and, if older, fixated in this psychology; if he comes from the upper classes, then he regards himself as *déclassé*, as having broken with his social roots, and as taking up ideas aimed to overturn his parents' class; if he comes from the lower classes, or some alien religious culture, he finds himself culturally removed from the parental attitudes and traditional religion; he then regards himself as an aristocrat, of nature born, who thus far has been denied membership in any house of social lords. The emotional vector of generational rebellion is engraved in the unconscious of the intellectual. The intellectual's challenge to society, as the projection of such emotions, usually has only a peripheral foundation in any scientific study of relevant facts, or in the domain of his professional qualifications. Rather, the intellectual is defined by an *emotional a priori*. He has what might be called a 'dialectical personality', that is, he is under a compulsion to see the existing system in its entirety as doomed. No matter what reforms may be proposed, the 'dialectical personality' is emotionally cast to demonstrate anew his 'dialectical proofs' that they cannot possibly work, that the system must break down. He and his fellow intellectuals will be the redeemers fashioning the new society.

As a branch of science advances, its logical content becomes ever more divested of ideology. Pre-scientific philosophical circles in Asia and antiquity tended also to be political-ideological groups. To the modern intellectual, likewise, ideology is the focal center of his spiritual life. What the future of ideology will be is then inextricably tied to the existence of a class of intellectuals. Are they then a social formation which is now permanently part of our society?

The word 'intellectual' (as a noun) first acquired its vogue during the debate which divided French society over the Dreyfus Case. On 14 January 1898, the newspaper *L'Aurore* published a protest against the conduct of the trial in 1894; it was signed by distinguished names in French letters and science, Anatole France, Zola,

P

Charles Seignobos. The editor, Georges Clemenceau, by a historical inspiration, gave it the title 'Manifesto of the Intellectuals' (Manifeste des Intellectuels). The next day, the anti-Dreyfusard critic Brunetière attacked the Intellectuals. This 'recently created word', he wrote, designated a would-be aristocracy of individuals, researchers in laboratories and libraries, who looked at themselves as 'supermen'. The next month, he wrote that he could not see 'that a professor of Tibetan has the authority to govern his fellows'. The word quickly crossed the Atlantic Ocean, and in March 1898, appeared in the editorial columns of *The Nation* which deplored the sight of Brunetière 'sneeringly' calling the defenders of Dreyfus, of liberty and justice, 'intellectuals'.

From its inception, the word 'intellectual' had the connotation of a compulsive malcontent, a misfit, whose demand for moral authority was impeded neither by modesty nor scientific standards. It carried too, in America, the suggestion of the alien. For the first group to call themselves 'intellectuals' were the student children of Jewish immigrants in New York's East Side. Nowhere in the United States was generational conflict so intense as on the Jewish East Side, where the young, rejecting their fathers' religion, sought desperately for an ideology which would be its moral equivalent. Such visitors to the East Side as Hutchins Hapgood were entranced by the ' "Intellectuals" of the Ghetto', these young workingmen and workingmen who gathered in the cafés in the evening—anarchists, socialists, writers, arguing ideology endlessly, mixing Ibsen, Plekhanov, and Bakunin with their tea.[40] In the socialist political parties, heated polemics were waged over the place of 'intellectuals' in their movement; were the 'intellectuals' joining the cause because they hoped to rule the workers' party? The 'intellectual' now had a dual referent; it referred, on the one hand, to those who had rejected their upper class origins, but secondly, it also denoted those with lower class origins whose reading had liberated their political and cultural

---

[40] Hutchins Hapgood, *The Spirit of the Ghetto: Studies of the Jewish Quarter in New York*, 1902, Rev. ed., 1909, pp. 38–43. Lewis S. Feuer, 'The Political Linguistics of "Intellectual" 1898–1918', *Survey*, No. 1 (78), Winter 1971, pp. 161–3.

ambitions. A leading socialist intellectual wrote in 1910 that 'the very use of the term "intellectual" as a name here in America is ignorant and absurd. In France, where numbers of educated men come into the movement for the sake of personal advancement, there is some justification for using the term in a depreciatory sense. It was there that the term was first employed.... But there is no justification for its use in that sense in America.'[41] The following year in 1911, John Spargo, the most widely read socialist expositor in the United States, further defended the intellectuals;[42] while conceding that they came mostly from the privileged classes, they had provided the movement, he emphasized, with 'most of its philosophers, economists, orators, artists, poets and political leaders'; to them, he said, the proletariat owed its sense of 'mission'. And who were the anti-intellectuals? Their chieftains were themselves 'nearly always unsuccessful "intellectuals"—lawyers without clients, authors without publishers, professors without chairs, ministers without pulpits and so on', declared Spargo.[43] It seemed that if the Socialist ideologists were marginal intellectuals, then the sub-marginal intellectuals contributed the anti-intellectual intellectuals. In any case, both groups were equally ideological, though they differed in their location of the mission-mantled elite.

It was noteworthy that those countries were most 'ideology-prone' which likewise had the greatest occasion to use the category of 'intellectual', Russia, France, Italy, Germany. The Russian loan-word from the German, the 'intelligentsia', for a while vied with 'intellectuals' for adoption in the United States, but it was even more foreign-sounding than 'intellectual'. The latter word was already used as an adjective, and less redolent with overtones of the nihilist and bombs.

The word 'intellectual', however, retained the connotations of the social misfit or maladjusted. During the first twenty years of its use in the United States, it was prefaced in the overwhelming

[41] W. J. Ghent, *Socialism and Success*, New York, 1910, p. 165.
[42] Ibid., p. 147.
[43] John Spargo, *Sidelights on Contemporary Socialism*, New York, 1911, pp. 10, 67–74, 84.

majority of instances with the derogatory 'so-called' or enclosed in warning quotation marks.[44]

The relationship between the intellectual class and ideology perdures. 'Intellectual' was delayed in its reception in the United States for the same reason that Americans had less of a need for ideology. Educated persons in the United States, the small number of college graduates, found places in social life which corresponded to their ability and ambitions. Before the Civil War the abler students were generally at college to prepare for the ministry. Restless persons went to seek their fortune in the frontier commonwealths of the West. There were safety-valves which afforded socially useful outlets to rebellious generational energies.

The revival of ideology today is fed by the emergence in America of a huge class of intellectuals, with a heavy representation of the marginal and sub-marginal kind. In the Roman Empire, the relative prosperity enabled a class of 'philosophers' to exist; the word 'called up the vision of some anarchical Cynic, with a long untidy beard and rough cloak, savagely preaching against all human institutions.'[45] In latter Hellenic times too, the Cynics with their diatribes against civilization, and their deliberate violation of all decorum in personal behavior, affirmed their contempt for the total structure and achievement of society. The vastness of American technological achievement has likewise brought into existence a huge class of intellectuals, that is, persons who have a surfeit of aggressive, rebellious energies especially so because in the American case economic history seems so largely to have come to an end. The stability and productivity of the American economy guarantee livelihoods even for the non-working. The nine millions at the colleges and universities have a considerable number who are unable intellectually or

[44] Lewis S. Feuer, 'The Political Linguistics of "Intellectual": 1898–1918', *Survey*, No. 1 (78), Winter, 1971, pp. 156–83. As late as 1919, Veblen referred to ' "the Intellectuals", as a late and perhaps vulgar designation'. Thorstein Veblen, *An Inquiry into the Nature of Peace and the Terms of its Perpetuation*, New York, 1917, p. 109.

[45] Martin Percival Charlesworth, *Five Men: Character Studies from the Roman Empire*, Cambridge, Mass., 1936, p. 101.

emotionally to fulfill the requirements of modern science and scholarship. Bereft of religion, and without material challenges to their existence, seeking a purpose in life, they find that ideology offers them a vocation—one of destroying the system which fed and comforted them too well. And ideology closes their minds still further to social reality, and provides a socio-theology to justify their generational hatreds.

The Jews for hundreds of years solved the problem of ideology by discouraging the advent of intellectuals; everyone had to earn his living by a trade or vocation. Today, the colleges and universities in the cases of hundreds of thousands heighten the sense of super-fluousness which nurtures the need for ideology. The curriculum in liberal arts, which once provided the preparatory years for the small corps of clergy and civil servants in Britain, often leaves its American graduates with a sense of vacuity. Efforts are being made to remedy this situation by making education more ideological. If anything, the current educational reformers will contribute even more to the emotional vacuity of the next generations. What is required indeed, is to join all the curricula to actual professions and jobs, and thereby to assure the students that jobs, hard and necessary, and important, await them. The old curriculum, modelled to the preferences of a small aristocratic elite, should be largely reformed. Curiously what is needed is more of the ethics of work and sense of pride in one's job. And it is work, above all, which holds man fast to his sense of reality, giving significance to his energies. The workless man loses his sense of time and self-significance. 'To do one's thing' as a universal maxim is finally to do nothing, and one cannot discover one's vocation in an educational system which is weak, flabby, and enervating.

One cannot predict 'an end to ideology'. But one can state the conditions for its efflorescence and decline. For there will always be ingredients in the generational unconscious that will find myth congenial though their potency varies with social conditions. So long as a society engenders intellectuals, dissociated from work-realities, generational rebellion will tend to issue in ideology. A society which is rational and work-occupied is one which has men of intellect, but not intellectuals. Jefferson, Franklin and Lincoln were men of intellect, but always putting ideas to the test of reality, they never became intellectuals. Meanwhile, one can mitigate the consequences of ideology, by analyzing its appearance among intellectuals as scientifically as a medical scientist would study recurrent fevers, and noting how they can be alleviated. Then, when intellectuals cease to be ideologists, that is, cease to be 'intellectuals' and become instead scientists, scholars, teachers, they will find a vocation more enduring than any that myth can confer, more sincere because without self-illusion.

Bibliographical Note

Students of ideology might well begin with the letters of Friedrich Engels which dealt with the concept. They are reprinted in Marx and Engels, *Basic Writings on Politics and Philosophy*, ed. Lewis S. Feuer, New York, 1959, pp. 395–412. The pamphlet by V. I. Lenin, *What is to be Done?* (1902), tr. New York, 1929, is important for its transformation of the meaning of 'ideology' to denote any set of class-sponsored ideas and its dropping of the notion of 'false consciousness'. Karl Mannheim's *Ideology and Utopia*, tr. L. Wirth and E. Shils, New York, 1936, awoke the interest of American and British sociologists in the subject, though its actual substantive contribution was slender. Robert Michels' essay 'Intellectuals', in *Encyclopaedia of the Social Sciences*, Vol. VIII, New York, 1932, pp. 118–126, was a magisterial analysis of the bearers of ideology; Joseph A. Schumpeter's *Capitalism, Socialism, and Democracy*, 2nd ed., New York, 1947, has become a classic on the theme of the sociology of intellectuals and their ideology. Raymond Aron's book *The Opium of the Intellectuals*, tr. T. Kilmartin, London, 1957, initiated a discussion concerning the end of the ideological age; the theme was pursued in Daniel Bell, *The End of Ideology; on the exhaustion of political ideas in the fifties*, Glencoe, 1960. A controversy developed in which the advocates of ideology assailed its critics in terms which were perhaps more verbal and vehement than factual and scientific. An anthology edited by Chaim I. Waxman, *The End of Ideology Debate*, 1969, is useful for this episode of intellectual history. A bibliography of ideology for an earlier period is contained in a report entitled 'The Sociological Study of Ideology (1940–60)', published in *Current Sociology*, Vol. IX, No. 2, 1960. Among later important works are Maurice Cranston, ed., *The New Left: six critical essays*, London, 1970, which evaluate the ideologists of the new wave; John Plamenatz, *Ideology*, London, 1970, a careful survey of the career and classical usages of the term; a volume of studies by political scientists, David Apter, ed. *Ideology and Discontent*, New York, 1964; a group of discerning essays in Donald G. MacRae, *Ideology and Society*, London, 1961; a series of important articles in Philip Rieff, ed., *On Intellectuals, theoretical studies, case studies*, New York, 1969, and the erudite analyses of George Lichtheim, *The Concept of Ideology, and other essays*, New York, 1967.

Index